On South Africa's Secret Service

On South Africa's Secret Service

An Undercover Agent's Story

Riaan Labuschagne

GALAGO

GALAGO BOOKS

Galago books are published by Galago Publishing (1999) (Pty) Ltd
P O Box 404, Alberton, 1450, Republic South Africa

Web address: www.galago.co.za

Galago Books are distributed by Lemur Books (Pty) Ltd
PO Box 1645, Alberton, 1450, Republic South Africa
Tel: (Int +2711 — local + 011) 907-2029, Fax: 869-0890

Email: lemur@mweb.co.za

First published by Galago, October 2002 as
On South Africa's Secret Service
by Riaan Labuschagne, October 2002

© Riaan Labuschagne, 2002
ISBN 1-919854-08-8

Riaan Labuschagne has asserted his moral right
to be identified as the author of this work

Typeset in 11.5 Times Roman by Galago

Colour and black and white photographs reproduced by
Full Colour Graphics, Johannesburg.

Layouts and colour corrections by Galago

Printed by CTP Book Printers

Electronic DD20: 355.496

Book design: Francis Stiff and Madelain Davies
Dust jacket design: Francis Stiff, Justyn and Madelain Davies
Dust jacket conceptualisation: Justyn and Madelain Davies
Dust jacket photography: Justyn Davies

For my father, for my wife and best friend Liesl, and for Estiaan and Margit. For times lost

Acknowledgements

'Ignorance is bliss', my friend Billy advised when I embarked on the project of writing this book. As I toiled what seemed to be endlessly to complete it, I came to appreciate the important roles that others were playing in its completion. I would consequently like to acknowledge and thank the following, in no particular order of importance, for their invaluable contributions.

Firstly my loving wife Liesl and my children, Estiaan and Margit, for their exemplary patience in providing me with the personal space that allowed me to submerge myself once more in the shadowy world that was once my life.

I thank Bettie for believing in me.

There was: Peter and Elsabe, who not only shared my dream but had also shared my profession; my good friend and top journalist Dawie who remained passionate about my endeavours and helped me to place events of the past into correct historical perspective; and my former colleagues of the National Intelligence Service who shared details of what were often truly amazing operations with me. There are other former members of the Service, now with the new National Intelligence Agency, who helped, but wish to remain anonymous and to whom I am grateful. I am grateful to Patsi and Billy for their friendship and professional advice. Heinrich and Liesl are thanked for their love and dedication.

Last, but by no means least, I wish to thank Peter Stiff, my publisher, friend and mentor, for going far beyond the boundaries of the conventional and making an all-out effort to assist me with the makings of this book.

Contents

Colour and black and white photographs

In-text illustrations

Foreword

On South Africa's Secret Service reveals for the first time sensational details of South Africa's ruthless secret intelligence war as conducted by the National Intelligence Service. It is told by Riaan Labuschagne, a man in the maelstrom of events during the 1980s and 1990s.

In 1981, while still a university student, he was persuaded to take diving parties to the Seychelles during vacations to collect 'routine low grade intelligence on the islands to build up the Service's information bank'. He wasn't told that the intelligence was required in connection with a pending coup attempt by mercenaries that NIS was supporting. While he was there the coup attempt exploded into action and he was fortunate to escape.

Later, after the conclusion of his university studies and two year's national service as a naval officer, he was accepted into the Service's Counter-Intelligence Division as an undercover field operative.

The Personnel records showed him as Riaan Lesage, which allowed him to work openly under his real name. He found he had entered a world of lies and half truths, secrecy and stealth, evasion and denials, deceits and manipulations. It had little to do with the Calvinistic ethics of Christian nationalism that had provided the guidelines for his upbringing as a young Afrikaner.

He recruited the Soviet Military Attaché in Gaborone, Botswana, and gained valuable intelligence that allowed the SADF to pre-empt and defeat a major Soviet-supported attack on UNITA in Angola.

He subverted the Libyan Military Attaché in Gaborone — a married man with an eye for the girls. The Libyan was corrupted and turned by using a 'honey trap' in the form of a well-known South African television actress.

While Assistant Trade Representative (the cover used by intelligence agents) at South Africa's Trade Mission in Harare, he recruited a top MK (*Umkhonto we Sizwe* — Spear of the Nation — ANC's military wing) officer as an agent. The regular flow of information gained ensured that most MK groups who attempted to infiltrate South Africa were intercepted and shot.

Information from a top agent in Zimbabwe's Central Intelligence Organisation foiled a MK plan to launch attacks against the Swartkops and Waterkloof Air Force bases in Pretoria and resulted in the arrest of the culprits.

He explains how in the early 1990s, using the guise of an Afrikaner liberal, he infiltrated the top structures of the ANC in Durban and made friendships with men who later became cabinet ministers. The ANC's offices were not safe either, and his NIS teams equipped with portable copiers covertly broke into them almost weekly and duplicated every document they could lay their hands on.

He reveals, also for the first time, the existence of the sinister and deep cover Directorate K (for covert), formed by the NIS in much the same way as the SADF formed the notorious CCB. While the NIS did not possess 'executive powers' (an euphemism for a licence to kill) Directorate K probably did.

He tells how Directorate K, acting as an *agent provocateur*, supplied explosives to AZAPO's military wing, AZANLA, to blow up civilian targets in Port Elizabeth. The reason was to arouse the ire of white Afrikaner right wingers to provoke them into attacking black civilians. It would have provided an excuse to crush them and prevent a much feared attempt by the Afrikaner right wing to seize control of South Africa to stop a ANC takeover in the April 1994 elections.

There is far more than just that in this fascinating book.

1

The losers

It was sunset on the evening of 1 September 1996 — the official first day of the South African spring — and I was sitting in Joe Cool's Restaurant watching the Indian Ocean. In the background a female voice resonated:

'. . . had one of his informers persuade the five to rob a bank. He and his men then ambushed and killed them all. They murdered the fifth man in a car elsewhere so that he could not talk and they blew up his body so he could not be identified'.

The television got my full attention. A reporter was leading with a story that would irritate and open wounds from the past.

'Hit squad murderer Eugene de Kock, who was found guilty of 89 crimes this week, will spill the beans and name senior police officers who were aware of or involved in his activities when he leads evidence in mitigation of sentence in the Supreme Court in Pretoria on September 16.

'Some have already been named in the De Kock trial, including retired generals Johan le Roux and Krappies Engelbrecht. The special police squad led by Brigadier Ivor Human and Captain Mike Holmes that brought De Kock to trial on 121 counts is expected to pounce on several high-ranking officers after De Kock has been sentenced. After their arrest it's almost certain that De Kock will turn state witness against them to support his plea for mitigation of sentence.

'The former commander of the hit squad known as C10 feels he has nothing to lose and is angry because so far he has had to carry the can alone. This was confirmed by his counsel, Flip Hattingh, on Tuesday shortly after the marathon 18 month trial was concluded. He also said he expected his client to describe visits to the hit squad headquarters at Vlakplaas by former minister Adriaan Vlok who attended barbecues and social gatherings there.

'On Friday the African National Congress welcomed the guilty verdict in the De Kock case, but said the judgement and the evidence led during the trial challenged the veracity of claims made by former president FW de Klerk that his government had never sanctioned murder, assassination, assault and kidnapping'.

My gaze returned to the Indian Ocean as the newscaster switched to other news. I had resigned from the National Intelligence Service (NIS) two years before and had started a new life divorced from the realities of the world stage. I knew that the media and the general public would never learn the real truth about De Kock and the National Party government's campaign against the ANC. I thanked God I was no longer involved. I pitied De Kock for the situation he found himself in. He had been abandoned by his former masters who had given the orders and suddenly he was the scapegoat for all the evils committed by the apartheid regime.

The lives of luxury and comfort being led by the former political elite of the National Party were in stark contrast to the misery of the forgotten ones they had left to take the rap.

The story of Eugene de Kock had really disturbed me. I looked at the people outside, enjoying the last rays of the sun and the cool air that was blowing in from the sea. Couples were holding hands as they strolled along the beach. The promise of summer showed in the faces of young and old. It was a new beginning.

But it was not much of a fresh start for Colonel Eugene de Kock . . . poor bastard.

I swallowed the last dregs of beer and ordered a double whisky. I thought of assassinations, blackmail, lies and denial, the question of survival while on a quest to satisfy a thankless master. I was buried in an avalanche of recollections as my thoughts took me back on a road I had once travelled with such enthusiasm.

2

The islands
November 1981

1981 had been a good period for me. I had just completed the first year of my second degree and I was once more en route to the Seychelles for a working holiday as a diving tour leader and instructor.

I was sitting in the bar off the departure hall of Jan Smuts Airport (now Johannesburg International) sipping a scotch on the rocks. I was looking forward with excited anticipation to the arrival of my tour group. Only five of the 15 were divers. The rest, mostly students on their first trip outside the borders of South Africa, were girlfriends or had just come along for the ride.

Two hours earlier I had checked in all the diving gear on to British Airways Flight BA026 that would soon be departing for Mahé in the Seychelles.

The first to join me were Allan, an ex-navy diver; Frankie, a Portuguese restaurateur; Serge, a French diver and my diving partner Mariana, an ex-naval intelligence officer.

The waiter and a group of policemen eyed us with a mixture of jealousy and distaste as the number of empty beer bottles on our table multiplied. Gerhard and Barbara Olivier arrived with Hilton — our doctor for the trip. In January Hilton would be inducted into the South African Army for his national service, but would act as a dentist. Gerhard, who had married Barbara a week before, had only just completed his final veterinary exams. The rest of the party had arrived by 15:00 and, after finishing our drinks, we boarded.

The sun was just above the horizon as we passed over the coast of Madagascar at an altitude of 10 000 metres. I stood alone in the tail section of the aircraft looking through a porthole at the green land below. Serge, Frank and Allan had boisterously relieved the cabin crew of their duties and were lightheartedly serving drinks in abundance to both themselves and a group of passengers.

Although I was enjoying their company, their reasons for being there were different to mine. I pondered my own motives. It had been at the start of the summer holidays more than twelve months before. It all began with an unexpected phone call.

'Riaan, telephone — it's Tersia.'

I took the call on the other phone in the study.

'Hi, Ters.'

'Hello, Riaan. It's my company's year end dinner party on Friday night and I don't have a partner. I've been wondering if you'll come with me.'

We had been friends since schooldays and had an easy relationship. There were no strings and no romantic connotations. Tersia was just one of the boys.

I had hesitated for a moment, looking for an excuse as I did not really feel like going.

'Please come. There are people I want you to meet. I promise that you'll enjoy it. Besides there'll be free food and drink and dancing afterwards. It should be fun.'

What the hell, I thought. Why not?

'Okay Ters, I'll go.'

As I replaced the receiver I wondered briefly about Tersia's employer. It certainly seemed to be a strange sort of outfit. I recalled an odd incident involving a fellow employee of Tersia about eight months previously. A neatly dressed woman in her late twenties had arrived at my parents' home after requesting an interview with me. She had introduced herself as Marelize Nel and said she was doing a character reference on Tersia who had applied for a position in the government's information service. In a casual but very purposeful and efficient way, she had milked me of details about Tersia's family, her personality, her friends, her loyalty and even her sexual preferences.

I thought at time that it had been a remarkably clinical way of getting into the core being of someone's life. I was astonished at her depth of knowledge about my friend. She even knew about Tersia's father, an executive with one of South Africa's top insurance companies, who habitually got pissed at major functions and regularly made a fool of himself. Marelize thanked me as I walked her to her car. It was a metallic blue VW Passat. A real fancy car for so young a woman, I remember thinking.

It was her parting words, however, that had surprised me the most.

'Thank you for your co-operation, and remember, not a word to Tersia.'

I watched her car disappear down the street. I suddenly felt ignorant — even stupid — which I knew I was not. I matriculated at 16 and had successfully completed a Bachelor of Arts degree and was on my way to a degree in theology — a seven-year study course in total.

But I had never before come across anyone tapping information from me quite so blatantly. And what the hell was this so-called company that Tersia had spoken about? Was it a company or was it really part of the government? It certainly went to extraordinary and underhanded lengths to check out and scrutinise prospective employees. And why was it all so confidential?

She got the job and now I was invited to a staff party. I was intrigued, speculating what it was all about. I wondered if the mysterious Marelize who had so efficiently interrogated me would be there.

That Friday evening while getting dressed for the party, I thought about Tersia. She seemed to be happy, well paid and more purposeful than before. She had also given up socialising with the boys in our group.

I left my old 1972 Volksie Beetle at her parent's house and we drove to the function in Tersia's company car — a brand new red VW Golf. From Pretoria she drove out on the Ermelo Road.

'Where are we going?' I asked.

'The function is at our training facility. We call it "The Farm". It's adjacent to the Rietvlei Dam and Nature Reserve', she told me.

About ten kilometres outside Pretoria she turned left off the main road that link the capital city with Delmas to the east. There was small signboard outside that read, *Ons Plekkie* (Our Place). All I could see in the gathering darkness were high electric fences to my left and a few small labourers' houses to my right. The narrow tarred entrance road continued for 800 metres before it split. The entrance to the main training facility on the left was blocked by a guardhouse and by booms. I could vaguely make out a large complex behind a double row of electrified fencing. We took the road to the right that led to the recreational facilities.

Another large gate manned by men dressed formally in dinner jackets blocked our way. They checked Tersia's 'company' identity card and waved us through into the facility. The building and the grounds were carefully maintained. The recreation hall was a circular building surrounded by rolling green lawns.

The welcoming party at the door seemed to consist of manager types and security guards. Even the guards appeared to be university graduates and of a much higher status than usual in the security profession.

The mood at the party was festive. It was more like the wedding reception of a wealthy uncle. Everyone knew everyone else and greeted each other cheerfully.

As we walked slowly to our table, Tersia briefly explained that we were at the National Intelligence Service's training and recreational centre.

The staff party was their end of year function. The guest of honour was Prime Minister PW Botha, who was personally responsible for South Africa's secret intelligence service.

I found myself in the company of those at the nerve centre of intrigue in southern Africa. I was, at the time, however, ignorant of the true function of an intelligence service.

It turned out to be the last function of its kind that I would attend at The Farm, despite my eventually pursuing a long career in the NIS. That career would be as a member of the Service's covert structures. As such, I would be excluded from attending such events. Contact with other declared members of NIS, either professionally or socially, was forbidden.

The ten or so couples around the table greeted us with smiles. They all knew Tersia. She guided me to an older man with a much younger wife.

'Riaan, I would like you to meet Mr van Tonder and his wife Hester.'

'This is Riaan, my friend I told you about — he's the one who's always off diving in Mauritius.'

Many years later I discovered that it was Tersia who had suggested my recruitment into the Service. Like its British counterpart, MI6, the National Intelligence Service was a very restricted club. Invitations to join its ranks came only on the specific recommendations of serving members.

Nico van Tonder, or 'Sokkies' as he was commonly known in the Service, had just completed a spell as First Secretary at South Africa's embassy in Rome. I found out later that 'First Secretary' is the diplomatic position allocated to intelligence personnel in embassies. It is common practice amongst intelligence services throughout the world.

'Pleased to meet you, Riaan. What's the surname again?'

'Labuschagne.'

He stood up and shook my hand.

'Tersia, sit here next to Hester and we'll get some drinks.'

On approaching the bar with Nico I noticed an obvious hierarchy, although not as pronounced as it was in the South African Police from which my father had retired as a major. Certain people at the bar, including Sokkies, were addressed as 'sir.'

I felt flattered. I was chatting easily on first name terms with a senior man who was almost my father's age. I felt stimulated and far removed from the conservative world that I had been brought up in.

A sudden bustle heralded the arrival of Prime Minister PW Botha (dubbed the Great Crocodile by the media) and his wife Elise. Deferentially ushering them in was Dr Niel Barnard, Director General of the National Intelligence Service.

Botha came into power after the National Party government of John Vorster was rocked by a major scandal. At the beginning of 1971 Eschel Rhoodie, then press officer at the South African Embassy in The Hague in Holland, clandestinely negotiated an agreement with a Dutch publisher, Hubert Jussen, for the establishment of a new magazine in South Africa. It would be published on the lines of *Time Magazine* and would be called *To the Point*. It would be financed secretly by the South African government for the purpose of countering the unfavourable press coverage that South Africa was getting abroad.

The project was approved by Prime Minister Vorster, Chief of the Bureau for State Security (BOSS) Intelligence Services, General Hendrik van den Bergh; the Minister of Information, Dr Connie Mulder; and Gerald Barrie, Director General of the Department of Information.

Rhoodie was appointed Secretary of Information in July 1972. From 1973 on he worked in close co-operation with General van den Bergh. This resulted in various new schemes and projects being introduced into Rhoodie's Department of Information.

In February 1974 Vorster put his official stamp of approval on covert action that led to *Project Annemarie* towards the end of 1975. The action also targeted the English language press which the government regarded as the enemy. The objective was to introduce an English language newspaper into the South African market to counter attacks on the government.

The man chosen to front the operation was Dr Louis Luyt, a millionaire South African businessman. *The Citizen* was launched in his name as a daily newspaper in the second half of 1976. Finance to fund the project was channelled to the Department of Information by the Department of Defence.

The Citizen's growth rate fell far short of expectations. Furthermore, PW Botha, then Minister of Defence, was unhappy about his department's money being used to finance a secret information project. The relationship between Luyt and Rhoodie deteriorated rapidly.

In November 1978 the so-called Information Scandal broke. Evidence, mainly assembled by investigative journalists, revealed beyond all doubt that *The Citizen* was being financed with state funds.

Louis Luyt named Prime Minister Vorster, Connie Mulder and General van den Bergh as key figures in the secret project to finance the newspaper. In the subsequent commission of enquiry, PW Botha denied any involvement in the affair and was found blameless.

The stress resulting from the affair proved too much for Vorster and it impacted negatively on his health. In September 1978 he was forced to resign as prime minister when it was established that he had lied to Parliament about the scandal.

The National Party caucus conducted two votes to choose a new prime minister from candidates nominated for the office. In the first run off, PW Botha got 78 votes, Connie Mulder 72 and Pik Botha 22. Mulder would have been the natural successor to Vorster, but with the Information Scandal also hanging over him his election became unlikely.

In the second round of voting PW Botha scored 98 votes, gaining virtually all of Pik Botha's support votes.

PW Botha took office as Prime Minister of South Africa in 1978. Connie Mulder, also because of the Information Scandal, lost his position as the provincial head of the National Party in the Transvaal. On hearing the result, General van den Bergh immediately tendered his resignation as head of BOSS. A mutual dislike that verged almost on hatred existed between himself and PW Botha. Behind the cover of Premier Vorster, he had frequently undermined PW's position as Minister of Defence. Both Van der Bergh and Vorster, as members of the *Ossewa Brandwag* movement, had been detained by the Smuts government for pro-Nazi activities during World War-II. It took little guesswork for him to realise that with his protector gone, he would soon have been sacked by PW Botha if he did not go voluntarily and quickly.

In August 1979 Prime Minister Botha appointed Niel Barnard as Director General of the newly formed National Intelligence Service that Botha created to replace BOSS. Barnard replaced Alex van Wyk, a seasoned career officer, who had taken over from Van den Bergh.

The appointment of Barnard, a young academic in his early thirties at the University of the Orange Free State, came as a shock to the hardened intelligence community and everyone else. With PW being the former Minister of Defence, the intelligence community was expecting Botha to favour the military.

It soon became evident that the NIS would play a major role in Botha's decision making in future. By choosing Barnard, a non-career intelligence officer, PW knew he had someone independent of the power struggles within the intelligence community on whose loyalty he could rely.

PW's autocratic style of government soon became evident. He certainly had no intention of being bound by cabinet decisions only. He preferred a cabal or inner circle of ministers advised by the security services through the organs of the State Security Council and the Security Management System. He preferred to surround himself with government officials like Barnard, the Chiefs of the SADF and the Army and the Commissioner of Police, rather than the politicians of his own party.

In the years that followed, this aspect of Botha's leadership would create huge divides within the structures of the National Party and the cabinet.

Because of Barnard's influence, the Service's recruitment sources moved more towards university campuses and away from the South African Police, which had been the preferred area of recruitment in Van den Bergh's days. Until then the Service had a culture and mentality that made it almost an extension of the SAP's Security Branch.

The remuneration packages and privileges for officers of the new National Intelligence Service far surpassed those of the police. Field officers were issued with cars which automatically became their property after a certain period of time. They would then be issued with a new 'company' vehicle.

This sort of thing contributed towards the jealousy, strife and competition that came to exist between members of the two services. The security policeman resented the former because they felt they often did more dangerous and dirty work than their NIS cousins.

By the time I joined, a university degree or college diploma was a pre-requisite for admission into the Service.

Through a policy created by the vision of Barnard and his leadership, the Service moved away from the often ruthless, brutal and ham-fisted image that BOSS had portrayed. Barnard believed in stealth, diplomacy, outwitting and out-thinking the enemy. He placed a high premium on intelligence analysts within the service and on the value of validated information. It therefore became inevitable that a more refined culture would set in. Brutality, womanising and excessive drinking were frowned on by senior management. Repeated abuses of this nature could and did lead to the termination of a member's security clearance — which effectively meant the end of his career.

A full-time social worker and a Dutch Reformed Church minister were appointed to the Service's permanent staff.

Under Niel Barnard's leadership, the Service strove to become a professional first world intelligence service, not the typical secret police-type organisation that was common in Africa and Eastern Europe.

Considerable emphasis was placed on the training and psychological evaluation of members. The establishment and development of the National Intelligence Service's Academy on The Farm became living proof of Barnard's philosophy. Intelligence training there was provided not only to members of the NIS, but also to personnel in the intelligence services of the independent homelands of Venda, Ciskei, Transkei and Bophuthatswana. In many instances, training material was provided in liaison with intelligence services elsewhere on the continent.

In his speech at the function I attended, President Botha thanked the Service and its members for their product, loyalty, commitment and sacrifice during the past year. He stressed that the New Year would require more commitment and greater innovation than ever before.

With formalities concluded, the higher echelons of the service's command structure left the hall. It was time to play— time to let your hair down — something I would hear on many occasions in the future.

*   *   *

Mariana found me lost in thought and staring at the sea below.

'Come on, Riaan. Have a drink — we're going to land soon.'

'I'm sorry, I'm just unsure about my future. There's a lot on my mind.'

'You know, you are made for these islands and you're such a good diving instructor. You'll never be satisfied, so leave South Africa, settle on the islands and then you'll be happy.'

'I can't Mariana. I haven't completed my studies. I can't just give it up. My family is badgering me to stop travelling and grow up. They think I'm a professional beach bum.'

The plane was on finals approaching Mahé airport. The sea was magic — flat, smooth, and eternal. As we disembarked, I could smell the tropics, the plants, the salt of the sea and the humidity. As always, it was the real thing for me.

Everyone was energetic, vibrant and loud. The group was in abundant high spirits. The island's ambience had already touched their souls.

Outside the terminal building I caught sight of Jacques and Jacky.

'*Comment Sava*, Riaan.'

'*Sava bien*, Jacques.'

I embraced them both. I had met them on the islands three months earlier when I had brought another group of South Africans. I called the party together.

'Listen, folks, these are my friends Jacques La Vigne and Jacky Hunt. They will be spending a lot of time with us and Jacques will be taking us diving from his boat every day. The hotel is expecting us. Decide amongst yourselves with whom you want to share a room. The bus is outside. I'll meet you at the hotel.'

I took Jacky by the hand in a friendly gesture and headed for her vehicle. I immediately sensed a disproving reaction from the rest of the group, especially the girls. Although undoubtedly beautiful, in South Africa Jacky would have been classified as 'coloured'. Back home, just holding her hand in public might well have been deemed a transgression of the Immorality Act. This ridiculous legislation of the apartheid era outlawed any kind of sexual flirtation or intimate friendships between whites and non-whites, no matter how innocent. Jacky was the daughter of an English father and a Creole mother. Her father was not short of money and his house had been rented out to the Soviet embassy.

I smiled to myself. Thank God Seychelles was not Pretoria.

I was a typical Afrikaner male, conceived by a teacher mother who had been fertilised by a policeman father. All the right sentiments had been slotted into my mind at an early age. God, country, education, authority and the big brass-balls of a macho-manhood. The Afrikaners as a nation, including myself, believed they had been chosen by God to uphold their teachings and values amidst the barbarism of the African continent. Included in this God-given mission was the duty to protect the National Party government from the total onslaught of communism spearheaded by the ANC. The Afrikaners never harboured a doubt that they would win the war against the godless liberation movements. South Africans, we knew, could never lose. They would always fight and survive. God and our own strengths and abilities inherited from our Voortrekker forefathers would ensure that.

This philosophy had been the backbone of my traditional upbringing. But in small ways I had already begun to rebel against the creed that had been drilled into me. As I matured, I found it difficult to accept the unappetising, dogmatic conservatism of dos and don'ts that Afrikaner group identity found it necessary to comply with, in order to feel secure.

My attitudes had begun to change after my first visit to the islands. Through my exposure to the Seychellois people and their way of life over the past year, I had started to become more cosmopolitan and inquisitive. My style of living was being subtly shaped in this paradise and a quality was beginning to emerge that would one day become my trademark in the espionage game.

For the second time that year I shared room 39 at the Reef Hotel with Allan. The porter was stowing the diving equipment in the hotel's storeroom, which allowed time for the new arrivals to freshen up for dinner.

Feeling refreshed after showering and some generous tots of scotch, we rejoined the others downstairs in the open-air restaurant by the pool. After dinner there was dancing, talking and a lot more alcohol. The long flight had tired everyone out. By midnight almost everyone had retired to bed after making arrangements to meet for breakfast at 07:00 the next morning.

Jacques had been surreptitiously signalling me and when the others had gone we went to the pool, ostensibly for a swim to escape the heat. I could see that something was bothering him. He was not only my contact on the island, but he had also become my friend and mentor and had done much to minimise the conservative Afrikaner influence on my life. Jacques epitomised the islanders — no inhibitions or restrictions. Although only a fisherman with little formal education — a man who had never left the islands — he had nevertheless subtly begun to shape my thoughts about life and self.

'What's on your mind, Jacques?'

'Riaan, it's a year now since you first came here. Our hopes rise every time we hear that you are returning. There is so much tension and frustration. We desperately want to get rid of René — he's fucking up paradise!'

The Seychelles had received its independence from Britain in 1976.

In 1977, while President James Mancham was attending the Commonwealth Prime Ministers' Conference in London, his own prime minister, Albert René, had staged a coup and had taken control of the country with the help of Tanzanian troops.

His stringent 'African Marxist' philosophy and the deterioration of the local economy had led to an estimated 10 000 islanders fleeing the country. By the 1980s unemployment and poverty had increased dramatically. People lived in fear as the slightest criticism of the René regime could lead to arrest and imprisonment.

I shared his sentiments but said nothing.

'Is your group up to something that I should know about?' Jacques demanded. 'It has been said in resistance circles that we can expect help from South Africa. Is this true? Is that why you are here?'

26

I had never admitted a connection with National Intelligence, or with the South African government. Why these sudden probing questions? I was about to answer when the picture came together in my mind. How could I have been so stupid? My first meeting with Jacques eight months before must have been pre-arranged. Nico had liaised with Ian Hunter of Holiday Hunter — a tour operator in Johannesburg. He had obviously contacted Masons Travel in the Seychelles which had introduced Jacques as a dive operator and my guide. While I had known that Nico was in National Intelligence, it had not occurred to me that everyone right down the line to Jacques was also involved.

Jacques, it seemed, knew more about what was going on than I did. He had been briefed to assist me, but had not been told who or what I was. That is why, on my first visit, he had taken me all over the island and had complied with my every request. He had exposed me to knowledgeable people, divulged inside information on personalities, loyalties and subtle undercurrents on the island. He had helped me to take photographs of America's NASA (National Aeronautics and Space Administration) satellite tracking station, the airport, the water reservoir, the radio station, military bases, the harbour and even President René's residence. It embarrasses me to remember that in my naivety I had assumed Jacques was only a helpful tourist guide who was merely assisting an inquisitive tourist.

That explained the questions. Jacques needed answers that I couldn't give because I knew as little as he did. I had been briefed that the gathering of intelligence, the taking of photographs and so on were routine and required simply to build up records on a country hostile to South Africa. I suddenly realised that I had been used to gather tactical information for military purposes. The reports that I had unwittingly compiled and the photographs I had taken and submitted to Nico — all with Jacques' help — would probably be used in an attempt to overthrow René's government. It was time for me to be straightforward with my friend.

'Jacques, the truth is that I am here to gather more information about the islands. The people I have brought with me are genuine tourists. They are here on holiday and know absolutely nothing about my real purpose. Apart from that I can truthfully say that I know nothing. Maybe there is going to be a coup attempt, maybe not. I really don't know.'

'I believe you', Jacques said doubtfully, his voice lacking conviction. 'I must tell you that the uncertainty of waiting for South Africa to make a move is killing me.'

He left me at the pool, my thoughts in turmoil.

You bastards, why didn't you tell me you were planning a coup? I thought to myself, suddenly realising how vulnerable I was.

*   *   *

My involvement with National Intelligence Service had been initiated by Nico on the night of the dinner party at The Farm a year before. It had been finalised a few days after that.

It was a Wednesday evening when I pitched up at Nico's house in response to a dinner invitation. Nico excused us from his wife Hester and his daughter and led me to his private bar. He switched on some classical music and turned up the volume, giving me the impression that he had no wish to be overheard by anyone, including his family.

Previously while making small talk at The Farm, I had mentioned to Nico that I had been taking diving parties to Mauritius to earn extra money. He had asked if I had ever thought about taking such parties to the Seychelles. When I asked why he wanted to know, he said that the National Intelligence Service was engaged in routinely collecting low grade intelligence on the islands to build up the Service's information bank. He stressed that it involved no danger and that being a non-member of the organisation minimised the risk. After all, what difference would it make if I took divers to the Seychelles instead to Mauritius? National Intelligence could also assist me with expenses, he added as an aside.

I was not particularly keen to switch to a place that I was unfamiliar with. Besides, I liked Mauritius.

'Think about it', he said.

I was being mind-fucked and I didn't realise it.

As the days passed I began to regret that I had turned Nico down. I should have accepted his offer. Opportunity rarely knocks twice.

Then came the invitation to dine at Nico's house. I realised immediately what it was all about and I accepted casually but with alacrity. The romantic notions of espionage had proved too great a temptation. I could dive and also get expenses. Besides that, I had read up on the Seychelles since the offer and the diving there was supposed to be great.

'So what did you decide?'

'Why not. Yes, I'll switch to the Seychelles.'

It was a 'yes' that would change my life. It would be my first step into the labyrinth of espionage. Without realising it, my introduction into a career with the National Intelligence Service had begun. From then on everything would be different. My seduction into the spying game would go slowly at first, but after that the virginity of my mind would be lost in a rush.

'Will you be able to take your first tour in March or April?'

'I'm sure that will be fine.'

'Okay then, get your group together and let me know when you're ready. After that you can phone Ian Hunter, he's the owner of Holiday Hunter, a travel agency in Johannesburg, and he'll make all the arrangements. I've already spoken to him and he's expecting a call. Keep me up to date with what is going on and give me a call if you need anything.'

The music had begun to play and I was following the conductor. It would be my first performance in the dark with the orchestra.

'One important thing, Riaan. Our relationship is between you and me and must remain completely confidential. What we discuss stays between us. For the record, you don't even know me. No one must know of your involvement with National Intelligence, whether they are your friends, your parents or even members of the Service whom you might know— like Tersia for instance. Our friendship and any future contract that enables you to continue in the Service, will depend on your ability to keep your mouth shut.'

'Our government has numerous enemies both inside and outside the country,' he continued. 'You hardly need me to tell you that we are fighting a war in South West Africa and Angola. It's our job to gather information and secrets about the enemy so that we can beat them. One of our tasks is to infiltrate perceived anti-government bodies, organisations and institutions to facilitate the control of our enemies. Surely you don't want the kaffirs, the communists and the liberals to take over this country, do you?'

'No, I don't.'

'That's why we gather information required by the decision makers. Look on yourself as a journalist. The only difference is that you'll be writing stories for only one client — the Service — and not for the public at large. The information you gather will belong to the Service and we have to protect the substance and detail of such information with the greatest secrecy. The Service falls directly under the office of the State President. We work directly for the great man himself — that's why he was at our function the other evening. A breach of secrecy might embarrass or compromise him. We don't want that to happen, do we?'

'Certainly not', I said with conviction. 'What do you want me to do?'

'I need a story about the Seychelles and its people, supplemented with photographs. I'll provide you with a more detailed briefing before you leave. You'll be paid R1 000 for the story. That's far more than the average newspaper reporter earns. Make it a success. This is a privilege. Remember that very few people get an offer like this.'

My private domain had been created and its boundaries drawn. It was something I would have to protect with secrecy, stealth, evasion and half-truths. In future years lies, secrecy and denial would come more naturally to me. I would learn that this is an agent's first line of defence and the reflex response to any question. It buys time to enable one to evaluate and formulate the right response.

When I left Nico's house I felt a changed man. A barrier had been effectively erected between myself and my friends and family. It was a barrier that would prevent me from discussing the many questions raised, the opportunities that might present themselves and the direction that my life was taking. I was on my own.

In the weeks that followed I took countless photographs of government buildings, police stations, military installations and even the NIS headquarters in Pretoria, perfecting my skills and my ability to remain undetected. I wrote reports conveying useless information, learning to incorporate the who, what, when, where, how and why. I submitted everything to Nico for his scrutiny and comment. I never went to his house again and our meetings were always at different places and at different times. We used public places like coffee shops, restaurants and bars.

I was undergoing a crash course in intelligence tradecraft.

In March 1981 I had led the first group of holidaymakers to the Seychelles. The tour was packaged by Holiday Hunter. Mason's Travel, Hunter's contact in the Seychelles, arranged a boat and for us to stay at the Reef Hotel. They introduced me to Jacques Lavigne who would be my general guide and dive master.

The absolute beauty of the Seychelles astounded me. The islands showed no signs of volcanic rock and they abounded in dense natural vegetation. The calm transparent waters and the diversity of sea life made for magnificent diving.

I completed my assignment for Nico while enjoying the holiday of a lifetime.

On my return to South Africa I compiled a written report about the island, its infrastructure and influential personalities. I met Nico at a coffee shop close to the University of Pretoria on the Monday following my return. My report and two spools of film went into Nico's ostrich leather satchel. This and the meetings that followed were always short and to the point.

Nico slid a white envelope and a folded sheet of paper across the table.

'Here's R1 000. It's a one-off payment for the trip and your report. You've done a good job.'

```
ATTN IAN

RE LABUSCHAGNA DIVING GROUP

PLS DISREGARD COSTING FOR BOAT AS WE FIND IT RATHER EXPENSIVE STP
HAVE MADE ALTERNATE ARRANGEMENTS WITH MR FLAAM FROM SOUTHWIND
WHO WILL MEET WITH YOUR GROUP ON SUNDAY 28MAR AT 10-.,-.-.AM
TO DISCUSS STP PLS NOTE ALL EQUIPMENT CAN BE SUPPLIED LOCALLY STP

BEST REGARDS
DOREEN MASON

2230 MASONS SKKKKC
3-7751 SA
E
```

Telex from Mason's Travel re the booking for the yacht *Southwind*.

I pocketed the money, feeling proud of my achievement and glad for the remuneration.

'Thanks for the money', I said and unfolded the sheet of paper.

'What's this?'

'It's a receipt. Just fill it in and sign at the bottom.'

Seeing it as merely a part of the procedure, I complied and handed it back to him.

*   *   *

With my feet dangling in the pool of the Reef Hotel I stared up at the clear Seychelles sky and accepted my current situation. I was acting on behalf of an intelligence organisation against a foreign sovereign state. My recruitment was complete. I had received money for services rendered and acknowledged it by signing a receipt.

Years later I would use the same strategy when recruiting agents from other intelligence services. The first step was to bond with the target and get him to provide you with any written information of significance that he might have. Then one would compromise him by paying him, arrange for the transaction to be photographed and casually request him to sign for the money. Such evidence would often prove useful later.

It was only then that I began to realise that my innocent reports on the

Seychelles and its people were more important than I had thought.

* * *

At 07:00 the next morning everybody started to drift into the breakfast area where a spread of fruits, cheese and bread was laid out.

'When you've finished breakfast meet me in the parking lot.'

Jacques was already loading diving kit into a Mini-Moke which he'd rented for me for the duration of my stay. Jacky led the rest of the group to the bus stop across the road from the hotel. We had to travel to the other side of the island to get to Jacques' boat which was anchored at Beau Vallon Bay.

A green medium-sized bus with some locals aboard pulled up at the stop.

'Are we going in this? It's a kaffir bus,' one of the girls whispered.

Frank, who had accompanied me on a previous trip, laughed.

'Welcome to paradise, baby. You can walk if you like, but this is the only transport you are going to get.'

In South Africa where apartheid ruled, there were separate public transport systems for blacks and for whites, but the majority of whites never used public transport anyway. Riding on multi-racial public transport was the last thing they expected. The learning curve was steep, but I knew from experience that the island and its people would begin to engrave new values about life and people onto their minds.

With a typical no-hurry island attitude, the rest of the passengers happily accepted the delay in getting this rowdy bunch and their equipment on board. Jacques, Serge, Mariana and I followed in the red Mini-Moke cabriolet.

My South Africans gathered on the beach at Beau Vallon Bay. They were amazed at its beauty. Fine pure white sand stretched away in both directions and one could hear the whisper of small waves as they floated across the sand. Two Seychellois girls and a guy walked up to me, hugged and kissed me French-style on both cheeks. Jacques had told them of my arrival in the Seychelles and they had been waiting since early morning.

I introduced them to the group as Placid Andre, Nadia and Jacky's sister Jane.

* * *

A year later, after the coup attempt, Jane married a Tanzanian army officer seconded to René's government so she could distance herself from her anti-government activities in the past. Many years later when I was serving in Natal and she was visiting her family in Durban, I tried to recruit her. She feared her husband so much, however, that she not only declined but also skipped the country the next day.

*   *   *

The days passed idyllically.

Jacques, Placid Andre, Nadia and Jane loaded the diving equipment, crates of beer and picnic stuff onto two boats — one for the divers and one for the others. It was already 30° Celsius with a humidity of 92%.

The absence of breaking surf made it easy for everyone to board the two ski boats. The powerful engines sliced through the transparent blue water towards Intendance Beach or *Anse Kaple* — translated directly as 'sex beach'. The rest of the party raced on as the divers and I anchored about two kilometres offshore for the first dive. Jacques chose a reef about 18 metres down. I buddied up with Mariana, Gerhard was with Barbara, and Serge with Allan.

'Okay, guys. Go in pairs — see you at the bottom. You can stay down to the limit of your tanks.'

We fell backwards into the transparent blue, descending weightless through crystal silence. I reached the bottom with Mariana at arm's length to my left, skimming the bottom in awe and admiring the exotic sea and fish life.

I bagged some crayfish and when we broke surface the others were already having their first beer. A bonita of about six kilograms lay wriggling in the bottom of the boat. Allan had a magic touch with the spear gun.

A braai fire was already burning on the beach. Placid was marinating an octopus in coconut milk to prepare it for a curry dish.

Most of the group stayed together. The spontaneity and uninhibited focus on pleasure and fulfilment by the locals was a culture shock for these conservative South Africans. As the tour leader I was the bridge between them and the locals.

The unashamed sensuality of the topless local girls was an issue for both the female and male South Africans. The men finding themselves surrounded by bare-breasted women, thought, of course, that they were in paradise. The women disapproved, but it was clear that they were well aware of the attitude of the men. As an onlooker I could not help thinking that they were also tempted to remove their tops so as to compete with the island girls. But they didn't do it having grown with the belief that stripping off was an unchristian thing to do.

About an hour before sunset, while the others were loading the boats, Jacques called me over.

'Riaan, something is going to happen. We need to talk about it. Come to the Katiolo Restaurant later this afternoon. Don't tell anyone where you're going. You can bring Allan if you trust him because you might need him. Otherwise come alone.'

*   *   *

I decided not to invite Allan and just made an excuse to get away. Jacques' mood and his assumption that I was a full-blown intelligence operator directly involved in their struggle to get rid of René concerned me. I had a feeling of dread that something was about to happen over which I would have no control. I needed advice and needed it in a hurry, but contacting Nico was out of the question. Seychelles intelligence might well be eavesdropping on all telephone calls to South Africa. I just had to fly by the seat of my pants.

The Katiolo restaurant, on the beach halfway between the airport and the Reef Hotel, was a well-known watering hole used by the locals. It was a semi-circular building with a palm-thatched roof. Local Seychellois music was playing. An old-fashioned roof fan was circulating the humid air.

Jacques and Placid were standing with their backs to the entrance and looking out to sea. Jacky was talking to people at the bar. Everyone seemed to know everyone else and there were no tourists.

There was a seriousness about Jacques that was out of character. On my first trip the year before when one of his boats had been washed onto the beach during a storm his only reaction was: 'No problem.' Now there was an agitated edge to him and he was speaking from the soul.

'Riaan, we trust you and regard you as one of us.' He took a deep breath. 'We are going to overthrow René by force. If the coup attempt fails and something unpleasant happens to us, you will be our only link with the outside world. None of our people, even if they escape arrest, will be able to get out of the country or make free contact with the outside world. If that happens, get the full story out to your government and to Gerard Hoarau in Durban. Hoarau is leading the move to reinstate the previous government. If things go wrong, we will need help from the outside world. Don't speak to anybody else on the islands, not even to those Seychellois whom you know. You cannot trust anyone. If for any reason you lose contact with Jacky or me, come to this restaurant and ask for the owner, Tom, or his wife Amelie. They will give you the contact details for Gerard. Just be careful. These are strange times and the islands are small.'

'Fuck, Jacques, how and when? Where are you going to get weapons? You're a fisherman and a bloody gigolo. You're not a fighting man. You can't do it.'

'I can't give you any details. It's better you don't know in case things go wrong,' Jacques responded.

'Jacques', I said, 'I've never signed up with your bloody resistance. I've got nothing to do with this shit. What you are planning is for trained soldiers and people who know what they are doing. You'll end up getting all of us arrested or even killed.'

'You are part of it and it seems you didn't even know!'

I was stunned. His words confirmed that Nico, National Intelligence, Holiday Hunter, Jacques and some Seychelles were all linked to a pending coup. I had already provided information and photographs to Nico. It obviously formed part of the overall planning to overthrow Rene's government. I had suspected it but having it spelt out to my face was another thing altogether.

This was more than I had bargained for. The intrigue of being on an island holiday, taking photographs, writing reports and playing at being a spy was one thing. But suddenly realising that there were consequences involving personal danger made a huge difference.

'Okay, Jacques', I said regaining my composure, 'just remember that if there is a fuck-up, there is only one way off this island and that's by an aircraft. You'll never make it in your boat.'

Breaking the tension I said jokingly: 'If the coup is a success you can appoint me as the Seychelles' Minister of Sport and Recreation.'

I realised that there was nothing I could do to change the situation and the last thing I needed was to alienate Jacques.

Suddenly the unthinkable happened. There were sporadic bursts of automatic rifle fire. It took a few stunned seconds before there was a universal recognition of the unfamiliar sounds. The firing stopped for a few seconds and then started again. The music had stopped and everybody stood frozen.

All hell broke loose as the patrons stampeded for the doors en masse. Jacques was by my side within seconds.

'Riaan, take Jacky and go to your hotel. Don't leave there and keep your group together. Don't leave the hotel until you've heard from me.'

'What the fuck is happening, Jacques?'

'There's fighting at the airport. We are taking the country. Now get out of here!'

The customers began to disperse. Those who had to travel in the direction of the airport where the firing was coming from hung around in the car park in groups, too scared to leave.

I grabbed Jacky and bundled her into the front passenger seat of my Mini-Moke. I followed Jacques' instructions and pushed the Moke to its limit in a dash back to the hotel. News about what was happening had beaten us to our destination. People were huddled in groups discussing the latest developments and how the coup could impact on their personal circumstances.

The hotel staff were attempting to calm people and allay their fears, urging them not to leave the hotel grounds. There was nothing anyone could do and, in fact, no one really knew what was happening, except that there was fighting going on at the airport. While the locals obviously had no details, they certainly were aware of the significance of the events.

Jacky and I joined my group who were gathered around the pool bar.

'There is nothing we can do now', Allan was saying. 'We have no idea what is happening, but we are safe here at the hotel. We're tourists we didn't do anything. This is not our fight or our country, so let's do what we came here to do. Everyone get a drink and let's sit by the pool. I'm not going to spoil my holiday for nothing.'

He ordered a double scotch, walked over to a table at the pool and sat down.

I could hear the almost continuous crackle of rifle fire and explosions penetrating the night. Some of our girls were close to tears. Not only were they strangers, but their immediate environment was pregnant with hostility. But Allan's act of bravado had paid off and everyone, including Jacky and myself, joined him at the table by the pool.

Mariana voiced what was on everyone's mind.

'Riaan, how are we going to get off the island? Aggro towards whites is bound to develop over this and being South Africans will probably put us at serious risk. You know as well as I do that this is a communist government and anti-South African.'

Mariana was a former lieutenant in the South African Navy.

'First and foremost let's stay calm and stick to one plan', I said. 'I'm also pretty scared, but we don't know what's happening. Let's wait until morning when we'll probably get the facts. Whatever happens, just remember that we are not involved.'

We cannot just get off the island either. There's only a flight to South Africa every fortnight. There are still quite a few days left before we go. We'll have our dinner together and stay together afterwards. There is no reason why we shouldn't all crash in one or two rooms.'

Stephanie was still upset.

'I'm going to phone my father.'

She had to be stopped. A wrong phone call to South Africa under the present circumstances could well endanger us all.

'No, you're not. You don't even know what's going on. The last thing we must do is attract unnecessary attention. Wait until we know, okay? Now let's go to my room.'

After dinner Jacky walked to my room holding Stephanie's hand to reassure her. Nevertheless it was quite obvious that she was still on the verge of panic.

I wondered what had happened to Jacques and Placid. It was clear that the coup had not been quite the pushover expected because there was no lull in the firing.

With everyone in room 39 it was so crowded that Allan and I had to stand on the balcony. We heard what seemed like a large jet coming in to land at Mahé.

What timing that they should fly into this, I thought.

With 12 days left before the next flight out I decided it would be best to get the group off Mahé for a couple of days. This would get us out of circulation and break the tension that was evident in everybody. I got the most sensible of them — Serge and Mariana, together with Jacky — to join us on the balcony and discussed it with them.

I suggested I arrange for us to sail to some of the outer islands, like Praslin and La Digue, for a few days until things settled down on Mahé.

There was unanimous agreement.

Serge was the first to notice the silence.

'There's been no shooting for the last three quarters of an hour or so. Do you think it's over?'

We decided to go ahead with our plans, agreeing that whoever had come out on top, as South Africans we would be better off out of the way. Jacky said she would arrange a yacht.

She took the phone and cryptically finalised arrangements with a close friend, Robert Flaam. He agreed to charter her a 12-metre long double-hulled catamaran that sailed under the French tricolour. I had used it during my earlier visit in March.

While Jacky was talking, we heard the screaming jet engines of a large aircraft taking off over in the direction of the airport.

It gave us purpose.

'Okay, guys', I said, addressing the group, 'tomorrow we're going on a four-day cruise to see the islands. We'll stay on the yacht and basically all you need is a costume and a T-shirt. Food and booze will be supplied. The boat might not have enough bunks for all of us, but the nights are warm and there is no reason why some of us cannot sleep on deck. We'll leave very early — the idea is to be at the harbour at sunrise. I'll arrange some extra Mini-Mokes and get the hotel to make us sandwiches for breakfast. We must get some sleep and as I said before, we should all sleep in a couple of rooms — maybe just in this one.'

Everyone agreed to stay together and sleep in my room. They were all preoccupied with the day's happenings and settled down to find a corner to sleep in. There seemed to be people everywhere trying to sleep, seeking comfort in numbers and the support of each other's presence. I couldn't sleep. I was too much aware of what had happened and the possible consequences. Had the coup been successful or not? My mind was full of questions.

It was still dark when I got up, stepped over the sleeping bodies and left the room. I collected the sandwiches from the kitchen, then checked on the Mini-Mokes that the rental company had left in the parking lot the previous night.

Before leaving I scribbled a message on hotel stationery for Jacques and left it at the reception desk.

'We're on Robert's yacht, see you in a couple of days.'

Allan had got to the parking lot before me and the rest came drifting down from the room soon afterwards. They had either been awake already, or had been awakened when either Allan or I had stepped over them. They stood around the vehicles, red-eyed from lack of sleep.

Serge busied himself organising the transport arrangements.

'Let's move guys. We don't want to miss the boat.'

The small convoy of red Mini-Mokes started up and headed towards the hotel's gate. A truck loaded with heavily armed soldiers drove in and passed us as we left.

My heart skipped a beat. It was going to be a nerve-wracking time before we got off the islands.

I realised Jacques might be looking for me, but I had to get the group out of the mainstream of events in Mahé for a few days until things cooled down. Robert's yacht, *Southwind*, provided the perfect hideaway.

Making use of the pre-dawn light while en route to the harbour, I managed to photograph the bullet-ridden front entrance of the military base. I also filmed the effects of the fighting that had taken place at the airport terminal building as well as a Royal Swazi National Airways

60-seater F28 Fokker Friendship aircraft with a huge whole blown right through its cockpit area.

The rising sun peeked over the horizon as the *Southwind* cleared the harbour entrance under power. She left behind at their berths two small unmanned Seychellois naval vessels.

Pedritto, the cook, served chilled Seybrew beer the moment the sails had been hoisted and the motors cut. The song 'The beer I had for breakfast was not bad', came to mind. It certainly helped to take the edge off shattered nerves. I sat on the bow deck, legs stretched out in front of me looking beyond the stern at the foamy wake created by the yacht's passage. I could see the white satellite dishes of the US tracking station on the hillside behind Victoria.

There had certainly been a coup attempt. Whether there had been outside — specifically South African help — it was impossible to say. Obviously, though, it had been a fuck-up. I faced the problem of being on the communist-ruled islands with a group of South Africans after a possible South African-backed coup attempt.

I felt sure that my photographs and reports had been used for reconnaissance and planning. If any of those involved in the coup attempt had been captured and mentioned me — especially in the light of my links with the resistance — then I was in grave danger and by association so were the lives of the other South Africans in the group.

On top of that many locals, including the Seychelles government, were aware that I made regular visits with South African tour groups.

For four days we sailed aimlessly through the island group, lazing in the sun, scuba diving twice a day, drinking bottles of Seybrew and feasting on seafood. At night we anchored close to shore and most of us slept on deck. We were cut off from political developments on Mahé because nothing came over the radio about it.

We anchored off La Digue Island on the last night before we returned to Mahé.

'Riaan, what's going to happen tomorrow?' Mariana asked, venting the question on everyone's minds

Robert answered with typical French savoir-faire.

'No problem, *cheri*, we're flying the French flag. My boat is like French soil. If you're worried just come to me on the *Southwind* and I'll take care of you.'

Smooth words in a smooth accent. But I knew it was not true — not here and not under these circumstances. I just hoped the Seychelles Security Forces did not conjure up a reason to suspect us of involvement. I knew that nothing would stop them from acting against the despised white South Africans and definitely not a French flag on a yacht in their own territorial waters.

'We'll be back in Mahé by midday tomorrow,' I said. 'For the record we'll pretend to be ignorant of anything that happened, having just returned from a four-day cruise. Once back, I think we should spend most of the time at the hotel behaving like tourists until we are sure everything is back to normal.'

The next morning I conferred alone with Jacky.

'I'm going to stick to the group at the hotel. I think you should try to make contact with Jacques and then meet me back at the hotel and you should sleep there with us tonight.'

Jacky nodded her agreement.

'I think the coup failed,' I continued. 'I'm sure that if it had been successful Jacques would have contacted Robert via the yacht's radio. If it failed and he has not been arrested, he'd be afraid to use the radio in case his transmission was picked up by the military. If the coup was unsuccessful we can be sure that the government will be conducting a witch-hunt. I've no idea where I'll find Jacques, but someone will know where he is. Don't worry, I'll find out and let you know.'

Allan and Serge came to me on the afterdeck.

'Riaan', Serge said, 'both Allan and I've done our military service. We have experience with the SADF in the Angolan Bush War which makes our situation here precarious. There's obviously been a failed coup and they are going to look for culprits. We probably fit the profile they are looking for. Especially you. You've been here a lot and people who you know, like Jacques, are obviously anti-government. And we are South Africans and you know what that means.

'If the shit really hits the fan and we have to get off the island,' he added, 'there is only one way and that's this boat. We have already spoken to Robert and he's willing to give it a try. You probably don't know it but he was a legionnaire and he hates the communists. He says he's willing to smuggle us out of Seychelles territorial waters. After that we can sail to the Comores where there's a French Foreign Legion base.'

I was unhappy, not about Serge's suggestion but because the reality of the situation had finally been forced on me. I had to face what I had been trying to avoid. We had to make emergency arrangements in case the situation soured.

'What do we tell the others?' Serge asked.

'Nothing', I decided. 'We are not going to tell them anything. If we do, it will create a panic that might be difficult to control. Keep the idea amongst the three of us. If a dangerous situation develops we'll go ahead as you suggest — provided there's no other choice — but we'll only tell the others at the last minute. Just keep things natural and do everything you can to avoid panic. Meanwhile, Allan, you've been in the Navy, so work out details with Robert in case we have to make use of his offer.'

At 10:00 the *Southwind* was under full sail and heading for Mahé. Pedritto, the cook by night and the lookout by day, called a warning.

'Boat approaching. It's about two kilometres off our starboard bow.'

Robert focussed his binoculars on the vessel, which was coming at speed.

'It's a military gunboat', he announced.

For the moment there was a stunned silence.

Jacky was the first to react. Her yellow bikini top fell to the deck to reveal her small honey-coloured breasts.

'Come on girls, it's the fucking army, tops off. Show them what you've got. It will keep their minds busy.'

Fear and the sense of survival outweighed modesty. Mariana immediately followed Jacky's example, then the others did. A yacht flying the French flag with topless girls on deck in skimpy bikinis completed our disguise.

I retrieved three films from my camera case in the wheelhouse and handed them to Mariana.

' Just drop the films overboard if there's any trouble.'

Allan raised the music level and broke out fresh beers for everybody.

The gunboat was small. A single-barrelled 12,7mm machine gun was mounted on its starboard side. It passed the *Southwind*, circled and signalled Robert that he should heave to. The mainsail was hauled in and the gunboat came alongside. Two men armed with AK47s and wearing Tanzanian Army uniforms boarded the yacht. Their eyes darted continually towards the women.

Serge, Robert and Jacky, the only French speakers, stood strategically at the wheel. The others on the foredeck ignored the soldiers and spoke to each other in English. They carefully avoided using Afrikaans.

Jacky spoke to the gunboat's skipper in Creole. He was obviously a Seychellois. The Tanzanians' French was so poor it verged on non-existent and having noticed the French flag they seemed unsure of themselves. I deliberately turned away from the boarders afraid that something in my eyes might give me away. I could feel sweat pouring down my back.

Robert provided them with a brief outline of the yacht's movements in the past few days and told them we were on our way back to Mahé. They conducted a cursory search below deck which, of course, produced nothing. Finally, satisfied that Robert had not encountered any other vessels recently they terminated their interrogation and climbed back aboard the gunboat.

'*Merci — au revoir, Capitan.*'

They pulled away with arrogant flair, waving to the girls.

Everybody was visibly shaken. It accentuated our vulnerability to a hostile situation in a country that we were stuck in. Robert broke the spell of the unwelcome hostile visit.

'Set sail for Mahé. We're going home.'

The *Southwind* entered Mahé harbour with sails stowed and under power. A strong military presence was evident and armed soldiers were checking the departure and arrival of all vessels. They were even checking the locals going aboard the government ferry to other islands.

I got off first and waited on the quay as the others nervously walked down the gangplank and towards the Mini-Mokes parked nearby.

'Thanks, it was great', I said, giving Robert a casual wave.

Allan and Serge remained behind to finalise any possible contingency plans with Robert.

Jacky chatted briefly to some locals, then went back up the gangplank and spoke to Allan. A few minutes later she joined me in my Moke.

'What's wrong, Jacky?'

'The government has instituted a curfew from sunrise to sunset. They say the *Seychelles Movement de la Resistance* supported by South African soldiers tried to grab control of the island. The attempt failed after a shootout at the airport. The South Africans hijacked an airliner and fled the islands. The troops are searching for South African spies, members of the resistance and Seychellois with known anti-government sentiments. I warned Allan to be sure he gets back to the hotel before the curfew starts at sunset. Apparently some Seychellois and a few foreigners, probably South Africans, have been arrested and are in custody.'

It was a crazy situation. It felt as if they were looking for me. I knew I was guilty, but it didn't weigh on my conscience. After all they were the bad guys who deserved to be overthrown. Whatever the case, I realised that even innocents could be nailed in a hostile environment like this.

There would be no help from Nico or the National Intelligence Service if things went wrong. They would not even acknowledge my existence. I was part of the orchestra but I was playing solo. No one could help me. They must have known there was going to be an attempt to overthrow the government, but had just kept quiet and sent me headlong into the situation regardless.

When we walked into the hotel lobby, the receptionist called Jacky over. I continued to the pool bar area and joined some of the others at a table.

Gerhard and Barbara, both keen divers, were frustrated at the thought of being stuck at the hotel without being able to dive.

'Riaan, what now? What are we going to do with the rest of our holiday? Can we dive tomorrow?'

'I'm not sure yet. I'll ask the hotel management. There's a reef in front of the hotel that's about four metres down. Maybe we should just snorkel there. I don't think we should go into town at this stage.'

Jacky joined us at the table. While the rest continued talking in Afrikaans, Jacky handed me a hotel envelope.

'Here are your South African passports. Tell everyone to keep them on their persons — it's safer.'

I took the parcel from her and stuffed it into my camera bag.

'Okay, I'll hand them out tonight.'

'Come, let's go for a swim', she suggested.

She grabbed my hand and I followed her into the pool. Other guests were already splashing about. When we were waist-deep in the water, she put her arms around my neck and whispered in my ear. Anyone watching would have thought it was a romantic interlude.

'Two nights ago while we were on the yacht, government agents questioned the reception staff about you and your group. They demanded your passports which they had for safekeeping. Fortunately she's a friend of mine and she told them you hadn't handed them in when you arrived. She told them you had checked out for a four-day cruise.'

'What else did they say?'

'Nothing — they just left. Just keep your passports with you. They are probably running checks on names, passport numbers and faces.'

'What's happened to Jacques?'

'I've no idea. I'll try and find out and I will see you later.'

There was something of a party that night. The large number of people attending and the exclusiveness of the hotel grounds gave everyone a sense of security.

It was late, after 22:00, when Jacky reappeared.

'Jacky, how did you get here? What about the curfew?'

'Don't worry. I drove here on a moped without lights. I've located Jacques. He's hiding on a yacht anchored in the harbour, not at one of the berths. He's about 500 metres beyond Robert's boat. It's called *Madonna* and is flying the Australian flag.'

'What did he say?'

'I didn't even see or speak to him, but he left a message that you should come and see him. It may be the only opportunity you'll get. I'm sure it's really important both to him and to the Seychelles.'

'When should I go?'

'Tonight.'

'You must be crazy. If they catch us we'll have no excuses. They will just shoot us!'

'Riaan, maybe the islands and their people will be lost. René is well aware there's resistance to his rule amongst the Seychellois — particularly now after the coup attempt. He won't stop until he has stamped out and neutralised all signs of opposition. The outside world needs to be told the truth. You must help us.'

I crumbled before her plea.

'I'm not going alone,' I said reluctantly. 'I'll speak to Allan.'

I was concerned. Until then my involvement had been indirect. Now I was being asked to put myself at risk and deliberately break the law by ignoring the curfew and assisting an enemy of the state on the run. The penalty would be death if I was caught. This mission was not observing and gathering information — it was collaborating and actively participating in an attempt to overthrow René. My introduction to the tradecraft of spying under Nico's tutelage within the safety of my own country's borders suddenly seemed pathetically inadequate.

When I approached Allan for assistance, his reaction was simple and to the point.

'Let's do it. Fuck the commies, their curfews and their fucking laws. We don't fall under their laws. Whether we fight the commies in South Africa, Angola or here, it's still the same thing. We have a duty to help Jacques.'

Serge joined us.

'What's up, Riaan?'

'The local resistance movement attempted to overthrow the government', I explained. 'South African soldiers, probably mercenaries, were compromised in a shootout at the airport and the military base. They failed to gain control but managed to escape by hijacking an airliner. The government is hunting down perpetrators and collaborators.'

'Jacques is one of them and he's hiding on a yacht in the harbour. He wants to see me.'

I had no intention of telling them everything, particularly about my involvement with National Intelligence. But I needed their help and they were both keen to assist. Both had completed national service and were trained and experienced soldiers who had been involved in military action against FAPLA and SWAPO in the bush war in SWA/Namibia and Angola.

I explained our plans to Jacky and she agreed to stay with the group and cover for our absence.

We made our plans carefully, talking at the pool bar and not in one of the hotel rooms. Considering our status as suspects, they might have bugged the rooms. We set our time of departure for 01:00. The party would be over by then and most of the guests would be sleeping. Hopefully too, so would the guards at the military base and at the airport which were both en route to the harbour. There was a full moon and it was almost like daylight, which was bad news but we could do nothing about that.

It was past 01:00 when we reached the clump of palm trees that overlooked the hotel parking area. Allan selected a Mini-Moke that was parked near the exit and ran towards it. Serge and I headed for the bush area next to the road that we were taking.

We had decided not to use my Moke, but to steal someone else's. Then, if we had to abandon the vehicle for some or other reason, it would be impossible to trace it back to us. While we waited for Allan to appear in the stolen vehicle, it occurred to me that by stealing a vehicle, I had crossed the legal line for the first time. Our actions might well implicate an innocent too. If the Moke was later linked to any criminal action against the state, it might well cost the person who had hired it his freedom.

I would not be so innocent in years to come. I would learn that the rules by which ordinary people live do not apply when one's survival or the success of a mission is at stake. Breaking the rules, endangering one's own life and the lives of others is justified. The mission must succeed, regardless of the consequences. One could beg, borrow or steal — methods were unimportant — only success counted. The only rule was to never get caught.

Allan appeared, driving slowly and without lights. We crept from the bushes and he stopped briefly while we boarded. Loose wires hung from the ignition where he had hot-wired the vehicle to start it. He drove on at a snail's pace, ready to turn into the roadside bush at the slightest sign of life.

We didn't talk. The island seemed deserted, with no lights and not a sign of life. We heard an occasional dog barking in the distance. Close to the military base Allan suddenly braked and killed the engine. He pointed towards a clump of trees about 100 metres to the right. We could see in the brilliant moonlight that three camouflaged figures were reclining against palm trees at the entrance to the base. Maybe there were more. We could not see if they were armed or not, but they seemed to be asleep.

My immediate thought was to run and get the hell off the island. We were sitting ducks in a stolen vehicle in the middle of the night, ignoring a military curfew.

Allan rejected a suggestion that we abandon the vehicle. It was too far to walk to the harbour and an abandoned vehicle would draw negative attention.

'There's only one way', Allan said. 'Let's push the vehicle until we're out of sight of the guards. Fast, let's go!'

There was no argument.

A Mini-Moke has no roof, doors or side windows and is also relatively lightweight, which made pushing easy. Serge and I shoved from behind while Allan steered and pushed from his side. Our adrenaline levels made it seem as if we had trained for this event all our lives.

Our pace picked up until we were at a jog, anxious to get past the sleeping guards. We were too scared to look towards them, in the fear that a stare might wake them. As we came around a bend that would put us out of sight of the guards, Allan somehow tripped, lost his grip on the steering wheel and crashed heavily to the ground. Serge tripped over him and also fell. With nobody steering, the adrenaline-powered vehicle veered off the road, its momentum neutralising all my efforts to stop it. The noise as it crashed to a halt against a coconut palm prompted Serge and me to dive for cover. Allan recovered from his fall and caught up with us, blood oozing from his leg and hands. A nasty bruise on his forehead added to his discomfort.

Minutes of silence passed, but nothing happened. They had not heard us. Stars were visible through the palms. It was such a beautiful night, I thought.

'Guys, I need a holiday', Serge said in a stage whisper.

His attempt at humour released some of our stress.

Thirty minutes went by and still nothing happened.

Allan assessed the damage to the Moke. There was a dent in the front fender and the left headlight was broken.

'It's fine — let's go, guys. We can't wait any longer.'

We eased the Moke slowly back onto the road and pushed it for another 200 metres. By then we were sweating heavily from the humidity and the physical effort. Allan abruptly quit pushing.

'I think it's safe enough to drive again.'

The Moke's engine caught and we drove off towards the harbour. There was not a soul to be seen along the way. It was as if we were the only living people on the planet.

We reached the entrance to the harbour area in about 15 minutes. I was wary. Where were the soldiers guarding the harbour?

Allan manoeuvred the Moke under overhanging palms adjacent to the main parking area that hid the vehicle from view. He jumped out the vehicle and gave a wry smile, giving the impression that he was enjoying the excitement — a remnant of his military past.

'Riaan, you and Serge wait here. I'll scout the area and see if I can find the yacht that Jacques is staying on.'

To our astonishment Allan then retrieved a bottle of white rum from under the front seat. He took a swig and splashed some of its contents on the front of his shirt.

'If I'm caught, I'll say I got pissed and passed out. Take a shot — it will calm your nerves.'

We gratefully obliged. The alcohol was raw. It burned my stomach and gave me instant heartburn.

'I'll be back. If anything goes wrong, wait till sunrise before you show yourselves. Don't worry about me. I'll be fine.'

He set off into the darkness, bottle in hand, moving from tree to tree in a manner more sober than the rum bottle implied.

We stretched out on the ground to minimise the chance of detection.

Time dragged by. The illuminated dial on my diving watch screamed at me. Allan had been gone for more than 30 minutes.

'The waiting is killing me. Another slug of that rum is what I need', Serge whispered.

'Ssh, someone's coming.'

We pressed our bodies to the ground. We heard the sounds of closing footsteps and then saw the dark outline of a figure. Moonlight reflected from an object in the figure's hand, indicating it was most likely Allan and his bottle of rum.

'It's Allan.'

'Wait', I said gripping Serge's arm. 'Let's make sure. He might be under duress and leading them to us.'

'Fuck off, Riaan, Allan is my friend. He will never betray us.'

Serge started to get up, but I grabbed him and held him down.

'Get off me, you bastard!'

'Shut up.'

'What the fuck are you guys doing?' Allan asked. 'You're waking the whole island. Do you want to get us killed?'

Serge and I got up, glaring at each other.

'Riaan said you would betray us.'

'Bullshit!' I said angrily. 'I said he might have been captured and forced to betray our position.'

'Riaan is right', Allan said, 'anything is possible. Now let's leave it. I've found the yacht. It's about a 400 metre swim. There are no soldiers anywhere around.'

Warming to the situation, Serge vented his disgust.

'Lazy complacent bastards. You'd hardly say there had been a coup attempt here in the last few days, would you?'

Something had been lost in the relationship between Serge and me and we ignored each other. Despite Allan's all-clear, we still moved with caution but reached the quay in ten minutes. We found ourselves out in the open. There were no shadows, only glaring lights. We hastily stripped and slipped into the water to get out of sight.

Our naked bodies glided through the water. Allan had tied a rope to a watertight bag containing our clothing and the little that remained of the bottle of rum. He pulled it along with every stroke, trying to minimise the noise created by the drag.

We approached the yacht from the port bow. The name *Madonna* was stencilled above the water line. She flew no flag as far as I could see. The lantern hanging from the mast threw a sliver of light onto the afterdeck. We circled to the stern and found a ladder that reached down into the water. Everything seemed to be in place and the name was right. But what if it was a trap? What explanation could we give for being there? I shrugged mentally. It was too late to think about that. I followed Serge and Allan up the ladder. Water dripped from our naked bodies, forming puddles on the deck.

I heard footsteps on the ladder leading from below and Jacques' smiling face appeared at the hatchway.

'Welcome, friends, thank you for coming. I've never had naked visitors before.' Jacques' levity eased the tension. 'Come below, I've got some dry clothes down there.'

In the cabin a dim light was burning on the bulkhead. Maps and navigational charts were scattered across the bureau. We changed into loose fitting island-style shorts and eyed the generous tots of Campari and orange juice that Jacques was pouring.

Avoiding specific details, he outlined events since the abortive coup. The morning afterwards, numerous Seychellois suspected of harbouring anti-government sentiments had been arrested, including Jacques' friend, Placid Andre, who was now in detention. Jacques had fortuitously avoided arrest by arriving at his house after the police had raided it. Since then he had been in hiding on *Madonna* which belonged to a friend. He had been living on dry rations that friends had managed to smuggle aboard.

He slid a sealed white envelope across the table to me.

'Don't let it fall into enemy hands. If need be, destroy it.'

He tossed over a book of matches showing the three-fish logo of the Reef Hotel.

'A Durban telephone number is written inside. When you get to South Africa, phone it and tell whoever it is that answers that you've an envelope from me. They are ex-Seychellois and will tell you what to do.'

Jacques was unsure about his future. The coup had failed and the dream of a unified Seychelles had disappeared for the time being. Armed conflict was inevitable — the government of Albert René versus the people and their democratic wishes. But when that would come about was anyone's guess.

It was almost sunrise and time to go. Words in a situation like this were futile. Allan and Serge hugged Jacques' bony figure and climbed the ladder to the deck.

I kissed Jacques on both cheeks and left without a word. We had become close friends and I felt empty. Jacques was in an awful predicament, but there was nothing I could do to save him from possible imprisonment and maybe even death.

It was after 06:00 when we got back to the Mini-Moke. The curfew was no longer in effect so it was safe to drive openly. It was important we get back to the hotel in a hurry before the guy whose vehicle we were using found it was missing and reported it stolen.

Nobody noticed us as we parked the Moke at the same spot we had found it. The hirer would have a hard time explaining the damage to the rental company when he returned the vehicle.

Allan and I parted from Serge in the hotel foyer. Before going up to our room I turned to Serge.

'Thanks for helping, Serge — I'm sorry about last night.'

'That's okay, but it's bloody awful leaving that guy behind.'

I had been awake for more than 24 hours but I found it difficult to sleep. The events of the night were playing havoc with my mind. Survival, I realised, was the natural instinct of the predator. Surviving at all costs. It had nothing to do with right or wrong. Fatigue eventually overcame my thoughts and I slept.

At midday I woke up alone in the room. After a cold shower, I dressed and strolled down to the pool bar where I found Allan, Mariana and Frankie sitting at a table drinking Seybrew beer.

We spent the afternoon packing our belongings and hanging round the pool, drinking and making small talk. It was evident that everybody was eager to go home and apprehensive that something could still go wrong at the last minute.

The hotel's traditional farewell dinner that evening was disastrous. At about 22:00 it was spoiled by soldiers armed with AK47s disembarking from a truck at the entrance.

Without saying a word they deployed around the hotel's perimeter, their figures throwing dark shadows in the night. This blatant act of intimidation frightened everyone and anxiety levels rocketed. Their very silence was threatening. No one including the hotel staff knew what they wanted. I wondered if the whole group of South Africans was in danger or whether it was only Serge, Allan and me they were after. Perhaps Jacques had been arrested. Maybe they had found out about our visit to the yacht.

Whatever else, their very presence was a sure party killer! The dancing stopped and everyone sat around whispering at a table by the pool, just getting comfort from each other's presence. Some of the girls were crying. They did not even bother with the futile question about what was going on. They just accepted that nobody had the answer.

The flight to South Africa was scheduled for 04:00.

Nothing happened and the predator just watched its prey. There had been absolutely no action on the part of the phantom soldiers for two hours, which made the situation even more intimidating.

At 01:00 I told everyone to vacate their rooms, deposit their luggage at reception and return to the table by the pool. Avoiding a general exodus, two or three people left at time to create the impression that no one was in a particular hurry to go anywhere.

I called for an 'absolute bloody final round' of drinks for everyone, acutely aware that the hotel bus would be leaving for the airport in 20 minutes. We would soon know our fate. Would it be arrest, interrogation and a cell on a lonely island, or would it be a safe departure for home?

Just after 02:00 we left the pool area and walked towards the hotel entrance, saying our farewells to the reception staff en route. We went outside and began to board the waiting bus. We were a rowdy bunch, defiant in the face of the enemy, some of us still with drinks in our hands to indicate a cool that we didn't possess. I was the last to board. I forced myself not to look towards the soldiers, knowing it was important to stay cool, calm and collected.

I paused in the open doorway and addressed the driver in French.

'*Aller*' (Go).

Armed soldiers were deployed on both sides of the road as the bus passed through them out of the hotel grounds. It turned right onto the main road and headed for Mahé International Airport. We encountered no traffic en route. It seemed the curfew was still being strictly adhered to.

The bus drew up in front of the entrance of the airport terminal just before 03:00. Armed soldiers were hanging around the entrance to the departure hall. There was no reaction or heightened alertness as we walked by.

Escape and freedom suddenly seemed possible. But there were more soldiers inside the building. We began checking in, queuing to receive our boarding passes. Barbara at the front of the queue placed her bags on the scale. A customs official reached for her green vanity case. My heart missed a beat.

Descent into hell lay concealed in that vanity case. Jacques' white envelope and the three spools of film I had shot were hidden there. It was devastatingly incriminating evidence which, if discovered, would lead to Barbara's immediate arrest and the rest of us coming under immediate suspicion of being involved in the coup attempt.

I watched, frozen by shame, guilt, and mounting concern for the unsuspecting Barbara. It was too late to reverse my actions of a few hours ago. Whilst packing my luggage in the privacy of my room, I had thought about how to smuggle Jacques' letter and my films off the island without endangering my survival. Fearing compromise if the material was found in my possession, I had decided on Barbara as the unwitting courier. I had slipped into her room while she was at the pool, found her vanity case, hidden the envelope in the bottom of a tampon box and covered it with the original contents. The films fitted snugly into the nozzle of her hair dryer. I had replaced the tampon box and hair dryer, expecting she would not disturb or find them.

The vanity case, now in the official's brown boney hands, became the focus of my existence. He opened the lid and scrutinised the obviously intimate female contents. It seemed like an eternity before he eventually closed the case, seemingly in slow motion, locking its secrets inside.

I cleared customs without difficulty and walked out into the night to board flight BA025 for Johannesburg.

The thrust of the powerful turbines lifted the Boeing off runway 07. As its wheels raised and locked into place, the South Africans burst forthwith into a spontaneous cheer.

The only thought in my mind was that we were free and heading for home. Champagne flowed freely for the duration of the flight. Everyone was hugging and kissing each other. Survival had created a special bond between us.

It was early morning and raining softly when we stepped off the plane at Jan Smuts (Johannesburg International) Airport. The news of the attempted coup had made international headlines and there were joyous reunions with waiting family and friends. During emotional rounds of hugging and kissing as we said our goodbyes, I secretly retrieved the envelope and the films from Barbara's vanity case.

The bulky figure of my father caught my eye. We shook hands.

'Welcome back, son. Are you ready to go home?'

'Sure Dad.'

We left the airport building, walking side by side.

3

What I hadn't known about the Seychelles

During the late 1970s and early 1980s the Seychelles became of increasing strategic importance. Their geographical position made their political allegiance a prized jewel in the Indian Ocean.

For each predator and competitor there was a different attraction.

The US satellite tracking station on Mahé, representing a US$14 billion investment, facilitated naval surveillance of the African coast, the Persian Gulf and the Indian sub-continent.

The Soviets needed influence in the region to counter the threat posed by the US Naval base on Diego Garcia. At the 26th Communist Party Congress in Moscow the Soviet Navy hailed the USSR's foothold in the islands as a stupendous achievement.

For South Africa, on the other hand, a foothold meant a positive voice in the OAU, landing rights for South African Airways, trade links and a route for oil from the Middle East.

As always this world of international politics is bizarre, devious and despicable.

In 1977 Albert René toppled Seychelles President James Mancham in a coup with the assistance of Tanzanian soldiers. René's policies and affiliation soon fell within the cradle of Soviet influence which posed a threat to the American presence on the island and to the region in general. His pro-Soviet African Marxist regime soon negatively affected the lives of the Seychellois. In 1979 the Seychelles Resistance was born and the games began.

Exiles living in South Africa and Europe contracted mercenary leader Colonel 'Mad Mike' Hoare to lead a counter-coup and install the cabinet in waiting. In May 1979 Hoare met the Director General of the National Intelligence Service, Alec van Wyk, in South Africa. After negotiations, the secretariat of South Africa's State Security Council (SSC) turned down Hoare's request for assistance.

This didn't deter Hoare who continued his quest and compiled a

US$5 million plan based on reconnaissance trips to the islands and the local knowledge of expatriates. His idea was to infiltrate weapons and men separately into the islands. They would then link up with the island resistance for D-day and restore the exiled government to power.

Unbeknown to Hoare, intelligence information about the Seychelles crisis was already being independently gathered and evaluated by the National Intelligence Service. In 1981 Mr Rothmann, commonly known as 'the Arab' and later to become Deputy Director General of the Service, relayed the cabinet's approval for the coup to Hoare. Jimmy Claasen was assigned as case officer.

A shoestring budget of $300 000 was approved. Hoare's acceptance of the proposal scuttled his idea of sending in weapons and mercenaries separately. As was par for the course, infighting developed between National Intelligence, Security Branch and Military Intelligence, which resulted in the project being handed over to Brigadiers Hamman and Knoetse of the latter organisation. MI supplied weapons to Hoare in abundance. Mercenaries were recruited, a safe house was established in Mahé and a sprinkling of weapons was smuggled into the islands by various couriers.

The South African contingent included some ex-Recce Commando members. Some, like Johan Fritz, had returned to their studies at university after completing national service in the SADF. The principal obstacle faced by the mercenaries had been created by the parsimonious budget. Each mercenary had to separately clear customs at Mahé Airport with his unassembled AK47 hidden in a false bottom of his hand luggage. It was a risky proposal.

As luck would have it and through no fault of the mercenaries, all hell broke loose when fruit, a forbidden import, was discovered in the hand luggage of another passenger as he passed through Seychelles customs.

This prompted a more stringent search of luggage which resulted in the discovery of an AK47. One thing led to another and an accidental discharge in the arrival hall killed Fritz. With the plan compromised, the mercenaries had no option but to start the assault there and then. They were, of course, in disarray without communications or assistance from the resistance movement and with the element of surprise having been lost.

They took control of the airport but could not extend their influence beyond it. Although the initial onslaught had failed, the situation was not lost. Events took an unexpected turn when an Air India Boeing later landed at Mahé Airport. The aircraft and its passengers were in grave danger, as one stray bullet could have sent it up in flames.

President René granted permission telephonically to Colonel Hoare for the plane to refuel and take off and a temporary cease-fire was arranged to facilitate this.

While thanking Hoare for his arrangements, the captain of the Air India flight was persuaded to offer passage to Hoare and his men. Most opted to go and not fight it out the following day. The main body of the mercenaries, accompanied by a reluctant Hoare, boarded the aircraft and took off under cover of darkness for South Africa. A few of the mercenaries decided to remain on the island.

South Africans awoke the next morning to the news of an abortive coup in the Seychelles and a hijacked plane at Durban Airport. It was an international incident par excellence. For a time, because government involvement was suspected, it seemed that South African Airways would lose its international landing rights. The book was closed on this, however, with the arrest, trial, conviction and sentencing in South Africa of Hoare and his men for aircraft hijacking. Those who remained behind on the islands were also weeded out and arrested by the authorities there. One of them, Martin Dolinchek, who was National Intelligence's representative at the coup attempt, sang like a canary to save his skin. Most were convicted of high treason and some were sentenced to death.

The South African Government, the National Intelligence Service and Military Intelligence denied involvement.

On 28 July 1982 those involved in the hijacking were charged under the Civil Aviation Act, 1972. After a marathon trial all but one were convicted. Colonel Mike Hoare was sentenced to ten years imprisonment. Tullio Moneta, Peter Duffy and Pieter Doorewaard each drew five years, Ken Dalgliesh and Charles Goatley got 30 months and Vernon Prinsloo 12 months. The other 34 were given six months with another 54 months conditionally suspended for five years.

The SADF was sympathetic towards the plight of their own and they secretly moved their former Recce operatives from prison to a Security Branch camp north of Sodwana on the Natal North Coast. The wooden bungalows are situated between Mabibi and Black Rock and can only be reached by driving a 4x4 vehicle along the beach. The husband of a former colleague of mine at the Service's regional office in Durban told me about this 'holiday camp.' He was amongst those sentenced to imprisonment and who had served his time there.

The men got the short end of what was commonly known and used by intelligence services throughout the world — a government's right of denial.

The death sentences on the mercenaries captured in Seychelles were never carried out. In April 1982 President René appealed to Prime Minister PW Botha not to execute three MK guerrillas sentenced to death for an armed attack on Soekmakaar Police Station in January 1980. President Botha uncharacteristically commuted the sentences to life imprisonment in June 1982 — before the sentences of death were passed on the mercenaries in the Seychelles.

In a move of apparent largesse, President René pardoned the raiders in July 1983. They were freed and allowed to return to South Africa. The reason behind René's benevolence remained concealed for nine years until July 1992, when he revealed that South Africa had paid a ransom of US$3 million for the reprieve, release and safe return of the mercenaries.

In testimony to South Africa's Truth and Reconciliation Commission on 14 October 1997, ex-Foreign Minister Pik Botha confirmed that 'between US$3 million and US$6 million was paid to the Seychelles for their release.' He confirmed that the National Intelligence Service and/or the SADF was involved.

In his TRC testimony, the former Director General National Intelligence Service, Niel Barnard swore that neither he nor the Service had prior knowledge of the coup attempt. He said he had met Colonel Hoare during a routine visit to the Service's Durban offices. Hoare had explained his plans and asked for assistance but Barnard said he turned him down. He also said that Dolinchek's involvement had been unauthorised.

He testified that he and a senior colleague had sought an interview with Prime Minister PW Botha, told him what they knew and explained that there was a possibility of military involvement. 'He told me that he would discuss this on a political level with his colleagues, because this could have negative results for South Africa. That was the last I heard about the Seychelles incident.'

His denial was in the best traditions of the Service!

*   *   *

In the mid-1980s a senior National Intelligence Service operator recruited President Albert René himself in the mid 1980s as an agent. I became aware of this while serving in Division 031 before my service in Zimbabwe. Dr Daan Opperman, head of Division 031 was the president's handler. The objective of Rene's recruitment was not to gain intelligence on the Seychelles as such, but on the goings-on at the Organisation for African Unity (OAU). The West, at the time, regarded the Seychelles as a Soviet client. In fact, the whole of the Indian Ocean region including India was leaning towards the Soviets. René provided National Intelligence with volumes of information on the OAU. He was simultaneously also used as an agent of influence within that organisation.

Opperman's man on the islands was an Irishman, Ian Douglas Withers alias John Douglas, who became René's National Security Advisor. He was a long-time agent of National Intelligence and had first worked for General 'Lang Hendrik' van den Bergh when the organisation was still called BOSS. Withers admitted devising a system of 'pre-employment screening' of members of the British Anti-Apartheid Movement. His career was chequered and convictions for bugging telephones were recorded against him in London and Hong Kong.

He had used the cover of Christopher Robin Investigations in London and also that of another detective agency in Dublin. This cover fell apart when Gerard Hoarau, who had been plotting President René's overthrow, was gunned down in a quiet London street. It was the second attempt on his life. The first had been an assassination bid in Cannes, France, that was bungled.

MI5 (in its guise as the Anti-Terrorist Branch of Scotland Yard) swooped on Withers' London offices. He had, however, done a runner and the only staff member left was his unfortunate 17-year-old receptionist who was roped in for interrogation at MI5's detention centre — the Paddington Green Police Station cells. Later, three men — Bill Underwood, Dave Coughlan and Dave Richards — who described themselves as security consultants, admitted having been employed by Withers to bug Hoarau's home before he was killed. They claimed that Withers had told them the bugging was being done on the behalf of Britain's Foreign Office. The court, nevertheless, did not accept this and they were jailed.

Meanwhile in Dublin, the 'To let' signs had been put up. Withers reappeared in Mahé where he opened the *La Perle Noire* (The Black Pearl) restaurant. Whether the assassination of Hoarau was a National Intelligence operation designed to demonstrate to President René that the Service was truly on his side remains a matter of conjecture.

Recruiting René was certainly a better option than trying to kill him. It seems, though, that Military Intelligence, through a front company called Longreach that was run by Colonel Craig Williamson, eventually stole a march on the NIS.

Williamson told author Peter Stiff that he had used controversial Italian billionaire Giovanni Mario Ricci, a good friend of President

René, to gain an entrée for Longreach. During negotiations Williamson had played on René's paranoia about his fears of a coup d'état. He insisted Longreach was not a South African Military Intelligence front, but said its employees were professionals and well connected in intelligence circles. If the South Africans, the British, the Yanks, the Soviets or anyone else began planning a coup he would find out and tell him.

Although René might well have suspected that Longreach was indeed a South African Military Intelligence front, on Ricci's recommendation he took it on to handle all security matters and intelligence for the Seychelles. The price for this service was a miserable US$40 000 a month, which was all that the Seychelles could afford. Craig Williamson and his Military Intelligence superiors would, of course, have done it for nothing. Ant White, a former captain in the Rhodesian Selous Scouts, became Longreach's director of operations in the Seychelles. He also became the de facto Director General of the Seychelles Intelligence Service.

This was a truly amazing situation where two intelligence agencies which were highly competitive of each other had taken over the intelligence of a Soviet-leaning state. It put South Africa in an unbelievably strong position when dealing with the CIA, MI6 and other Western intelligence agencies. If they wanted to know something, they had no option but to come cap in hand to the South Africans.

It also gave René, a mere minnow in an Indian Ocean that was awash with sharks, the comfort of knowing that he was being looked after by not one but two South African intelligence agencies.

4

The offer I couldn't refuse

I tried to contact Nico for two days after my return. He was not answering his phone nor responding to my messages on his pager. The lack of communication was pure frustration. Jacques' envelope, my completed report and the films were worthless if they remained undelivered.

On the third day Nico phoned, apologised for his silence and arranged to meet me at a coffee shop in Pretoria's Sunnypark Centre that afternoon.

I wove in and out of the busy afternoon traffic on my XT 500 Yamaha Scrambler, worried about being late for the meeting. I parked on the kerb outside the centre, a common practice by Pretoria's motorbikers.

Nico was sitting at a table in the far corner. His companion was a lean middle-aged man with a prominent Roman nose and streaks of grey in his long black hair. He was neatly but casually dressed and projected a cosmopolitan air. By his looks, his southern African or Afrikaans origin were not obvious.

They stood up when I reached the table and we shook hands. Nico introduced his companion as Phillip Swart, deputy head of National Intelligence's Counter-Intelligence Division.

As we sat down I passed Nico an envelope containing my report, the films and Jacques' letter. He took it without comment.

They listened intently as I spoke about my Seychelles trip and the attempted coup. When I mentioned Jacques' letter and said it had to be forwarded to someone in Durban, Phillip responded.

'Other intelligence services, related formations and their agents are my division's responsibility. That includes the resistance movement in the Seychelles and its members on South African soil. That envelope concerns information in that category. I must see what it contains and identify the addressee before passing it on.

He took the envelope and asked me for the Durban contact telephone number.

'I'll take care of this — you've fulfilled your commitments to Jacques. I'll brief you on the outcome later. Don't worry, we'll phone and forward it. What are your personal feelings about what you've done for us in the Seychelles until now?' he asked changing the subject skilfully.

'I'm comfortable about it now, but it was stressful. I might add that I was totally pissed off at one stage.'

Phillip and Nico smiled.

'Why were you upset?'

'I went into a situation without knowing what was about to happen. I had no communication facilities and no backup. You could have briefed me. I might have ended up arrested.'

'I understand', Nico said, 'but I've no wish to discuss details of this specific situation. I can only say you will have to get used to it and learn how to deal with it. Nothing is about to change. Next time you must expect the unexpected. Welcome to the world of espionage.'

I did not realise the full import of his words at the time. Fear, loneliness, lack of backup and the omnipresent chance of compromise would become the foundation for my future with National Intelligence.

I would also learn that if an agent is compromised or attracts media attention towards the intelligence community, it's his head that goes on the block. The system will deny all knowledge of a compromised agent — as they initially did with Martin Dolinchek.

*   *   *

I was due to report for two years national service in the South African Navy in two weeks. Phillip wanted an answer from me before I left. A phone number scribbled on a napkin was the only evidence of his confidential proposal.

The procedures for my recruitment into the Service, it seems, had been completed. I had been spotted by Tersia and suggested as a likely candidate. I had been tested and used in the Seychelles, but I was still an outsider. Now a window of opportunity had opened for me. I had been made an offer. Years later I discovered that most recruits were either related to or a friend of a serving member. You could not just apply for a position and expect to be accepted.

In the late 1980s a close friend of mine who was serving in the South African Air Force applied directly to join the Service. He was flatly rejected. A year later, as a serving member, I suggested him to the recruitment office. Six months later he was offered a post and a few years after that his brother also joined. They are still serving members of the National Intelligence Agency.

The similarity to the British MI6 in talent spotting is staggering.

Stephen Dorril in his book, *MI6 50 years of Special Operations*, wrote:

'Agent D/813317 Richard Tomlinson joined MI6 in 1991. Born in New Zealand, he read aeronautical engineering at Cambridge and was a Kennedy memorial scholar at the Massachusetts Institute of Technology. Fluent in French, German and Spanish, Tomlinson was approached at university where he gained a first. A lecturer had asked him if he wanted to do "something stimulating" in the Foreign Service. Despite modern recruiting methods, the trusted old-boy network is still a favoured option at Oxbridge and at a number of key universities, such as Durham and Exeter, they still have a contact group of lecturers on the lookout for "firsts" as suitable recruits.'

I was offered a full-time career with the National Intelligence Service to commence after I had completed two years national service. My appointment would be subject to a final selection process, psychological testing, top-secret security clearance and a vetting of my background and family. If successful, I would be appointed as a junior officer on a 12-month probation period. Initially I would work with a permanent and seasoned officer as my mentor.

Selection is a six months process at the least. The NIS would commence the process in the final year of my national service. My permanent appointment would become effective only after the 12-month probation period and would be subject to the approval of the divisional head. I was being recruited specifically for the undercover section of the Counter-Intelligence Division of which Phillip was deputy head. Given the sensitive nature of the division's activities, my identity and appointment within the Service would be classified as secret. My ties with Nico, as a known officer of the NIS, would end.

I examined the paper napkin with Phillip's fading phone number and for no specific reason I memorised it. I still had plenty of time to go with two years' military service ahead of me, so there was really no hurry. I decided to sleep on it and make my decision in the morning.

I awoke just before midnight and knew with certainty what I wanted to do. I padded barefoot over the clay tiles of the corridor to my father's study and picked up the phone. I knew the slight tremble in my hand was caused by excitement. I regained my composure and when the phone was picked up at the other end my voice was level and controlled.

'Hello', a male voice answered curtly after the second ring.

'Who's speaking?' I asked, although I already knew.

'Who would you like to speak to?' the voice countered.

'Phillip.'

'That's me. What can I do for you?'

'It's Riaan Labuschagne.'

'I know that.'

'Yes. I've decided to accept.'

'I thought you would.'

'What happens now?'

'Nothing', was his flat reply. 'Congratulations. Enjoy your national service and we'll be in touch with you after your officers' course. You'll be based in Durban.'

I somehow expected more, but he replaced his receiver abruptly.

I went out into the night. I pushed my motorcycle out of the drive and into the street to avoid waking my sleeping parents. I kick started the engine and with my crash helmet dangling from my arm, I set out for Pretoria's nightspots.

It was not a time to be alone.

5

National Service

I spent the last couple of days before my induction into the South African Navy at my parents' home in Pretoria. In South Africa military service brought a two-year interruption in the lives of most young men. Not only was I leaving home, but I was also entering a new life. I said my goodbyes to my friends and became almost saturated with farewell parties.

I could sense the emotionally charged atmosphere when I reached the departure platform of Pretoria Central Station that morning. It was the January intake of new national service recruits. Thousands of them, with friends, family, wives, girlfriends and an assortment of military personnel, were standing around in groups.

The recruits ranged between 18 and 25 years of age. The public address system croaked into life and announced the departure of the train to Cape Town. Frantic last minute farewells were interrupted by smartly uniformed soldiers herding the recruits into carriages. More recruits would be collected from the line of rail stations on the route south. Others would be dropped off to go to various destinations. All the naval recruits — that included me — headed for Cape Town.

It was time to leave.

'Thanks for dropping me off', I said to my father and we shook hands.

'Make the best of it, son.'

As a retired officer in the South African Police he was familiar with the training programme and he knew what lay ahead for me.

After a two-day rail journey I disembarked with 19 other recruits at the tiny railway station outside Gordon's Bay, 25km east of Cape Town. We were met by a chubby figure wearing the white uniform of the South African Navy. Before we could blink he bellowed at us.

'You — new recruits. I'm Petty Officer van Breda. For the next three months your arses are mine. I really don't how I'm going to make officers out of such a sordid bunch of wankers as you lot, but I'll do my best. Get your things and follow me.'

He turned on his heel in one controlled movement, his hobnailed boots crashing on the cement floor. In Van Breda's world, long-haired college graduates were the lowest form of life at the bottom of the feeding chain.

For me as a dyed-in-the-wool civilian, the situation was laughable. I regarded Petty Officer van Breda as a thick and ignorant fool who would be incapable of making his way in civilian life. Now, in this new world of the navy that I was joining, his word was law — according to the law of the land and the South African government. We had to submit and conform to become sailors, officers and gentlemen. There was no alternative. For two years I would be nothing less than government property and this awful Van Breda individual would ensure that I knew it.

Van Breda ordered us into the rear of a military truck and we set off for Gordons Bay. He gave us a typical 'rofie' (new recruit) ride. The truck swerved, skidded and braked continuously without any warning or reason. Bodies, equipment and luggage were thrown about as if we were on the inside of a tumble dryer. The process to unnerve us had begun.

Gordons Bay is a small one-hotel town on the north-eastern side of the Cape Peninsula. It's dominated by a high mountain range. The small harbour and immediate surroundings belonged to the South African Navy and the Naval College was the training facility for officers.

Van Breda drove his new recruits through the gates of the Naval College. The security boom dropped behind us signalling that our new life had started.

To make short of it, three months of controlled personal destruction and restructuring, accompanied by plenty of blood, sweat and tears, completed my transformation from a civilian to an officer of the South African Navy. I graduated from Naval College with the rank of ensign and was assigned as chaplain to the Durban Naval Base.

The sailors and base personnel were my responsibility. I had to ensure and enhance their religious and emotional well-being. The SADF held the firm belief that a serviceman's mental and emotional fitness were as important as his training and physical condition. It had instituted a spiritual and mental resilience and awareness programme amongst its members. This was designed to boost morale and ensure servicemen's belief in and commitment to the war against the total onslaught of communism.

The chaplains and the social and psychological service units of the SADF executed this responsibility. The programme was introduced during a soldier's initial basic training and was continued throughout his two-year national service.

The SADF comprised a Permanent Force (PF) of career soldiers, national servicemen and a Citizen Force (CF) comprising volunteer part-time soldiers and those who had completed their national service. National service was nine months at first, but this was soon extended to a year. When the war in Angola and SWA/Namibia escalated, it was extended to 18 and then to 24 months.

Military service was compulsory for all males between the ages of 18 and 65 years. In their initial period of service the vast majority of recruits spent time in the operational area in Angola or SWA/Namibia fighting South Africa's war against the Soviet and Cuban-backed SWAPO liberation movement.

Exemption from military service was only granted to men found to be physically or mentally unfit for duty. A minimum of four years' service in the South African Police, the NIS or other strategic government departments within the armaments and nuclear industry exempted men from military service. This was well known to South Africa's enemies. This was the reason for me serving two years in the military as an ordinary citizen without exemption, although I was slated to serve within the Service's covert structures. An exemption, it was thought, might have compromised me as another intelligence service could have noticed the gap in my curriculum vitae and guessed correctly about my affiliations.

Most church denominations in South Africa — Catholic, Methodist, Anglican and Dutch Reformed — sanctioned the induction of their ministers into the uniformed services. While each denomination catered for the religious needs of its members, they were all actively engaged in promoting the SADF's special awareness programme.

After three months at Naval Base Durban I had fully settled into the military lifestyle. I was comfortable in my role as an officer and as the base chaplain. I ran my own department — that of a spiritual cum political commissar. I put my heart into my work and gave it total effort and commitment. I was responsible for ensuring that the troops maintained a mental state of combat preparedness. This was nurtured by their belief in God, the South African government and in the justness of the war they were fighting.

As far as I was concerned, my responsibilities were more than just a duty. I believed implicitly in the South African government's philosophy of Christian Nationalism and my commitment was apparent. I befriended the troops, socialised with them after hours and accompanied them on operational missions.

Naval Base Durban is situated on Salisbury Island, a landlocked piece of real estate in the harbour that's linked to the mainland by a causeway built in the late 1940s. With Japan's entry into World War-II the war and the loss of Hong Kong and Singapore, the Allies required a naval facility in the southern hemisphere. The construction of a support base on Salisbury Island began in 1942 after negotiations between the British and South African governments. By the time the base was fully operational, though, the war had ended. It was handed over to the South Africans as a fully-fledged naval installation in 1945.

In my time the base was the command and support centre for the Strike Craft Flotilla, known as *SAS Scorpion*. A contingent of marines was also stationed there, tasked with general security of the base, the harbour and oil storage facilities. They also did tours of duty in the operational area on the SWA/Namibia -Angola border.

At the height of the border war in the 1980s the Strike Craft Flotilla was used to infiltrate Reconnaissance Commando operators into enemy countries like Angola and Mozambique.

Southern Africa's extended and virtually unprotected coastline is ideally suited for commando type operations. Strike craft and the Daphne class submarines were able to use all the South African naval installations along the coast as springboards for Recce raids. The vastness and scarcely populated coastline of southern Africa's east and west coasts made detection of these vessels highly unlikely.

Usually, the 'mother ship' would come close to shore under the cover of darkness to discharge its lethal load. A South African designed launch craft called the Barracuda was used to beach the troops. Two Scorpion missile pods on the strike craft's after deck would be removed to accommodate the launch craft. After destroying strategic installations or human targets on land, the launch craft would carry the troops back to the mother ship.

Such missions took place amidst great secrecy and the naval crew was only briefed once they were out to sea. These missions were carried out with great success, without compromise and with minimum loss of life. In the 1980s, however, a submarine was used to infiltrate Special Force units into northern Angola to attack the American owned Cabinda oil installations. The Americans, however, got wind of the operation and warned the Angolans to be on their guard. The South Africans were ambushed on Angolan soil, which led to the capture of Captain Wynand du Toit and the death of two of his men. The rest, some wounded, made it back to the beach and were extracted safely to the mother vessel. Despite intensive efforts by Angolan MiGs to track down the aggressors, low cloud cover, stealth and a degree of luck assured their safe return to a South African base.

```
BT
G E H E I M
1.                          . ANGOLESE UITSPRAKE NAV RSA VERKENNING
IN CABINDA
2. DIE ANGOLESE MINISTERIE VAN VERDEDIGING HET OP 22 MEI 85 IN
N COMMUNIQUE VERKLAAR DAT DIE ANGOLESE MAGTE OP 21 MEI 85 KONTAK
HET N RSA ''KOMMANDO'' ELEMENT GEMAAK HET
WAT NA BEWERING GEPOOG HET OM N OLIE-INSTALLASIE BY MALONGO TE
SABOTEER. VOLGENS DIE COMMUNIQUE IS TWEE RSA LEDE GEDOOD EN EEN
GEVANGE GENEEM
3. DIE ANGOLESE MINISTERIE VAN VERDEDIGING BEWEER DAT DIE VOLGENDE
UITRUSTING TYDENS DIE VOORVAL GEBUIT IS:
A. ''SINCAL SHORT WAVE RADIO''
B. TWEE ''ULTRA-SHORT WAVE A-84''
C. ''FAROL RADIO SET''
D. ''WALKIE-TALKIE''
E. ''TWO BOMBS''
F. ''FOUR BAGS OF HIGH POWERED EXPLOSIVES''
H. MEDIESE VOORRAAD
4. ANGOLA HET OOK VERKLAAR ''SOUTH AFRICA HAS BY SUCH ACTS,
DEMONSTRATED THAT IT HAS NOT YET RENOUNCED ITS INTENTION OF
DESTABILISING ANGOLA, THIS, VIOLATES THE PRINCIPLE OF INTERNATIONAL
BEHAVIOUR AND SOUTH AFRICA'S MUCH TALKED ABOUT NORMALISATION OF
THE SOUTHERN AFRICAN SITUATION'' ...''AFTER SOUTH AFRICA'S PHONEY
WITHDRAWAL, SOUTH AFRICA IS ENGAGED IN OTHER BELLICOSE ADVENTURES
IN THE NORTHERN PART OF OUR COUNTRY, WHICH CLEARLY CONTRADICTS
WITH ITS FALSE PROPAGANDA, WHICH ALSO STRIKES AGAINST THE VIGILANCE
OF ALL ANGOLAN PEOPLE AND OF ITS ARMED WING, FAPLA, WHO ARE
COURAGEOUSLY PREPARED TO DEFEND THE GAINS OF INDEPENDENCE''
5. OPMERKING. VOLGENS DIE AMPTELIKE SAW PERSVERKLARINGS WAS
VERKENNINGSELEMENTE IN DIE NOORDE VAN ANGOLA ONTPLOOI
BT
```

The intercepted signal that revealed the failure of 4-Recce's Cabinda raid.

The incident made international headlines. The fallout created considerable embarrassment for the South African government and for the until-then infallible reputation of the Recces. Shame, anger, guilt and feelings of failure were rife amongst those members of 4-Reconnaissance Commando involved in the operation.

The men believed — rightly — that the operation had been compromised in advance and that the enemy had prior knowledge of their arrival. Future operations were viewed with uncertainty, suspicion and fear. The operators suspected the politicians, the navy and any other outsider. After that episode, they asked for the exclusion of everyone not in the task force from the planning of future operations.

In the aftermath, the Recces mourned their dead and fought the ghosts of the unit's first major operational setback. To make matters worse, Wynand du Toit's wife, Louwna, was employed on the base and knew the families of the casualties and the survivors who had accompanied her husband.

My approach was to try and exorcise the guilt, however tragic the incident had been. I was personally convinced that there was nothing anyone could have done to prevent it.

The months dragged by. Louwna visited her incarcerated husband in Angola and returned home desperate. Neither the military nor the South African Government knew if the Angolans would ever release him. In the event, it took two years imprisonment, deprivation and torture before he was finally released in a prisoner swop and returned to South Africa.

I worked and lived on the base. The officers' mess on Salisbury Island was my home. I visited my parents and friends in Pretoria every few months for a weekend only. My exposure to civilians and the world outside the navy was minimal. Eventually my military and personal life became integrated into one world. I rubbed shoulders daily with professional soldiers; I met war heroes and listened to their tales. There were submariners, intelligence unit operatives, 32-Battalion soldiers and the Recces. The respect they commanded within this macho almost exclusively male environment conscripts like myself lived in, was awesome. To us they epitomised the pinnacle of manhood.

I had still not received word of my future job with National Intelligence as I had expected. I wondered what I would do if the promise came to nothing. I was torn between staying in the navy, returning to the Seychelles or going to some similar island as a diving instructor.

6

Counter-Intelligence Division

There was a sharp rap on my cabin door.

'Yes, it's open.'

'Good evening, lieutenant, there's a phone call for you downstairs.'

'Thank you AB (able seaman). Tell them I'm coming.'

It was close to 22:00 and I wondered who would be phoning at that time. I feared that there might be trouble at home. My father had been admitted to hospital a few days before with a stomach ulcer. I rushed downstairs to the duty room of the mess and took the call.

'Labuschagne', I said.

'Lieutenant Labuschagne?'

'Yes'.

I didn't recognise the voice and there was a moment's silence.

'My name is Steven van Zyl. I'm an associate of Phillip Swart and he has asked me to phone you. Does that ring a bell with you?'

I was taken by surprise. Only a few moments before I had been making alternative career plans and for a moment I remained silent.

'Are you still there?'

'Yes. I'm sorry, but I had expected a call six months ago.'

'So are you still interested?'

'Yes, I am.'

'There are some formalities that need to be addressed. Can we meet tomorrow?'

'Yes, where?'

'Be on the corner of Smith and Gardiner Street at 10:00. Someone will pick you up. Will you be wearing uniform?'

'Yes.'

'Don't be late.'

The phone went dead. It reminded me of when I had phoned Phillip to accept the offer to work for National Intelligence. Those guys didn't like becoming personal or making small talk on the phone.

It was 09:30 when I parked my military LDV in Smith Street. The rendezvous was two blocks away at the intersection with Gardiner Street. I joined the steady stream of pedestrians on the pavement. My white naval uniform stood out in the crowd of shoppers and tourists casually dressed to accommodate the sweltering and humid heat of Durban's summer.

I wondered for a moment if I was under observation, but I couldn't tell. A seaman passed in the opposite direction and saluted. I returned the salute. From where I was standing I could see the traffic lights at the corner of Gardiner Street about 30 metres away. I watched as a grey Volkswagen Passat left the flow of traffic and pulled up by the kerb. The driver remained in the car, but a middle-aged man wearing a dark business suit got out and stood expectantly next to the vehicle. I immediately knew he was there for me and I approached him.

'Lieutenant? We are to escort you to your appointment.'

I got into the back of the car. The driver, a man in his early 20s, was casually dressed in shorts and T-shirt and wore a pair of Ray-Ban sunglasses.

'Morning, lieutenant.'

'Morning.'

They made no attempt to introduce themselves and the driver eased the car back into the traffic flow.

'Where are we going?'

I immediately knew I shouldn't have asked.

'Just relax, we'll have you there in no time.'

They drove on in silence, but they were obviously uneasy about me. My uniform excluded me from their circle. I was not aware of it, of course, but what they were doing was routine. They had been told to pick me up but not to question me about my identity. They would take me to a certain destination and drop me, making sure that en route we were not followed.

I was uncomfortable with the enforced silence. I had expected a 'welcome to the club' sort of attitude — a sense of transparency. They drove aimlessly around the city for about half an hour with no apparent sense of direction or purpose. Having become used to the order of the military, it confused and irritated me, particularly when we passed the spot where they had picked me up for the second time.

The driver finally stopped in front of the Royal Hotel in Smith Street.

'Lieutenant, go to room 504. They are waiting for you,' the driver said turning in his seat.

'Thanks for the lift guys, but I could have walked here.'

The older man grimaced. It was not a smile.

I got out of the hot car, returned the doorman's salute, and walked into the air-conditioned foyer. The lift took me to the fifth floor.

My knock on the solid oak door of room 504 was quickly answered. It opened into a multi-roomed, exquisitely furnished suite, confirming the hotel's five star rating. The plush floor-length curtains were drawn and the only light in the room was provided by a standard lamp that was directed at the ceiling.

'Welcome Lieutenant Labuschagne.'

A short, clean-shaven man with blond hair and yellow-brown eyes, closed the door behind me. His body language and handshake, for a change, indicated a genuine welcome and the irritation I had experienced evaporated. He introduced himself as Steve.

A second man stood just behind him. He was tall with short cropped black hair. Intelligent eyes behind the John Lennon style spectacles gave him the appearance of an academic.

'I'm Pierre and I'll be handling the psychometric testing', he said, holding out his hand.

A good-looking woman was sitting cross-legged on a black leather recliner.

'Meet Layla du Toit', Steve said. 'She's also in Counter-Intelligence Division. New candidates are subjected to a polygraph test and that's her field of expertise. In layman's terms that's a lie detector test.'

'Riaan, I need to speak to you alone for a few minutes', Steve said.

He led me into an adjacent room and indicated that we should sit down on opposite sides of a coffee table. He handed me a form simply headed 'Application for Employment', a medical questionnaire and a covering letter on a National Intelligence Service letterhead. It was addressed to Lieutenant Labuschagne and briefly said that it had come to their attention that I was interested in a position and I should complete the attached documentation.

'Before you complete anything, I want to tell you what Counter-Intelligence Directorate is all about and where we would like you to fit in. The simplest way of describing our division is to by the slang terminology 'fly catchers', to be or more precise, 'spy catchers'.

'The Directorate is divided along functional lines, defensive and offensive. The defensive arm, code named Division 062, is tasked basically with the physical security of documentation, communications, personnel and intelligence installations. This protective function extends to our embassies abroad and includes VIP protection for the president and other senior government officials travelling outside the Republic's borders.

'The newly formed surveillance section or 'Watchers', as they are commonly called, also fall under this division. In short, their job is to pre-empt and neutralise foreign intelligence penetration of the NIS, the police, the SADF and other government departments. Pierre and Layla belong to the division's psychological unit and are responsible for personality analysis, placement potential and assessing the level of honesty of new applicants.

'You've been recruited for the offensive task force, Division 061. We focus on infiltration and recruiting foreign intelligence officers to spy for us. If it's found that you are suitable, you'll be assigned to the newly established deep undercover section', designated 061/01, which is headed by Phillip Swart. The aim is to infiltrate trained officers like you, with no known links to the Service, into enemy countries. You'll be established under a suitable cover to recruit and handle agents within government and the intelligence structures of the enemy state.'

For a moment I felt like a character in a John le Carré novel, but I had no idea how such elaborate plans could be implemented in an unsuspecting society.

'Sounds good, Steve.'

'Complete the application form and join us in the next room.'

The application for employment was a three-page document. It demanded personal details, academic history and qualifications, military background, language skills and extra-mural interests. It made no mention of the Service. At the base of the final page it asked: Position applied for, technical/personnel/analysis/field operative.

I ticked the box next to 'field operative', signed the form and rejoined the others.

In the next tedious two and a half-hours I went through a battery of psychological tests including the TAT (thematic apperception test), Wechsler Bellevue IQ test and Roscharch. I was a psychology major and familiar with the tests. In the background I heard Steve ordering drinks from room service.

It was Layla's turn next. She directed me to a leather Lazy Boy chair by the window. An apparatus that fitted into a brown leather case was placed on a table to my right. Layla mentioned casually that the Service had acquired the device from MOSSAD — the Israeli Intelligence Service.

She affixed small electrodes to the five fingers of my right hand and a blood pressure device to my left upper arm. Connecting wires led into the machine. She asked bluntly about my sex life, who I was currently sleeping with and whether I had more than one partner. She also asked if I had ever had a homosexual experience. I assured her that

I had not.

She delved into my political affiliations and beliefs. The session ended with me truthfully professing that I had never had any links with the ANC or the South African Communist Party. To stress the point I added that neither had anyone in my family or circle of friends.

I remembered what had happened with Tersia and I knew that the ten people on the list of character references that I had provided would be minutely checked out.

At the time the questions seemed absurd. I only learned much later how the Service emulated the British MI6 in its screening processes. This had stemmed from the infamous spy case involving Burgess and Maclean — both of whom had homosexual tendencies. Anyone showing the slightest sign of homosexuality was immediately disqualified. As the Afrikaner-controlled National Intelligence Service copied MI6, so would the ANC-controlled National Intelligence Agency adopt the practices of its predecessor.

It was a mentally tiring process that lasted for more than four and a half-hours. When it was all over, Layla and I joined Steve and Pierre for drinks.

Conversation was casual and touched on anything but work and the Service. For the first time I began to feel at home and a part of this mysterious society. I tried to understand their occupational code of conduct and separate it from their everyday views of things. There was already a developing camaraderie that took away my initial feelings of being the subject of scrutiny.

'Thanks for submitting yourself to the tests', Steve said wryly. 'You're almost there. If all goes well you'll get a written offer in the next day or two. You have to give your acceptance in writing.'

I returned to my normal military routine. Two days later, after the routine early morning heads of department meeting, I walked down to the strike craft berths for my ritual morning coffee. I climbed the gangplank of the *Oswald Pirow* and the guard sounded 'officer on deck.' I saluted as I set foot on deck in accordance with ancient naval custom. The ship was swaying on the incoming tide and there was a steady hum from its powerful diesel generators that provided it with electricity. There was the familiar revolting odour of diesel mixed with the smell of food being cooked in the galley, which followed me into the belly of the war machine.

I found the captain, Commander Steve Artman, bent over maps and technical drawings, preparing his ship for sea. I asked permission to join the ship's company for their daily sea trials. This was an infinitely preferable activity to routine meetings at the base.

'Morning, lieutenant', a galley hand said handing me coffee.

I accepted the steaming mug of black brew with thanks.

Unexpectedly, a petty officer from signals summoned me to the ops room. There was a call for me on the landline.

The ops room was illuminated by a single red light on the bulkhead. The green radar and computer screens glowed in the gloom.

'Lieutenant Labuschagne, morning.'

'Riaan, it's Layla, your offer is ready for signature.'

The *Oswald Pirow* returned to Durban harbour at dusk after a long day of comprehensive naval exercises in conjunction with the SAAF. The operation had been acted out beyond the 24km horizon to shield it from the prying eyes of the public. The ship and two sister strike craft had honed their skills of evasion and defence against the mock attacks of two persistent Mirage F1 fighters.

I went to see Layla.

'If you're happy with the offer, initial both pages at the bottom, but don't sign your name', she told me.

The document, printed on National Intelligence Service stationery, offered me an operational position on a salary of R12 030 per month with additional annual allowances of 12%. The second page committed me to accept any appointment within the boundaries of the Republic of South Africa and South West Africa/Namibia.

I initialled both pages of the document with the pen she had offered. She didn't touch the documents that lay on the side table next to her.

'Congratulations colleague', she said. Her eyes were teasing 'Would you not like to stay with me for a while?'

'No, thanks', I said, 'I'll see you around.'

Years later I would recall how close I had come to fooling around with Layla. The inherent secrecy of the profession and the close bonds between its members made the Service a breeding ground for extramarital affairs. Many officers commenced their careers while married, but finished up divorcing their spouses to marry someone in the Service. The general immorality surrounding much of the work that members were involved in, sometimes on a daily basis, had a lot to do with it.

Ten days after I signed the offer, a confidential signal from Naval Headquarters in Pretoria advised *SAS Scorpion* that Lieutenant Labuschagne was being released from national service two weeks early.

My discharge was celebrated at the officers' mess after 'stand easy' on a Friday afternoon. Most of my brother officers attended and some senior officers made token appearances but left after a short speech by the head of Natal command and some generous tots of rum. This was the signal for the ensigns, lieutenants and lieutenant-commanders to embark on a typical sailor's farewell party. My exit into civvy life was floated to new heights on a flood of war stories, a sea of liquor and much swearing of eternal brotherhood.

The next morning a pulsating headache and an excruciating thirst forced me from bed. A cold shower soon revived me. I dressed casually for the 700km drive back to Pretoria. With a last sentimental glance, I closed the door on the second floor room that had been my home during my short naval career.

The armed guards at the base's entrance lifted the security boom as my car approached. I drove past the checkpoint and the sentries, familiar with the car's occupant, saluted the lieutenant in mufti. I wound down the window and acknowledged their gesture with a casual wave.

It would be my last salute.

I moved into the garden cottage that my father had built ready for my return. The sweltering midday heat of the Highveld summer heightened my unease on how to handle my parents' inevitable inquisition about my future.

I spent my first day moving into the cottage. That evening's family dinner was supposed to be a celebration. My parents were hungry for details about my experiences and eager to hear about my future career plans. When my father asked me a direct question in this regard I knew I would have to brutally deflate their high expectations.

'I've accepted a position with an import and export company here in Pretoria.'

I lied with a straight face using a cover story suggested by Steve at that meeting in the Royal Hotel in Durban.

'An import and export company!'

'Yes, Dad, I'll be starting in a few weeks.'

'So you've studied theology for seven years to become a trader in oddities?'

My father made no attempt to hide his disappointment and annoyance.

'Yes, something like that.'

My father continued his tirade against my obviously inferior career. After all, I had the opportunity to become a church minister or, at the very least, to get an excellent job in any one of many government departments.

'What are you going to do, ship tea to China?' he asked sarcastically.

I kept my cool and eventually became obstinate.

'I'm not really sure. I'll know more about it once I've started. Can we talk about something else?'

They grudgingly left me alone and we reverted to discussing trivialities.

December dragged by without a call. Not being constructively occupied increased my restlessness and I became really anxious to start my new career. I spent my time exercising, taking an early morning run, or lying in the sun reading at the pool. I tried to rekindle past friendships, but with little success. I had been away for almost two years and the lives of my friends had drifted in different directions. Needless to say, none of this did anything to change my parents' minds about their dissatisfaction with my choice of a career.

Phillip Swart phoned me unexpectedly and invited me to his house for a social get-together. I gladly accepted, impatient to make closer contact with the new masters of my fate.

I was surprised to find that Phillip's home was in the same neighbourhood as mine, only a few blocks away. I arrived at his up-market townhouse just before dark, unsure what to expect from the evening.

Phillip, dressed in jeans and a black open-necked shirt, invited me in and introduced me to the other guests. There was Ron Sharlow, Divisional head of Counter-Intelligence and his two section chiefs, Steve van Zyl — whom I had met in Durban and Peter Whitehead. It was an all-male affair.

I accepted the short square glass filled to the brim with whisky and ice that Steve held out to me. He hadn't used a tot measure and I sipped it slowly.

The easy camaraderie amongst those present suggested mutual trust and much time spent together. Later everyone drifted out on to the patio where Phillip was preparing a meal on the braai.

Ron Sharlow, a thin greying man, interrupted the social chatter.

'Can I have a few words, please? It's been some time since we have had the opportunity to get away from the all the pressures and deadlines and socialise as a team. To Phillip, my deputy, thanks for the venue and the support you and your team have given me.'

We toasted that and waited for him to continue.

'Riaan, welcome to the Counter-Intelligence Division. You are now officially one of us. I'm well aware that you've waited a long time for this, although it has been on the cards for two years. I appreciate your patience.'

Phillip interrupted him and said to me: 'You could have been exempted from national service and joined us two years ago. You waived that right, however, and sacrificed two years to the military so as to fit the profile we needed. That's what I call commitment. Let's drink to that.'

The toast gave me a warm sense of belonging.

Ron explained what my duties would be.

'You'll be Steve's leg man. You start your duties next Monday. Come here at 07:00 and follow Phillip to the office.'

Later, in a private moment, Phillip told me the results of some of the tests conducted on me.

'Your psychological tests revealed a certain rebellious tendency which, if you fit our profile, is to be expected and is a common trait amongst our operatives. The analysts, however, are of the opinion that your commitment tends towards being conditional. This aspect was highlighted as a possible area of concern regarding your management and likely future assignments. They wanted us to know that you tend to obey the orders of only those people you perceive to be your superiors.

'This is not a criticism, but you should be aware of this trait, because there will be times when you'll have to follow orders blindly without knowing the plot.'

I started work with the National Intelligence Service on 1 January 1985. Unlike the South African Navy when I joined it as a national serviceman, I was not required to sign an oath of allegiance. This did not occur until almost two years later when I was ordered to attend the conference room on the 11th floor of NIS headquarters in Concilium Building, Skinner Street, Pretoria at 09:30 on 3 October 1986. In the presence of a few senior officers I took the 'Oath of Loyalty' before Director General Niel Barnard. Barnard liked to handle these sort of things personally and the fact that the oath was taken two years after it should have been, did not appear to concern either him or his administrators.

The Oath of Loyalty bound me in my loyalty to the National Intelligence Service and to South Africa — in that order. I was not given the certificate because I was working undercover and it was retained in my file at headquarters. Eventually it was given to me some years later after my cover was blown in Durban and I was moved to Port Elizabeth.

Perhaps I was lucky. I knew some officers — because of administrative oversight or inefficiencies or because they were in deep cover positions — never even took the oath. Others who did take the oath, were not given their certificates even when they left the Service.

This — whether oaths of loyalty were signed or not — made no difference to the control exercised by the NIS over the lives of its officers. Whether they were male or female, fiancees still had to be approved by the DG before a marriage could take place.

*   *   *

I followed Phillip's silver-grey Audi in the rush hour traffic. I hated the congestion and made a mental note to leave earlier in future, especially on a Monday morning.

Steve van Zyl's calling card for his 'employment' at PSA Enterprises, Imports/Exports.

I parked in a bay next to him in front of a double-storey shopping complex in Rietondale. Our offices were situated above a chain store. We rode up in the elevator and entered a small rectangular foyer beyond which were the undercover offices of Division 061/01. A metal security gate with a signboard blocked entrance into the passage. The sign said we had reached *PSA Enterprises — Imports and Exports*.

Phillip pressed the buzzer.

Steve's head appeared in an open doorway to confirm the identity of the visitors.

The gate clicked open.

'Morning, Mr Swart. Morning, Riaan.'

'Hi, Steve, I've brought Labuschagne. The first thing is to get him up to speed with the paperwork.'

'Yes, sir.'

'Riaan, it will be Steve's responsibility to teach you the day-to-day running of things. Your eventual posting and the operational planning connected to it is my responsibility. There's a lot of information for you to absorb and many skills to master. And we need you out in the field as soon as possible.'

He disappeared into the elevator. I was dumbfounded by the sudden formality. Steve calling Phillip 'sir' seemed so out of place. Steve smiled as he noticed my perplexity.

'Come on, let's get on with it.'

There were three offices off the narrow passage. The doors of two were closed. We went into the third, a large open-plan room. It was equipped with three computer workstations, a large Chubb safe, a paper shredder and telephones.

I was allocated a desk in front of the window from where I could see the street below.

Steve, my new mentor, was an unpolished rugged personality who expressed himself mainly in his daring and lack of personal boundaries. In later years I would learn of his career exploits. He had started out in the NIS as a bodyguard to the South African ambassador in Paris after which he was transferred to Division 061. He had proved himself an effective recruiter of agents — which he achieved with little finesse.

Throughout the 1980s National Intelligence struggled to produce a high-level product. Its regional offices were geographically divided and fell under the internal divisions of 041 and 051. Field operatives were posted to one of two sections, Political and Social. The Political Section attracted the more seasoned men and covered the activities of the ANC, Pan Africanist Congress (PAC), South African Communist Party (SACP), the various trade unions, radical organisations like Azanian People's Organisation (AZAPO), Black Consciousness Movement of Azania (BCMA), Muslim extremists and later, white Afrikaner right-wing organisations. Student organisations, pressure groups, NGOs, civic organisations and churches fell under the Social Section.

The NIS, under Niel Barnard's leadership, quickly realised that most information gathered internally only covered events historically. It provided little advance information of the enemy's activities and decisions. After analysing intelligence reports the management discovered that 80% of intelligence reports were, in fact, overt and only 20% were covert.

Following the examples of MI6, the CIA and the MOSSAD — with whom the Service regularly co-operated — a conscious decision was made to change the method of collection to become more covert. It was this decision that led to the inception of the undercover unit of Division 061.

Steve's briefing was informative rather than instructive. He was positioning my life within the intelligence domain. It was a strange world which he knew would be alien to me, despite my military background.

'Knowledge rules supreme in this game. Above all, know yourself. Only then can you master your craft and the enemy's.

'In the summer of 1984 the then chief of National Intelligence sanctioned the formation of a new desk that was designed to have a wide ranging remit that would span traditional frontiers. Opposition from the established desks, almost all of which had territorial fiefdoms spread across the globe, was ignored. The new desk, Division 061/01, was given the sole mandate to recruit foreign intelligence operatives. Hard-core intelligence from the heart of the enemy and from within its intelligence structures was needed.

'This office is the forward base for deep undercover agents like yourself. When ready, you'll assume an appropriate cover and settle in the field. You'll be handled by staff from this office which, as you'll have seen, uses the cover of an import and export company. This is an elastic arrangement and if the need arises, we'll simply relocate the office and assume a new identity. Peter Whitehead and I are the only case officers. It's our function to service you and other deep undercover agents in the field. The initial objectives of this operation are to establish you and three other deep undercover operatives in a target country. The other three recruits will be reporting here next week.'

'The Counter-Intelligence Division functions as a separate entity. It is compartmentalised away from the rest of the staff of National Intelligence Service. This is a necessity because of our watchdog function.

'Our installations and the identities of our members are concealed from other members of the Service. We monitor government officials, the police, the SADF and the greater intelligence community for possible espionage activities. Our section, however, specifically specialises in the recruitment of foreign intelligence operatives and diplomats, both locally and abroad.'

Steve familiarised me with the pecking order of the system.

'You'll find you are part of a highly organised and disciplined community. The director of the division, Dr Scholtz and his management staff of Ron, Phillip and Mike, plus the support team of typists, researchers and technical staff, are based at the Counter-Intelligence HQ which is in a building not far from here.

'Rank, chain of command and discipline are the same as in the military, but it's not so obviously flaunted. In the office environment

EED VAN GETROUHEID

INHULDIGING

van

ADRIAAN STEPHANUS LABUSCHAGNE

IN DIE NASIONALE INTELLIGENSIEDIENS

EK ONDERNEEM:

om die belange van die Nasionale Intelligensiediens te alle tye bo persoonlike belange te bevorder;

om in my soeke na die waarheid en die disseminering daarvan die hoogste graad van eerlike objektiwiteit, 'n gesonde analitiese ingesteldheid en geheimhouding na te streef;

om gesonde interpersoonlike verhoudings te handhaaf en te bevorder;

om die goeie interne orde in die Nasionale Intelligensiediens te handhaaf;

om nougeset die Wette, Regulasies en Direktiewe wat op die Nasionale Intelligensiediens van toepassing is, na te kom.

EN

Ek sweer trou in die teenwoordigheid van die Almagtige GOD aan die Republiek van Suid-Afrika en beloof plegtig en opreg om my te alle tye in my werksaamhede te beywer vir die handhawing en bevordering van die veiligheid van die Republiek; my aan die Grondwet te onderwerp; my werksaamhede getrou met al my kragte en talente na my beste vermoë en kennis uit te voer.

SO HELP MY GOD

Geteken op hede die............ derde ....dag

van Oktober ....19 86 .... te Pretoria

............Handtekening/Signature

OATH OF LOYALTY

INAUGURATION

of

IN THE NATIONAL INTELLIGENCE SERVICE

I UNDERTAKE:

to promote the interests of the National Intelligence Service at all times above personal interests;

to strive for the highest degree of honest objectivity, a healthy analytical approach and secrecy in my search for the truth and the dissemination thereof;

to maintain and encourage healthy interpersonal relationships;

to maintain good internal order in the National Intelligence Service;

to conscientiously carry out the Rules, Regulations and Directives applicable to the National Intelligence Service.

AND

I swear, in the presence of the Almighty GOD, to be loyal to the Republic of South Africa and solemnly and sincerely promise to endeavour to maintain and promote in my work at all times the security of the Republic; to subject myself to the Constitution; to do my work faithfully with all my strength and using all my talents to the best of my ability and knowledge.

SO HELP ME GOD

Signed on this the................................day

of.......................19..... in Pretoria

Direkteur-generaal/Director-General

S 105

The author's Oath of Loyalty to the National Intelligence Service and South Africa — in that order the management are addressed as 'sir', but as in all elite units there's a certain after-hours familiarity and friendship like you experienced the other night.'

Steve finalised his two-hour brief. 'Always remember that we operate in a public domain that's saturated by sensation-seeking media. Should you ever be compromised and your cover blown, it will signal the end of your stay in this section.'

He indicated the stacks of papers both on his desk and on the floor.

'We must convert all this into reports for the decision makers. In the end all your efforts in the field finally boil down to paperwork and intelligence reports. I guess we had better get stuck in.'

I examined what seemed like a mountain of documents. My eyes were drawn to one document classified as 'top secret'. It was headed 'Cabinet Brief: Zimbabwe Central Intelligence Organisation (ZCIO)'. The quality of the paper was poor — far coarser and darker than the local equivalent. It was dated 29 December and coded Bravo/D/21.

I looked at Steve quizzically and he responded nonchalantly.

'We have an asset inside ZCIO's Counter-Intelligence Division who has direct access to the Zimbabwe Cabinet and its deranged president, Robert Mugabe.

'Just remember, though, that everything you read is classified and you must not discuss it with anyone.'

I shook my head, totally absorbed in my reading.

'How did you manage that?'

'I can't tell you. All information is subjected to the principle of need-to-know. Stuff like that is only for the knowledge of those directly involved with the operation.'

I started the mammoth task of transforming the raw material into digestible, formatted intelligence reports. I rewrote the Zimbabwe cabinet brief, answering the stipulated structure of 'what', 'when', 'where', 'why' and 'how.'

I read secret information, treacherously exposed by someone in South Africa, that almost screamed at me:

> 'Intelligence of long-term operational value to the SADF indicates that the new MiG aircraft at Thornhill Air Base in Gweru are viewed as a threat. South Africa will not hesitate to launch a pre-emptive strike. The SAAF base at Louis Trichardt will most likely be used.
>
> 'The destruction of the Beira pipeline is imminent to make Zimbabwe more dependent on South Africa for fuel. Sabotage of the Rutenga/Maputo railway line will further increase

Zimbabwe's dependence.

'5-Reconnaissance Commando is fighting in Mozambique to topple the FRELIMO government and replace it with a pro-South African regime. South Africa is training RENAMO commando units at Entabeni, west of Phalaborwa, for this purpose.

'South African Intelligence has information on current ANC deployments from Zambia to Harare and to Bulawayo. They know that cadres are infiltrated through the border with Botswana, west of Plumtree and finally through the Botswana border into South Africa.

'South Africa's intelligence apparatus has commenced a definite campaign of assassination against ANC members in Botswana. Three people, Peter Ntiti, John Hnetsiwe and Moseki Jame, were recently targeted.'

I finished the report with an understanding of the strategic importance of high-level spies and the devastating damage they can cause. I wondered about forces that create the heart of a traitor. Steve's response was clinical and loaded with experience.

'Mice', he said. 'It's an abbreviation for money, ideology, compromise or ego. Those are the life forces that make people susceptible to corruption.'

'Look, you volunteered to become a spy for whatever personal reason you might have. But no one cares about your reasons or your honourable intentions. An intelligence operative is an expendable tool and his only worth to the system is his ability to recruit and handle agents. You'll find that demand always escalates. There's always an increasing need to infiltrate deeper and recruit someone higher up in the enemy ranks. Your response to this manipulation will determine your future value, promotion and status within the Service. Field workers who can't recruit agents are sidelined.'

I felt a sense of inadequacy bordering on panic. I wondered how I would master the obvious skills required to recruit top agents. It seemed to be beyond my reach.

'Don't worry, the system will do everything to ensure your success', Steve said, recognising my discomfort.

We toiled in silence, completing one report after the other. At 16:15 the shrill of the buzzer reminded us of the existence of an outside world. Steve got up and opened the front grill door and returned with a smartly dressed elderly lady named Celia. I learned that she doubled as a go-between, courier and an administrative gopher for the undercover section.

Steve's obvious respect stemmed from her ten years of dedicated professionalism in support of the 'men out in the cold.' She was one of them — a dedicated spinster married to the job who gave the division her all.

She welcomed me with an almost motherly touch, while taking a playful jab at Steve.

'He's one of the best in the business. Just don't learn his bad habits. Come boys, I'm in a hurry, they're waiting for these reports. The doctor is briefing the president tomorrow afternoon. I think Mugabe is on the agenda. All this must be typed and evaluated tonight.'

The reports and unprocessed documents were locked into two aluminium attaché cases. We emptied paper that we had shredded into a black plastic rubbish bag and handed this and the metal cases to Celia's young armed escort who was waiting for her outside the security gate. The documentation was kept overnight in a safe at divisional headquarters. As an additional security measure, the paper shreds were routinely burned at HQ to prevent possible reconstruction.

'I'll bring your documents back early tomorrow morning, Steve. I presume you'll be here at about 06:00?'

'Yes mother', he chirped.

The spy-lady and her escort left and we returned to our empty office. All signs indicating the nature of our nefarious business had been removed.

The wall clock showed 17:00, which was a fair indication that the working day had come to an end. Steve, however, frustrated my intentions of leaving. He produced a bottle of Bells and two glasses from the top drawer of a steel cabinet. The office fridge contained the ice and water.

He measured two tots for each glass and added ice and a splash of water.

'Cheers on your first day.'

'Thanks very much.'

'After work we always have a postmortem on the day's activities and a couple of drinks. It's an unofficial must.'

I was eager to get home. I needed time to myself assimilate my hectic first day in the espionage business.

Steve took a pager from his desk and gave it to me.

'You must keep this with you at all times. You're on call 24 hours a day, so always be available. The code is on the back.'

I toiled at the coalface like a slave. I was confined to my desk for eight to ten hours a day, seven days at a stretch, transforming secrets of the Zimbabwean government and its Central Intelligence Organisation into workable reports.

Peter Whitehead, accompanied by two men and a woman, walked into the Rietondale office a week after my arrival and the day before I was due to attend a six-week training course. The strangers were the new recruits.

I was briefed by Steve and instructed not to reveal my true identity. I was to use the *nom de guerre* Riaan Lesage, the name that appeared on my personnel records at headquarters.

Registering a member's appointment under a false name enabled an undercover operative to work in the field using his or her real name. This served a dual purpose. It protected the field operative guaranteeing that no official documentary connection with the intelligence community existed. It also protected the NIS and the state from embarrassment should an agent be compromised as a spy — in this event the Service would deny all knowledge of the member.

I introduced myself to the three new agents who were hiding behind their own fronts too. This game, where we all knew the others were flying false colours, cast an ambivalent shadow over our comradeship.

Phillip addressed the members of his newly formed unit and outlined the general structure in some detail was needed before we left to attend the module-one training programme that was commencing the next day.

My new colleague, Jean-Pierre, a freckle-faced man with a Parisian accent, was assigned to the African Desk. This section was responsible for active intelligence structures on the continent and in the Indian Ocean area.

Steve van Zyl headed this desk.

Paul and Tammy were assigned to the European Desk which Peter Whitehead headed.

The Americas and the Far East fell under Phillip and Ron Sharlow respectively. They operated from Counter-Intelligence Headquarters.

The covert activities of the liberation movements, spearheaded by their intelligence and military structures in those regions, were given priority attention.

As a former Security Police officer, Peter Whitehead's personality contrasted with that of his fellow section head. He was an amiable introvert with shoulder length blond hair. His eyes were distorted into slits by the thick lenses of his spectacles. After recovering from a devastating year-long battle with depression, he had resigned from the Security Branch an emotionally scarred man and accepted a lower profile appointment in National Intelligence. His emotional disintegration arose from his suspected involvement in the death in detention of Doctor Neil Agget — a well known trade unionist and political activist — who had been detained for questioning. Whitehead found him in his cell where he had apparently hanged himself.

As the officer responsible for Agget's interrogation and for his safekeeping, Whitehead was suspected of being involved in foul play or having knowledge of it. His identity was dragged into the public eye by the media. The incident was responsible for him becoming one of the top ten priorities on the ANC's assassination list. It contorted his personal life, and influenced his style of professionalism. In National Intelligence he was the proverbial lone wolf operating in isolation and he shied away from discussing his methods.

Phillip elaborated on the communal destiny of the new recruits.

'After completing your training course you'll be based in these offices. Here you'll prepare yourselves for settlement in the target countries. The history, politics and intelligence structures of the target countries are subjects you will study. In the first instance you'll pay regular visits to those countries as tourists, which will help to familiarise you with the scene. Before you settle there we will endeavour to recruit an agent in the target country's intelligence service.'

*   *   *

Botswana was significantly important in the struggle. In intelligence circles it was regarded as the listening post of Africa. Because of its geographical position bordering all the countries engaged in the southern African conflict — South Africa, SWA/Namibia, Angola, Zambia and Zimbabwe — it was swarming with agents and intelligence officers from all sides. Although ostensibly neutral, it was stable enough to provide safe haven for all the spies operating within its boundaries.

The concentration of MK cadres in Gaborone and the use of the country as an infiltration route into South Africa spurred the State Security Council (SSC) into action. In June 1985 it approved the major Special Forces raid into Gaborone under the code name *Operation Plexi* to eliminate MK cadres who had congregated in the capital. The raid killed 14 people — eight of them South African nationals. The others were Somali and Botswana citizens.

In the event that the Botswana government decided to launch a retaliatory counterattack into South Africa, another SADF force was readied at Zeerust. It comprised tanks, helicopters and jet strike aircraft. No counterstrike was mounted by Botswana.

The disaster occurred because of the way the Security Forces functioned. Security Branch informers pointed out certain houses and fingered their occupants as MK members. Informants were seldom paid a regular salary and their income depended on their level of their production. It's therefore not surprising that in many instances they reported unsubstantiated information and even fabrications as fact in order to increase their earnings. By the same token, career officers needed successes in the field to aid their own promotion.

The rationale for the Botswana raid was that the SSC was determined to send a strong message to Botswana that it should not harbour terrorists. There was an institutionalised and continuous flow of information obtained from informers or terrorist suspects between National Intelligence, the Security Branch and Military Intelligence. The transfer of such information from National Intelligence to the other two organisations occurred regularly from the Service's headquarters in Pretoria.

Field officers belonging to all three often exchanged information and co-operated with each other without telling their respective head offices. This arose because of animosity and professional jealousy that existed between the institutions at a higher level. They all had their own personal fiefdoms and 'a marble to polish' for their political masters. At ground level, though, the men usually had no problems with each other. They had a war to fight, sources to recruit and deadlines to meet, so they co-operated but it was often only in secret.

In the Botswana case there was no permanent professional member of the security services available to check, cross-check and confirm the validity of information on the ground. NIS, unlike the CIA and MI6, did not have an 'Authenticity Officer' to validate information. There were only analysts sitting at their desks in offices. They were university graduates, certainly specialists in their fields of study — whether it was economics, social sciences, politics, history and so on — but they were not intelligence officers. All they saw were the reports which they examined at their desks between 08:00 to 16:00, on Mondays to Fridays only. They were not field officers who often had to judge the truthfulness of information often by looking an agent or informer in the eye and making assessments. Nor did they have any understanding of the intricate dynamics of field officers, agents and informers. Often too, they got hold of the wrong end of the stick and presented the information incorrectly. The field officers, however, never got to know this. It was only in later years that they were provided with feedback on the results of the information they had provided.

The result of the Botswana raid was that 14 civilians died. They may have been ANC sympathisers, but most were not MK soldiers.

The Special Force operators, soldiers and Security Police members who conducted the attack were only following orders. They had nothing to do with the sources or accuracy of the information. A deep undercover agent who had penetrated the ANC as a spy, was living with a group of MK soldiers in a house nearby. That was the house they should have attacked, but they didn't know it.

The bungled operation almost blew the undercover agent's cover and placed him in extreme danger. At one point he could have killed two of the South African attackers whom he had in the sights of his AK47. His loyalty, however, prevented him from acting. He continued his operations in Botswana for a further two years before returning safely to South Africa. In the meantime, he had provided a wealth of intelligence on MK and the movement of its weapons and cadres into South Africa.

On the 20th December 1985 a similar disaster occurred in the mountain kingdom of Lesotho. An eight-man South African Police task force from Vlakplaas, led by Colonel Eugene de Kock, attacked an ANC safe house in Maseru West. Nine people died. Six of them belonged to the ANC but only two were senior MK members. The remaining three were Lesotho nationals.

Lesotho was of strategic importance to South Africa as it epitomised the proverbial Trojan Horse. The small mountain kingdom, an independent state within the borders of the Republic, is completely surrounded by the South African provinces of Free State and KwaZulu-Natal and the former Transkei. Lesotho allowed the ANC to operate on its soil, so the South African Government regarded it as a threat to its national security.

The government's avowed policy was to combat terrorists wherever they might be.

A police spy, Elvis McCaskell, a Lesotho national and a member of the ANC, supplied the Security Police with information that the ANC in Lesotho, under the leadership of Leon Meyer, was planning an attack in South Africa during December 1985.

McCaskell arranged a Christmas party for members of the ANC at his Maseru home. Effectively he was setting them up for the kill.

The planned attack was discussed at the State Security Council by members of the SADF, the South African Police, the NIS and the Department of Foreign Affairs. Either no record was kept of this meeting or the minutes were destroyed. The Commissioner of Police subsequently ordered the attack on McCaskell's house to go ahead. Leon Meyer and his wife, Jackie Quinn, were killed, but their one year old baby, Phoenix, survived.

The ANC members who died in the attack were Nomkhosi Mini, Vivian Mathee, Themba Mthembu, Joseph Mayoli, Lulamile Dantile and Moris Seabelo. Ironically, one of the two dead MK members was a top National Intelligence agent. The Service had waited ten years for him to reach executive level in MK.

After the raid, Colonel De Kock was awarded the Police Silver Medal for bravery by the Commissioner of Police at a secret ceremony.

The informer McCaskell was given R2 000 for each dead terrorist. The SADF denied involvement in the raid. An opposition group, the Lesotho National Liberation Army (LNLA) — a surrogate organisation of the South African Security Forces — claimed responsibility.

Interestingly, the minutes of a SSC meeting on 20 December 1985, authorised three government ministers — Pik Botha, FW de Klerk and General Magnus Malan — to 'use violence across the border' to end the Lesotho government's support for the ANC.

Three weeks after the raid South Africa imposed a blockade on all goods entering or leaving Lesotho. This resulted in its government being toppled in a coup led by officers of the Lesotho Defence Force. The blockade was lifted and the new military government promptly deported all ANC activists to Zambia.

In June 1985 the ANC had held a watershed ten-day conference in Kabwe, Zambia. It was officially called the National Consultative Conference, but it is generally known as the Kabwe Conference. It was the first such conference since the Morogoro Conference held in Tanzania in 1969. Amongst other things, the election of the organisation's national executive was on the agenda. Since Morogoro vacancies on the national executive had been filled by co-option and not by a democratic electoral process.

The venue was kept secret until the last possible moment, because of fears that the SADF would mount a strike with air or ground forces if it got known too early. Journalists were permitted to attend a limited number of open sessions. The NIS had advance knowledge of the planned conference, so they recruited a Reuters journalist to provide them with information. A foreign journalist was chosen as it was unlikely that a South African journalist would have been accredited.

The reporter in question recorded most of the conference. She also provided material on in-depth discussions with the ANC's leadership and also managed to take their photographs as well.

The photographs were particularly useful as most of those the Service had were fairly outdated and most had been taken from a distance. The journalist even managed to get a personal interview with the exiled ANC president, Oliver Tambo, in the Lusaka flat of Thabo Mbeki, who would one day become the South African President.

*   *   *

The embarrassing trend of South Africa's security services killing their own agents through negligent incompetence continued. This was highlighted by the assassination of a member of SWAPO's executive, Advocate Anton Lubowski, in front of his Windhoek home by agents of the SADF's deep cover CCB (Civil Co-operation Bureau) on 12 September 1989.

Lubowski was a deep penetration NIS mole at the time of his death. He was crucial in providing intelligence on SWAPO's positions and sentiments at the time when negotiations with the South African government were ongoing. In keeping with the Service's style, he was punted as an agent of influence inside SWAPO.

My knowledge of the affair stems from my contacts at Division 031. The foreign missions it was responsible for included the Service's Windhoek office. The two officers I believe were Lubowski's handlers expressed their dismay openly at the loss of yet another of their agents and railed against the idiocy of the military. One of his handlers continued to hold high office in the South African Secret Service (SASS) until the late 1990s.

In February 1990 following the assassination of Lubowski, Minister of Defence General Magnus Malan announced that the victim was a spy for South African Military Intelligence. This should have ruled out the fact that the military had any involvement in his killing. SWAPO and the Lubowski family, however, vehemently denied these allegations.

On 22 March 1990 evidence was led at the Harms Commission of Enquiry in support of Minister Malan's claim that Lubowski was a spy. Lubowski had two Nedbank accounts. One was in the name of Paradise Trust at the St. Georges Street Cape Town branch. The second was an account in Windhoek in his personal name. In June 1989 R40 000 and R20 000 respectively was paid into those accounts.

The fact was that Lubowski was a paid agent. Exposing him was not an impulsive move and the government deliberated for several months before outing him. Linking him to the military was a tactical move which suited them as it tended to get them of the hook on the reasoning that they would surely not kill one of their own. It also provided the Service with its traditional right of denial. It allowed the Service to remain unblemished by scandal and free to continue its then current role of negotiating with the ANC.

Yet producing records of cheque deposits hardly proved that Lubowski had been controlled by the military. The deposits could have been made by anyone within the security apparatus. The way things worked in the intelligence world was that for the sake of convenience, any National Intelligence agent could be made to appear as if he belonged to the military. The SADF was the effective ruler of SWA/Namibia, so from a logistical point of view, it would have been a simple matter for them to make the payments from their budget for later reimbursement.

The Service's office in Windhoek at the time was headed by Kerneels Uys from Division 031.

If Lubowski had been an agent for Military Intelligence, they could have produced his agent file on SADF stationery. Having decided to expose him after his death, there was no reason why they should not also have exposed the intelligence he had provided. It was all water under the bridge by then and would have been far more convincing evidence than the paid cheques.

7

Training

I left Pretoria in the early morning with Tammy, Jean-Pierre and Paul. We were collected by an operator from the Counter-Intelligence Division at a prearranged rendezvous opposite a coffee shop in the city centre. We travelled along Voortrekker road, passed through Wonderboom Nek and headed north. The gaiety in the vehicle reminded me more of a college student bash than a secret training mission for intelligence operatives. The driver kept his professional distance and maintained his aloofness.

We crossed into the so-called independent homeland of Bophuthatswana, run by a black Bantustan administration utterly dependent on the South African government. Its intelligence service had secretly provided a safe training base within its territory for its 'big brother'. We left the tarred regional road and turned onto a dusty dirt road which snaked through shoulder high buffalo grass that rustled in the breeze. The track ended at a whitewashed cluster of Cape Dutch style buildings and rondavels.

A bald, toad-like and obese figure in his 40s and dressed in a T-shirt and denim jeans, introduced himself as Jakes, the course leader. The trainees emptied the vehicle of food supplies and carried it into a primitive conference and kitchen complex. Facilities were limited to a gas freezer and a military field kitchen. There was no running water and a petrol generator occasionally provided electricity. The week's water supply was stored in 25-litre plastic drums in the kitchen. We were told that the divisional headquarters in Pretoria would resupply us on a weekly basis.

300 metres from the main complex, a long drop over a deep hole inside a wooden hut provided the only toilet facilities. At the back of the house a military-style cold water shower had been erected amongst the trees.

Our sleeping quarters were a scattering of thatched-roof rondavels.

I dumped my leather travelling bag, bought in the Seychelles, on the cement floor of the one I would share with Jean-Pierre. I opened the windows and curtains to get light and fresh air into the stuffy confines. A layer of dust indicated that it had seldom, if ever, been cleaned.

After settling in, everyone returned to the thatched 'lapa' for lunch. Jakes used the informal setting as a teaching opportunity and to get to know us.

'You can help yourselves to a beer — there won't be any classes today. We have to wait for a group of 12 youngsters from Division 062 who will be joining us for the introductory week of the course. As is routine, their true identities will be shielded from you and your's from them. They are recruits for the Counter-Intelligence Division's newly established team of Watchers.'

'This surveillance unit will be focussing its activities on foreign embassy staff and intelligence operatives suspected to be active on South African soil. They will also be used in all internal investigations, including against our own operatives. The team leader of this unit is Pete Richards. Pete is an explosives and close protection specialist. He has had extensive experience in surveillance techniques learned while he was working abroad.'

We students helped ourselves to food and while we were eating Jakes continued.

'The surveillance unit will be available to you to assist with any groundwork that might be required prior to a sensitive recruitment. They will be positioned to provide you with photographs, details of the habits, weaknesses and movements of your target to enable you to compile an informed pre-recruitment profile. They will also be able to assist and provide you with surveillance support for operations abroad.'

When Pete Richards' 12 watchers arrived later, Jakes performed the 'shaded identity' introductions between them and the four trainee spymasters. I was surprised to find four teenage girls amongst them — one an Indian fluent in Afrikaans.

The watchers had been together and under training for the past 14 days and they very much stuck together. They didn't suffer the double identity complication to the same extent as the four of us. They would function as a unit, so they were encouraged to bond and learn each other's intimacies. Nevertheless, they had to maintain their covers in the face of outsiders, including the four of us. We had to maintain our masks not only with the bigger group of watchers but also amongst ourselves. It was vital to protect our true identities and everything about ourselves in case one of us was later captured by the enemy or even turned and became a double agent.

I tried to commence a superficial conversation with Jean-Pierre, but being defensive about our origins and true identities, intelligent conversations involving little more than small talk were impossible.

Only Jakes and Pete could fully enjoy each other's company as they were the only declared members of the greater Service.

*   *   *

Jakes had a lot more wisdom to impart to us.

'In the next six weeks you'll have to master the basics of intelligence tradecraft before you are allowed into the field. That's my task. Your mentor in the field will play a big role in deciding your future deployment and its time frame. You might be put in to break new ground or you could be used to replace someone in an existing structure. On the other hand, there's a chance that you might not make it into an undercover posting abroad. You'll be moulded by the operations and those involved in them. The final decider is how you handle things in the field.

'You'll have to shape your own future once you are out there. Like a chameleon you can adopt any colour that suits you. If the information you produce is top grade you can live in virtually any country in the world. Everything is within your grasp. Never force your personality and always stay true to yourself, no matter what role you might assume for the moment.'

We learned the principles, or lack of them, that governed the art of espionage — how it was a game of wits, primitive instinct and survival. It was a profession that tapped into the diverse patterns of human behaviour.

Jakes shared some of his experiences with us, providing a broad outline of the type of skills we would have to master.

'I've worked undercover for most of my career. My last stint four years ago, code named *Project Cold Potato*, ended in disaster. I suffered a heart attack while I was living as an illegal in a certain African state. The head of the intelligence apparatus there had sanctioned my presence in the country without the knowledge of his president or the government of the day. With the assistance of senior officers under his command, he provided me with strategic and tactical information about the region as well as ANC operations in Zimbabwe, Zambia, Tanzania and Angola.'

I figured it had to be the DRC that Jakes was talking about. Many years later I learnt that National Intelligence had maintained a covert office in Zaïre (now Democratic Republic of Congo or DRC), with the

94

help of certain elements in the government. That office was still functional in the late 1980s.

Jakes continued: 'Being a confidant of the president, a head of state serving on the OAU, we had open access through his intelligence chief to priceless information on the region's political affairs. The arrangement was purely a financial one and the Service paid this prime source a fortune in US dollars. We even heard about Robert Mugabe's vanity, how he dyed his greying hair and how his late wife Sally kept him in complete submission.'

Jakes returned to the trauma that changed his career direction from operations to training.

'My heart attack threatened to compromise the ultra-sensitive understanding with the local intelligence chief. It had the potential of endangering the lives of our assets in that country. The heart attack happened late one afternoon. I must have lost consciousness because when I came to it was already dark. I was unable to walk and I crawled around groping for the telephone. My emergency communication, a UHF link with the South African embassy in London, was worse than useless for summoning help in time. In desperation I made a stupid and dangerous move to save myself. Ignoring the possibility of electronic surveillance, I phoned my agent the general, at home. He must have been utterly shocked because he just put the phone down.'

'What did you do?', Tammy asked.

'The pain was excruciating. I knew my false identity and the radio and photographic equipment in my house would compromise the general, his staff and our operation in the country. I managed to regain enough strength to destroy the evidence.'

After that, he said, he felt broken and lonely and began to wonder why he had never got married. He realised that the days of undercover work were over. Even if he survived, there would be no further foreign postings. Poor health would make it too risky. Then he lapsed into unconsciousness.

'When I eventually woke up,' he resumed, 'the lights were on and an elderly black man was inserting a drip into my arm. The pain and disorientation subsided. With the general's help, I transmitted an urgent request for evacuation to South Africa. The general and his aide put me on the back seat of his car, loaded the incriminating equipment still remaining into the boot, and drove me to the extraction point — an abandoned military airfield 50km south of the capital. It was an installation that I had identified as a future springboard for an emergency extraction, resupply or military strike. I had forwarded a code name and co-ordinates of the place to headquarters the week after my first arrival.

'The general and his aide made me comfortable in a broken-down hangar by the grass-covered runway. Before he left I assured the general that if I did not return, a suitable replacement would be sent to continue my work. We agreed on a message that my successor would place in the smalls of a local newspaper so that contact could be re-established. The aide remained with me while I waited for help to arrive. The following night, under cover of darkness and flying beneath the enemy radar, an unmarked SAAF aircraft landed and airlifted me to safety.'

I was curious to hear the final outcome of the episode.

'What happened to the general?'

'He certainly could not be abandoned. We needed him too much. I was replaced shortly after my evacuation by a French-speaking operator from Division 031, our Foreign Collection Department.'

'But how do we go about recruiting someone who is a traditional enemy?' Paul asked.

'Intelligence organisations in general, especially African ones, are very autonomous. The officers heading them don't necessarily support the policies of their political masters and even when they do, they are often just out to seek personal gain. In a continent where coups and counter-coups are commonplace, their jobs and their status might well be short lived. So they capitalise on their positions to enrich themselves while they can.

'Top-level agents like this secretly provide NIS with covert bases and infrastructure inside their countries. They also provide information on the region and the politics of our enemies. They don't regard the supply of intelligence on the liberation movements as a conflict of interest because they are not spying on their own countries. These countries are all former colonies.

'If you are fluent in French, English or Portuguese, are carrying the right passport and you are backed by a cover that suggests ample foreign currency, you'll more often than not be welcomed by such people. Once this has been achieved, our on-side host secures the necessary local documentation and ensures the day-to-day protection of the handler to our mutual benefit.'

He explained how spying is about ordinary people, their weaknesses and the innovative skill of the operator in luring a prey into the web. Spies are not recruited on the basis of their strength of character or virtues, but on their flaws and for their vanities. The weakest link in every espionage operation is the conveyance of your information without it being compromised.

'Communication is difficult, because in most cases countries in black Africa have no links with the Republic. Information has to be routed via one of our European embassies — the London station carries most of the traffic from Africa back to Pretoria.

He explained the dynamics with a factual event.

'The Zimbabwean Minister of State Security, without the knowledge of his dictatorial head of state, Robert Mugabe, has made subtle overtures to establish an unofficial link with the Service. Bob would have a heart attack if he knew what some of his top intelligence advisors think of him.

'Initiating contact with us in confidence and secrecy is complex and dangerous, especially for our biggest adversaries. The divide is great and trustworthy intermediaries are hard to find.'

'How do we establish secure contact then?'

'The shortest distance between two destinations is a straight line,' Jakes said, 'but in intelligence work there's no such thing as a straight line. There are what we call friendly intelligence services, perhaps a contradiction in terms. An operator from MI6, the CIA, the French service or whoever might be individually sympathetic to our cause and not toe the official line of his superiors thousands of kilometres away from Africa. Nurturing informal liaisons with such people is not a straight line but an indirect route to the target. It brings the parties together. In this particular instance the asset dropped a hint at an embassy function he was officiating at. He was overheard by a friendly who fed us the tip. We made an approach and the rest is history.'

*   *   *

I found my entrance into the world of intelligence extraordinarily difficult at first. I became constantly on guard and viewed anyone's interest in me with suspicion. As far as my private life was concerned I accepted that in the future, a lie would become my first response. This would buy time to analyse the question and the questioner's motives. In future, I would consciously suppress what often became a longing to discuss details of my career with people close to me. While I was thrilled and intrigued by the espionage profession and by my future prospects, at the same time I began to feel alienated from others. Erecting a stone wall around one's self and allowing in only those people I had to deal with was a high price to pay for a naturally gregarious person like myself.

In the first week we covered the origins and history of the profession, learning inter alia about Philby, Burgess, Maclean and the Israeli spy

Eli Cohen. We learned about basic intelligence tradecraft, dead drops, fleeting meetings, secret writing and surveillance. Techniques established as far back as the years before in World War-II were drilled into us. The writing of intelligence reports was of particular importance and training in this field became a daily activity. There was a large bundle of newspapers in the lecture room. In the afternoons, working individually, we converted the contents into intelligence reports.

The Watchers were excluded from the weekly project of compiling a defendable personal cover, with false name, a freshly minted childhood, geography of supposed living areas, higher education and professional qualifications. This subject occupied most of our evenings.

The Watchers left after the first week.

Expertise was drawn from the field to enhance our training. The Service's strongest players were brought in from all over the country to assist in getting the members of the new sub-divisions operational. Unnamed operatives, still active in the field, shared their knowledge and specific expertise. This included hands-on skills in all aspects of photography, lock-picking and matters like secret communication. We worked on assignments late into the night to digest information, talents, skills and values, foreign to the norm.

Towards the end of the course Division 061's management — Ron Sharlow, Phillip and Steve — visited the training camp. Each of us had a short, personal audience with the senior officers.

Steve buttonholed me and we spoke privately.

'There's been an interesting development since you've been away. A top- level recruitment might be in the pipeline for you. An official at the Soviet Embassy in Botswana has made two crossings into South Africa during the past week. He travels alone and appears to be pretty restless. We think he's KGB or GRU (*Glavnoye Razvedyvatelnoye Upravlenie*) — Soviet Military Intelligence. He's in the embassy's trade section under the name Anatoly Polozok.

Before we came here we had a meeting with CIA and MI6 liaison officers in Pretoria. They have no idea who he really is, but they will compare our photographs of him against their databases and will probably come up with an ID. If it seems positive and he does want to make contact, they want to be in on the act or, at least, share the information. You'll have to be pretty sharp with this one. We have a team on the ground on our side of the border. By the time you're finished here everything should be in place for the recruitment. Use the rest of your time here to make preparations and work on your cover for the field. This will not be a dress rehearsal but the real thing.'

For me it posed a thrill beyond comprehension — my first hunt would soon be a reality.

'Steve, please don't leave me out of this one.'

'Don't worry, this one is yours.'

The training became more focussed and personalised — each agent worked to perfect his own cover, building a fictitious legend for the field. We started to practise what we had learned in theory. During the day or at night, Jakes would cart us off to the busy streets of Pretoria, Johannesburg or the packed inner suburbs to complete assignments.

Some of it was a repeat of what I had learned before my Seychelles assignment. Armed with cameras, we would be dropped off at various places with instructions to photograph sensitive installations under a wide range of circumstances while remaining undetected. At the training base we had to develop and print the results of our escapades.

Much effort went into testing our cover stories. Our manipulative skills were used against unsuspecting patrons at bars and hotels. We would enter a public place alone and select a target. Using our skills in socialising, we would establish a bond that could be pursued in future and glean as much personal information from the individual as possible and commit it to memory. This kind of exercise also served as a practical test for the plausibility of the covers we had adopted and helped to identify possible weaknesses and loopholes.

In the evenings in the privacy of the training base, exhaustive postmortems would be conducted around the campfire with everyone offering criticism or praise.

Being an unaccompanied woman, Tammy's approach of male targets made her seem like an easy pick up. Her good looks and sexuality sometimes aided her schemes, but more often than not her efforts were nullified by male testosterone. Some of the stories she recounted around the campfire were hilarious and ranged from success to marriage proposals to outright offers of money for sex. As the course progressed, she left behind in her wake a string of frustrated males who were presumably ringing nonexistent phone numbers in a fruitless search to find her.

The system, in fact, would expect a female agent to prostitute herself as a recruitment option if faced with a top priority target. I remember Phillip saying that spying was all about power — those who are born to it and those who are bred to it through arrogance and ease. I made a note to beware of the dangers posed by a beautiful and well-trained female spy.

By the end of the fifth week I was accustomed to my altar ego. I could slip in and out of its character with ease and my two personalities had become entwined. Freelance journalism, specifically as a travel writer, was my cloak for operations. It would allow me to photograph and research political and economic matters across the length and breadth of Africa. I could travel either to exotic destinations or off the beaten track in Mozambique, Zambia and Zimbabwe to root out the enemy without raising suspicions.

In the middle of the night I was awakened by a knock on my door.

The potbelly frame of Jakes stood there.

'Your course is over', he said. 'Phillip has just phoned and said you're required in Pretoria. He said you'll know what it's about. Steve will fetch you at 06:00.'

'Good luck', Jakes added and stuck out a beefy hand.

To go back to sleep again was impossible. I had no doubt that the reason for my early departure was the Soviet agent, Polozok. I packed my gear and carried it to the dying embers of the campfire. I stirred it into life and warmed up a pot of coffee.

8

My first Russian

Steve arrived promptly at 06:00. I climbed into the passenger seat of his VW Jetta while the engine was still running.

'You've to be in Mafikeng tonight. You'll be meeting Polozok at the Red Lion Hotel at 19:00. The Yanks really came through on this one. They have confirmed his identity as Anatoly Polozok, a colonel in GRU, the Soviet Military Intelligence.

'Polozok enlisted in the Red Army at the age of 17 and worked his way through the ranks to colonel. It appears that he joined Military Intelligence as a strategic move to bolster his career. He supported and promoted the communist system with diligence and ruthlessly exploited the absolute limits of his power.

'His last known posting was as a military adviser in Afghanistan. He successfully infiltrated the ranks of the Afghan rebels and caused havoc for the undercover CIA operatives who were supporting the resistance on the ground. He then disappeared and nothing has been heard of him for 18 months until he turned up in Botswana.'

Recruiting a veteran intelligence agent like Polozok seemed a daunting task for a rookie like me.

'The Yanks know we're up to something and they're dying to find out where Polozok is', Steve continued. 'We'll have to be particularly careful — especially you on the ground. I know that by now the CIA will have alerted their field operatives in the Frontline States and told them to be on the lookout for him. They'll want him for themselves and they'll try to shadow us and grab him from under our noses, particularly if he's not on South African soil.'

We reached the Deputy Chief's townhouse in record time.

'Morning, gentleman', a stern looking Phillip said. Remember that you'll be up against an old hand and the possible presence of the active opposition. I'm not really concerned about the Bophuthatswana security people but I am about the CIA. If Polozok is under suspicion from his own side, there might be hoodlums around waiting to drag him back across the border into Botswana if he makes a wrong move. If you suspect that you might not be in control of your immediate environment, or that either he or you is being watched, don't make the meet. The last thing we need is to expose him by showing our hand prematurely. I must also remind you that while you are engaged in this operation, we don't know you.'

Phillip sketched the background to where the meeting would take place.

'Some years ago we acquired the services of the manager of the Red Lion on an ad hoc basis, capitalising on its strategic position so close to the Botswana border and straddling one of the ANC's infiltration routes. Six weeks ago he alerted us to Polozok's frequent visits. A team of Watchers was immediately despatched to the area to confirm the initial sighting and to take photographs so we could confirm his identity.

'They reported that Polozok had stayed at the hotel for the past four weekends. He normally breakfasts on the pool deck where he remains reading a paperback until about 14:00 when he returns to his room on the first floor. He goes down to the ladies bar, neatly dressed in an open-neck shirt and jacket, at about 18:00 for happy hour. He always dines alone, after which he enjoys a cigar and cognac on the terrace before turning in for the night. Until now he hasn't met anyone during his visits or left the hotel grounds.

'Our assessment is that we're dealing with a 'walk-in', Phillip continued. 'It seems that Polozok has placed himself on the market.'

The phone starting ringing inside the house and Phillip excused himself to answer it. He returned moments later.

'That was Ron on the phone. He needed to apprise the DG this morning about what's going on. I confirmed that we're going ahead.'

'Steve will share the nuts and bolts of the operation with you when I've finished,' Phillip continued. 'I need you to know that before I ordered your recall from the course, we tested our assumption that Polozok is engaged in marketing himself for recruitment. Celia spent last weekend at the Red Lion.'

'Which Celia?' I was surprised, even amazed.

'Yes, Celia the old spinster you met at the office', Steve laughed.

'Well, her cover as the hotel manager's sister on a visit worked like a charm. She mirrored Polozok's movements, having breakfast on the pool deck when he did, sunning on the pool deck while he was there, having cocktails at happy hour and dining at the same time as him. She made no contact, but just created a presence. Her behaviour was a signal that an operator of his standing would recognise. On the Sunday evening, as predicted, he asked her to join him for dinner.

'The colonel was not so blasé as to offer his services directly, although he identified himself as a Russian. Celia said he spoke in generalisations, voicing dissatisfaction with the domestic situation in the Soviet Union, the economic deterioration, escalating government corruption and favouritism.'

Phillip said Polozok's voice had been secretly recorded by Celia for forensic analysis and this had confirmed he presented an above average chance of recruitment.

The elaborate professionalism that was being used to snare a worthy target left me in awe. It was obvious that in the profession nothing was left to chance and that I still had a lot to learn.

'Polozok fears the approaching demise of the Soviet system, which for years had been his vehicle to personal gain, power and wealth', Steve added. 'I think he's disillusioned and angry with the communist system for failing him. He can obviously see that the GRU machinery is not going to fulfil his expectations. He's 52 years old and probably figures that this will be his last foreign assignment and the last opportunity he'll get to change sides.'

'We believe he's looking for a South African offer, but I think he suspects that we can't afford him,' Phillip continued. 'He's gambling that his co-operation will lead to a trade-off with the CIA or MI6, where he knows he'll be able to get his asking price, whatever that might be.'

'Although I think he's too expensive for us, let's humour him and help him to sell his birthright. When we've got what we wanted, we'll barter him to the Americans. They can either keep him or throw him back into the pond.'

It was an intellectual and mental skin trade, was the thought that occurred to me. There was no place for scruples or morals and the game was played strictly by the rules. He was the enemy, so fuck him.

Phillip excused himself to leave for the office. Steve took two cold beers from the fridge.

'Here', he said offering me one, 'have a drink.' It was 10:00.

'All right, relax', he said. 'I'll run through the plan step by step. Just concentrate and remember the specifics. Jakes has forwarded the final draft of your proposed cover which has been accepted in principle. You'll book into the hotel as Riaan Lesage, a freelance journalist doing an article on the feasibility of the area as a tourist destination. Riaan Lesage is accredited to the Independent Press Association (IPA) in Lusaka, Zambia. It's a black owned alternative news agency, but it's under our control. If anyone queries them about you, they'll backstop your story.'

He emptied an envelope on the table and I leafed through its contents. There was a press card and a South African passport in my cover name. The latter was complete with Zambian Immigration entry and exit stamps.

He slid a bundle R50 bills over to me.

I counted 20 of them and stuck them in my back pocket.

'That's for expenses.'

He passed a Volkswagen key ring with one key to me.

'Let's go. Your VW Golf is in Phillip's garage. It's registered in your new name.'

I gathered everything up, slung my travel bag and camera case over my shoulder and followed Steve outside,.

I left Pretoria at midday and headed due west for Rustenburg, the first major town en route to Mafikeng. I checked the rearview mirror for signs of surveillance but the road behind me was deserted.

I found the Red Lion on the north-western outskirts of Mafikeng. It was a whitewashed Victorian-style building dating from the early 1950s. I found an open parking space under a huge jacaranda tree on the far side of the packed parking lot.

The hotel's obvious popularity unnerved me. With such a crowd in the place it would be difficult to spot surveillance. I looked around but the Soviet colonel's desert-coloured Land Cruiser with its Botswana registration was nowhere to be seen. I climbed the wide slate steps and entered the reception through a set of heavy oak doors. I smiled at the receptionist as I confirmed my booking.

'Afternoon, Mr Lesage, we've been expecting you.'

I scribbled Lesage's illegible signature for the first time in earnest and accepted the key to room 202. I declined a porter's offer to help me with my luggage.

Room 202 was towards the back of the hotel. I dumped the Pentax and my hand luggage on the double bed and opened the windows to air the room.

I decided to go down to the pool for a swim and perhaps get a glimpse of the colonel. Ten lengths in the cold water cooled me down and restored my alertness. Not wishing to join a crowd of female reps and locals at the bar, I ordered a Bloody Mary from a roving waiter. From my vantage point on a deck chair by the pool I tried to spot the Russian amongst the crowd, but there was no sign of him. I was disappointed and began to have negative thoughts.

What if he doesn't show? How long should I wait?

104

My doubts echoed the torment of all field operatives in similar situations. There was always inherent danger in a face-to-face meeting with an enemy agent. Perhaps Polozok had been captured by his own side and broken in the interrogation room. Maybe the KGB was already setting a trap to capture a South African intelligence officer — me!

I didn't have the answers or the experience. It was my first exposure to the lonely and unaided pressure cooker world of counter-espionage. I finished my drink in the fading light of dusk, coming to grips with the only constant in the game — that there are no constants. I decided to wait and make a decision about leaving the hotel in the morning.

After a shower and a change of clothing I took up a position at the bar that gave me an unobstructed view of the reception area and the foyer. open plan downstairs area. I kept to myself and ignored the locals and reps drinking at the bar. After two whiskies I moved into the dining room and was guided to a table by a waiter from whom I ordered a bottle of red wine.

By 20:00 there was still no sign of the target and to avoid drawing attention to myself, I ordered a rump steak. While waiting for the meal and nursing my glass of wine, I became aware that the tables around me were filling up with diners, but there was still no sign of the colonel.

I had just started my meal when I suddenly became aware of the blue-eyed stare of Anatoly Polozok. He had positioned himself at a table in my direct line of sight. My appetite vanished as adrenaline coursed through me. I drank the rest of my wine in a few gulps and leaving what remained of my food, I got to my feet in an obvious demonstration of departure.

I could sense the target's eyes boring into my back as I moved through the sliding doors that led to the dimly lit patio. I deliberately stayed within his vision and moved to a table in the shadows by the pool. I knew that the colonel was monitoring my every movement.

He dawdled towards where I sat, moving slowly and carefully. I didn't doubt that he had made a positive ID of his opposite number, but he wasn't taking any chances. Face-to-face meetings like this were dangerous and to be avoided if at all possible. But he had initiated this one himself. He had things to say and needed to make demands and that could only be done one-on-one.

After I had been waiting in the darkness for half an hour. I heard rather than saw the Russian colonel approach. I listened to be sure that there were no other footsteps moving in my direction. The pit of my stomach was knotted like a fist and I wondered how many times I would have to go through this in my career.

Satisfied that no one else was around, I moved from the shadows. It also allowed Polozok to confirm that I was alone. I stopped about six paces from him.

We both had good reason to prefer the shadows. I was a spy and the colonel was both a spy and an almost-traitor. His Slavic accent was disguised but still detectable as he murmured the pre-arranged code: 'The smell of the frangipanis reminds me of home.'

I responded with my code word and dangled my room key in my left hand so that the white numbers on the perspex holder were clearly visible in the moonlight. My legs were shaking as I turned around and walked back into the hotel.

There was a single knock on the door of my room. The Soviet intelligence officer stepped into a den that I had prepared for secrecy. I had drawn the curtains and the only light came from a single bedside lamp. The television was on to confuse the substance of conversation from any hidden bugging devices.

We didn't embrace or shake hands. I merely introduced myself as Riaan.

Colonel Anatoly Polozok was a cold man, self-contained, aloof and arrogantly confident of himself and his actions — despite knowing that Mother Russia would not deal kindly with those of her military elite who turned traitor. I waved him to a chair next to a small table and sat down opposite him. I felt vaguely intimidated by the older and obviously more experienced agent. It was my first time to fraternise with a man who represented South Africa's arch-enemy. I decided that some drinks would probably relax us both. I decided against vodka as a matter of principle and instead ordered South African brandy from room service.

When it arrived I collected it outside the door. I passed him a drink and we sat in silence, like chess players awaiting the opening move.

'Do you mind if I smoke?'

'No, go ahead.'

The Russian removed a thick cigar from a metal tube and went into the ritual of lighting up.

He had been involved with specialised recruitment for most of his life so he knew what I wanted. He opened with his current intelligence access and background, which he knew I would require to brief my superiors.

'I'm responsible for the gathering of military-related intelligence in the region, with specific emphasis on the SADF's capabilities and its war effort in Angola. As you'll know, the Soviet Union provides the

106

South African liberation movements with advice, strategic information and weapons to aid their armed struggle. I'm the GRU liaison officer for this region responsible for Botswana, Zimbabwe, Zambia and Angola.'

He revealed his true status as a decisive move to promote his own value. 'I report directly to the Director Operations of the Joint Planning Staff in the Defence Ministry.'

I unwittingly gave the impression that I was more impressed with his access to the liberation movements and to the military arena in Angola than in the benefits of having an asset in Moscow's Funze Street. My inexperience didn't pass unnoticed.

Polozok felt that the South Africans had snubbed him by sending a junior officer for such a meeting, but he probably still felt confident that he was on the road to his ultimate goal — the capitalist riches of the Americans. He deliberately said nothing about his links with Minister of Defence Ustinov, the Moscow Party Chief, the communist boss of Leningrad and that outsider called Mikhail Gorbachev. He had no need to give away too much detail at such an early stage.

Having recognised my interest in the ANC, he began to relate some personal experiences.

'Years ago my friend Archie Sibeko was appointed the ANC's chief of logistics in Angola. We jointly established Bangu Camp, the ANC's main base in northern Angola. It's on an estuary of the Chicamba River and too far away for any possibility of South African interference. It's still being used as a secure site for sensitive KGB training and as a planning base for Spec Ops cadres before they return to South Africa.'

I was privately ecstatic with the progress we were making. I ordered another round of brandies to keep the wheels lubricated From Jakes' tuition I knew that the Soviets were commonly susceptible to betraying their country because of the pervasive corruption and nepotism that enveloped them.

Then came the clincher.

'There's a price, of course', the colonel said.

I recognised it in his eyes. He was planning to defect and he was determined that when he did it would make him rich.

'How much?'

'One million US dollars and an apartment in Florida. I love the sunshine.'

'Deal!' I said without hesitation.

It wasn't a deal yet, but I was determined not to let him slip through my fingers. I felt confident that the Service would find the money somewhere.

I did not realise it but my ready lie caused the intelligence veteran some amusement. Nevertheless, he was confident that his demands would be relayed to the right quarters.

He reached inside his jacket and produced a bulky envelope. He unemotionally explained its contents as I secreted it inside my travel bag. We agreed to meet again at the same venue in 14 days and he left the room.

Adhering to my training, I emptied the contents of the ashtray into a plastic bag and wiped the glasses clean of fingerprints. When satisfied that no evidence of our meeting remained and that sufficient time had elapsed since Polozok's departure, I packed my belongings and left the room. I checked out of the hotel at midnight and commenced the drive back to Pretoria. I stopped in Rustenburg en route and reported to Steve from a public phone. He said I should go directly to Phillip's townhouse.

It was 02:30 when Phillip slit open the envelope and examined the contents. The 89-page manuscript documented the information he had shared with me. It was my first intelligence product. Phillip read it aloud in amazed disbelief.

It contained a complete breakdown including the full names, postings international and national, of all South African intelligence personnel whether they belonged to NIS, Military Intelligence or Security Branch. It went into considerable personal detail even naming those who made a habit of swearing during general conversation and naming those at the opposite end of the scale who opened their meetings with a prayer. It named journalists who were NIS agents.

It was clearly the work of a mole and it came as a shock.

'I need a drink.'

Phillip poured each of us a shot of cognac. He said he had got the bottle while on a recruitment mission to Marseilles two months before. He had been saving it for a special occasion and this was clearly it. He raised his glass in salute.

'Well done, Riaan.'

We sipped in silence as Phillip continued.

'If what Polozok says is true it constitutes a major threat to our national security. The information will carry a top priority classification.'

Phillip picked up the phone and dialled the Divisional Director's home number.

'Sorry for waking you at this hour, sir.'

I glanced at my watch. It was 03:20.

Distrusting the security of the connection, his message was brief.

'The *Meerkat* (my in-house codename) has returned. I value his information as immediate.'

There were a few more 'yes sirs' before he replaced the receiver.

'There's a briefing at HQ in an hour', Phillip said turning to me. 'Stay here until you hear from me. I suggest you get some sleep. You're going to need it.

He nodded at Steve. 'Phone your wife and tell her we're having a crisis. You won't be home for at least a couple of days.'

'Phillip', I said insistently.

Phillip paused.

'He wants a million US dollars and I agreed.'

Phillip's face turned almost crimson and the veins in his forehead visibly swelled with anger.

'Are you out of your fucking mind? You haven't even got the authority to approve R100. You've only just started here!'

I blew up. The magnitude of Polozok's information pushed me over the edge and I leapt to my feet.

'Fuck, this bullshit! You sent me into this situation, so you must trust my judgement. If they want the information tell them to raise the money . . . or lose the bloody war!'

Steve reacted automatically and grabbed me.

'Relax buddy, relax.'

With me in his grasp he turned to Phillip.

'Its okay, just go.'

Steve and I killed Phillip's cognac in the early hours before dawn. After that we slept on the uncomfortable settees in the lounge.

'Where the hell do we get hold of a million dollars? I asked Steve before I drifted off to sleep.

'The short answer', Phillip told me three days later, 'is that we don't. I proposed it to Dr Barnard and the finance guys. Their decision is that he's too pricey for us.'

'But we need that sort of information', I protested. 'It's worth his weight in gold.'

'I absolutely agree', Phillip said with conviction. 'I understand the chief had the men from Langley [CIA] over for two days and they've been in contact with Washington. They've wanted him for a long time and they are willing to take him over, million dollars and all. Sorry about that, Riaan. The good news is that your work has impressed the management and they have decided to dispense with the rest of your probationary period and confirm your permanent appointment. Congratulations.'

'He might not work for anyone else', I persisted doggedly.

'You're the one who called him a mercenary. He'll go where the money is and we'll get the product anyway. When can you arrange the handover?'

'I'll be seeing him in two weeks, so it will be as soon as possible after that.'

The ease with which Phillip agreed to transfer the agent to the Yanks surprised me. Compared to the vast sums spent on the war in Angola, the price tag did not seem that exorbitant. The advance knowledge that he could provide would, in any case, save the military many millions of rands.

Looking back, my view is that we should have kept the agent and sold some of his information to the Americans to cover costs. Phillip, however, always had a high regard for the CIA and spoke of it as a bigger and better service which paid real money. We also knew that although liaison with officers of friendly services was sanctioned, it was no secret that the CIA made all-out efforts to recruit our officers. I could never decide if Phillip was working for the Americans, but I sure had my doubts at the time — and so did Steve.

Polozok's 89-page document on the organisation of the South African intelligence services caused a major stir in the NIS. In the end Paul Gough, Director Division 05 refused to accept its veracity. He believed it was the work of a single author, an insider who had openly defected, namely Martin Dolinchek

I had no feedback. I was too low down on the seniority scale and I was not even consulted. I only heard about it many years later. I could have told Gough, though, that his contention was impossible. Maybe he was whistling in the dark in the hope that the suggestion a mole was at work in NIA would just go away. Because of need-to-know only an officer from Division 031 or a very senior officer would have been able to put such detailed information together. Dolinchek was far to junior for that. He would have had no idea who was staffing the Paris or London offices or the DRC for that matter. And what about the information relating to Military Intelligence and the Security Branch? Where would he have got that?

I believe to this day that it was the work of a traitor — and a very senior one at that.

Arrangements for Polozok's takeover were eventually finalised four months later. I deliberately went out of my way to stall the transfer. When Polozok asked me why it was taking so long, I blamed the Americans for the delay in putting together his bride price. When Phillip asked me the same I blamed it on Polozok for procrastinating.

During this time Polozok and I became good friends, with him playing a bit of a father figure to me. In some ways I think our relationship reminded him of his son back home. In the end, I think he was also sad that he was not working for the South Africans. Naturally, though, the CIA money helped to mop up any tears he might have had.

I next saw Polozok on 19 January 1986. We arranged to meet unofficially at Lichtenburg to the east of Mafikeng. He said that Soviet General Konstantin Shaganovitch had arrived in Angola to take overall control of all forces operating in the country on behalf of the MPLA (People's Movement for the Liberation of Angola). This included Luanda's own troops.

950 Soviet officers had been posted to command and training duties in Angola. They included General Mikhail Petrot, First Deputy in the Soviet Politburo, who took charge of counter-insurgency policy. 2 000 East German specialist troops were deployed in the MPLA's intelligence and communication services. A further 3 700 Cuban troops had also been deployed.

The information came as a shock. The Soviet Union was a superpower and the magnitude of its military commitment against South Africa was frightening. The intelligence was vital to South Africa's security and it had to be relayed to the cabinet, the State Security Council and the SADF as soon as possible.

The last page detailed the military logistics that were being mobilised against us.

'Shaganovitch, a counter-insurgency expert, is planning a major offensive against the SADF in Angola. The following military hardware has already been shipped to Angola for this purpose:

'76 Ilyushin transport aircraft, 5 Antonov 22 'Cock' long-range heavy-lift turboprop transport planes, 27 Mi24 helicopters and 70 MiG21 fighters, 23 MiG23s and 10 Sukhoi 23s.

'T55 main battle tanks, PT76 amphibious tanks, BTR60 and BRDM2 armoured personnel carriers have already been airlifted from the seaports of Luanda, Lobito and Porto Namibe to the inland centres of Menongwe, Cuito Cuanavale and Luena.'

I took the information to Phillip. We were the first South African officials to see evidence of this massive Soviet military buildup. Somehow the top secret information seemed more sombre in the dead of night than it had appeared earlier.

On one occasion I helped Polozok out of a spot of bother he was having with his head office. They were pressuring him for information and had ordered him to step up his production rate.

I passed him a copy of the annual report of the Rössing Uranium Mine in SWA/Namibia. I knew that during the June 1985 SADF raid

111

on ANC safe houses in Gaborone, Botswana, a battle plan to attack Rössing Mine had been discovered. The annual report was a freely available overt document and it was loaded with figures and technical data. Polozok broke it up into several reports and submitted them as if they came from a South African agent he had recruited.

On the final occasion we saw each other, he told me that Moscow had given him a commendation because the Rössing information was so prized. We laughed and got seriously pissed on good South African brandy. He never drank vodka when he was with me. We exchanged contact details and promised to keep in touch unofficially. This was something I never shared with my superiors because after that Polozok was officially off-limits to me.

As a parting present he gave me some vital information to the effect that relations between General Shaganovitch and the top Cuban generals, Arnoldo Ochoa Sanchez and Rafael Del Pino Diaz, had become severely strained. Ochoa Sanchez, Del Pino Diaz and even Fidel Castro himself opposed Shaganovitch's planned offensive because they predicted defeat by the South Africans. The Russian, however, won the argument and was pushing ahead with planning for this campaign.

The South African war machine reacted swiftly and ferociously to the information. The SADF launched a strong assault against Cuito Cuanavale, Shaganovitch's main staging post for the offensive, and destroyed radar installations, artillery and bomb stocks. They killed scores of ANC cadres who were fighting alongside Cuban and FAPLA forces. The SADF won a major battle at the Lomba River, killing more than 600 of the enemy and capturing vast amounts of equipment including SAM 8 missile systems. It virtually destroyed FAPLA's 47th Brigade.

South African Special Forces slipped into Porto Namibe and sank a Soviet ship and badly damaged two others that were bringing in weapons for the offensive. They also blasted three petrol storage tanks in the harbour.

Douw Steyn, the 4-Recce officer who had led the assault, related to me what had happened.

They had approached the enemy harbour in a South African naval vessel in the dead of night. The assault teams, laden with equipment and explosive devices, had swum into the harbour to seek their targets, but found that only one of the targeted ships was in harbour. The operators had no intention of swimming back to the mother ship with the bulk of their explosives, so they decided to destroy infrastructure in the harbour area as well.

The Service's satellite eavesdropping station on The Farm intercepted a whole flood of Angolan telephone conversations about the bombing of fuel storage tanks, the blowing up of telephone and power lines and electricity sub-stations.

Douw Steyn was called in to explain the team's actions. He told them that, having gone to the trouble of infiltrating the harbour, he made the decision on the ground to destroy anything that might hamper the enemy's war effort.

He was given a halfhearted reprimand and excused.

Polozok's information had again turned out to be pure gold. Arnoldo Ochoa Sanchez returned home temporarily to become Cuba's deputy armed forces minister. He flew to Moscow to liaise with the Soviet Air Force where he found Perestroika and Glasnost in high fashion under the patronage of Mikhail Gorbachev. This was in stark contrast to what was happening to Ochoa Sanchez. Just over a month later, Ochoa Sanchez, his third wife and his three children boarded a Cessna light aircraft in Havana and flew to Key Largo, Florida. He was the most senior defector ever from Castro's Cuba.

Ochoa Sanchez had grown weary of government corruption in Cuba, of politicians accumulating fabulous riches in foreign banks for themselves while the young men were dying in the mud of Angola. In a media interview he was quoted as saying, 'I wanted to leave for many reasons, but Angola was one of the main ones. It had become a dead end street, Cuba's Vietnam. Only Fidel and his brother Raúl had any faith in victory.'

With Polozok and Ochoa Sanchez safe in the American intelligence arsenal, the South Africans were timeously informed of a pledge by Moscow to send another billion US dollars worth of arms to Angola.

This resulted in the US Congress voting out the ten-year-old legislation of senators Dick Clarke and John Turney and resuming American supplies to UNITA. The CIA by then was supplying the SADF with intelligence assessments on the FAPLA/Cuban buildup, based on General Ochoa Sanchez's debriefings after his defection. The product of Polozok, who remained active in the field, compared favourably with Ochoa Sanchez's.

9

The Libyan Connection

Two months later after the Polozok affair, secure in the knowledge that the SADF was getting the best intelligence possible, I took on my new assignment. I was to target a Libyan diplomat in Botswana.

I was dead tired. The muscles in my back and neck ached from being confined to a desk for most of the evening. I had been sifting through surveillance reports and listening to recorded telephone conversations of one, Al Jaghbub. He was a Libyan intelligence officer and I was compiling a recruitment profile on him. My eyes drifted towards the wall clock. It was just after midnight. It made no sense to go home and come back to the office at 06:00. The leather couch next to Steve's desk would have to do for the night, as it had for two other nights that week.

The offensive operatives of the Counter-Intelligence Division had been under pressure to recruit agents-in-place within the Soviet Block and in communist sympathising countries. The intelligence and military chiefs as well as the cabinet had expressed the urgency of confirming and complementing current information available on the Soviet and Cuban build-up in Angola. This, of course, is what was originating from the defector Rafael del Pino and Anatoly Polozok.

NIS wanted an independent source of information to corroborate what they received from the Americans.

Stationed at the Libyan Embassy in Botswana's capital, Gaborone, Al Jaghbub had come under the scrutiny of South African intelligence after a retired South African Army colonel had alerted an ex-colleague in NIS that the Libyan was a likely prospect. He had met Jaghbub quite by chance while they were holidaying in the Chobe Game Reserve in the north of Botswana.

When a whiff of suspicion about the diplomat's possible susceptibility to corruption arose, the task of recruiting Jaghbub

114

became my full-time responsibility.

Pete and four of his Watchers were infiltrated into Botswana to monitor Jaghbub's movements and establish the angles of attack on his personality that might compromise him into betrayal. To get a feel for his psychological make up and to gather information on his level of access, the electronic listening station on The Farm had been instructed to monitor his telephonic traffic. His number at the embassy and the one at his residence were monitored 24 hours a day. After a month of intense close quarter scrutiny a clear picture of the target's traits emerged. For a start he had an inferiority complex. This, the analysts said, led to him having an inflated and expressive ego which was manifested in his generally drunken and womanising behaviour. As a social flirt, he had access to a variety of embassies and intelligence personnel who were of definite interest to the South Africans.

Al Jaghbub had an above average command of the English language. He was outspoken in his aggressive defiance of conformity, rules and the religious policies of his Muslim leader Colonel Gaddafi — 'the mad dog of Africa', as the Americans called him. His profile revealed him as having the sort of manipulative and corrupt potential that intelligence services dream of.

I decided that Jaghbub was a definite hit. He was ready for the taking and his ego would be the primary soft spot to target. The proverbial wine, woman and song, I suggested, was the way to get him.

I ran through the last tape recorded from the Libyan Embassy the previous day.

Whrrr, click.

'Shit, he's on the phone to his wife again. She must phone the poor bugger 50 times a day from the residence. She's probably suspicious about his womanising lifestyle', I concluded.

The 8mm spools on the Rocs-machine kicked into fast-forward. I pressed the play button for the umpteenth time that evening . . . 'attack against UNITA.'

I only heard the last snippets of the sentence, but the words were enough to revive me from my fatigue. UNITA, headed by Dr Jonas Savimbi, was South Africa's military and political surrogate in Angola and our main ally in the fight against the combined FAPLA and Cuban forces.

I listened to the laboured accented English conversation between Al Jaghbub and his Vodka-guzzling Soviet counterpart, Yuri Bupka, at the Soviet Embassy.

'Yes, that's what I said. Moscow is planning a massive attack against UNITA at Mavinga south of the Lomba River. General Shaganovitch has mentioned something about chemical weapons. From Cuito Cuanavale he plans to advance to UNITA's main base at Jamba, 250km south-east of Mavinga.

My Libyan target voiced his astonishment.

'It will throw the whole region into turmoil. The South Africans will defend Savimbi's stronghold to the end.'

The Russian sounded tired. 'If we are ever to install the ANC government in Pretoria, we'll first have to kick the South Africans out of Angola and Namibia. If we destroy UNITA, it will lead to the collapse of Pretoria's military and diplomatic strategy for the whole southern African region. It will pave the way for the ANC and national liberation.'

'I hope you're right, my friend.'

'We'll have to wait for the dry season in a few months before we'll know.'

Steve reacted instantly to my alert. Thirty minutes later I was with Steve and Phillip at the Rietondale office discussing what was on the tape.

'We're very lucky to have picked this up.' Phillip lifted the phone. 'That puts an end to a good night's sleep.'

Ron was on leave, so Phillip was acting divisional head.

His conversation with the Director of Operations (DO) was cryptic and brief because of the unsecured telephone connection.

'Yes sir, in an hour.'

Phillip left to attend an emergency meeting in the situation room at the Union Buildings. He took the evidence along with him.

Steve and I shared the couch, attempting to get a few hour's sleep while we awaited further instructions.

While we slept the State Security Council plotted a vindictive response. An immediate increase in mechanised and heavy artillery support was ordered. Olifant main battle tanks and G6 155mm self-propelled super cannons would be committed in southern Angolan for the first time. To counter the enemy's superior MiG air support that would become evident during a ground offensive, the Americans would be alerted to supply UNITA with Stinger hand-held ground-to-air missiles. Plans were made for the declaration of a state of emergency in South Africa to counter possible local insurgency attempts and an aggressive programme of eliminating ANC bases, training camps and safe houses in regional African states was ordered.

Executive approval was also secured for the immediate go-ahead for Al Jaghbub's recruitment. I was instructed to direct my operation and assets, including the Libyan, against ANC targets on foreign African

116

soil. I was passed a request for information on ANC operations, operatives and support structures operating from foreign soil against the Republic. Within days, military action, covert operations and assassinations against both the internal and external wings of the ANC were approved.

10

The corruptor

'Top Secret' . . . I opened the envelope from Counter-Intelligence Headquarters sent to me by courier. I turned to the end of the two-page document to find the answers I was looking for. My proposal to recruit Al Jaghbub, now codenamed *Project Cuban*, had been recommended by Dr Schultz, the divisional director, and approved by the chief director of operations.

The power vested in me by the two signatures gave me a licence to reel in Jaghbub by whatever means I chose. I could use bribery, extortion blackmail — anything as long as I succeeded and left no trace that led back to NIS.

'I'm not sure how yet, but I think we should use a honey-trap to nail him. It's just an idea at the moment . . . I'm not sure if I can put it together.'

'I may be able to help you with this one', Steve said thoughtfully. He paused for a few moments. 'Every so often there are visitors to this country, diplomats, foreign dignitaries, international leaders in business and technology who feel the need for distraction . . . entertainment if you like.'

I nodded, guessing where he was going. Despite the veneer of Christian Nationalism that the executives in the system propounded, there were always surprises.

'Normally, the Watchers are the first to pick up their susceptibility to female company.

'Call-girls?'

'Well, if you want to call them that, yes. They're used by every intelligence service in the world and we are no exception. They say that spying and prostitution are the two oldest professions in the world, so we go nicely together.'

'So we run call-girls?'

'Run? No, definitely not. We don't run them because we don't pay them. The client does that. We only use them as a means to get to the target. Sometimes, though', he said correcting himself, 'there have to be exceptions . . .'

I digested the information.

'Okay, but I need someone a bit more intellectual and trustworthy than the average hooker.'

Steve rubbed the overnight stubble on his chin, contemplating and weighing options.

'I might have someone like that. We'll have to talk to her. Give me until morning to think about it. I guess duty comes before personal pleasure', he said wryly.

I didn't understand his innuendo.

The next morning Steve and I were driving up the hill towards the twin towers of the SABC in Auckland Park, Johannesburg.

'Turn right at the next street.'

Steve was in the passenger seat of my new Golf GTI — the latest symbolic reward for my successes.

We parked in the street by a terracotta-coloured cottage.

'Her name is Liz Bowe and she's an actress.'

The image of the timid blonde girl, the star of a number of local TV productions, came immediately to mind. I thought it inexplicable that a girl like her would consent to play the role we envisaged for her.

'It's a long story, don't even go there', Steve said, reading my mind. 'We've been having an affair for the past six months.'

I was shocked, but tried not to show it. How could he possibly prostitute someone he's sleeping with? I wondered.

The two white terriers that met us at the door yapped and wagged their tails, recognising the familiar smell and voice of one of the visitors.

'Hi.' Her voice was soft. 'Come in.'

She smiled and hugged Steve lovingly. I watched their intimate embrace and felt embarrassed about the pending discussion. It would change her from mistress to prostitute.

A maid brought glasses of freshly squeezed orange juice.

'Hello, Gladys.'

'*Môre, Baas* Steve.'

She greeted him as if he was a regular part of the household.

Steve, after a few uncomfortable minutes of small talk, opened the conversation that had brought us there.

'I discussed the basic outline of your requirements with Liz last night. She's agreed to work for us. She knows we're National Intelligence, by the way.'

I was shocked again that he had revealed our real employer.

'If you think she fits the profile for what you've in mind . . . I'll leave the details for you to explain.'

I smiled at her politely and glanced at Steve.

'Can we talk privately for a few moments?'

Steve stroked her hair reassuringly and got to his feet.

'Sure, let's go outside.'

We went through the back door onto a wooden verandah.

'What's wrong, buddy?'

'Why did you tell her we're from National Intelligence?'

Steve flicked his half-smoked cigarette into the garden.

'Listen Riaan, stop being a fucking James Bond. You're in the real world now. Your problem is that you are so bloody secretive you no longer know your real name. You can't always hide behind a mask. Sometimes, to get what you really want, people have to know you're a spy. This is one of those times. She'll be your go-between, so it's important for you to level with her. Is she what you need, yes or no?'

Steve simplified my choice.

'She's a pretty woman, an actress and I know her. I think that fits the job description. What's more she won't talk. If her links with us became known, she'd be ostracised by the whole bloody liberal art world.'

We moved back inside and I took the bull by the horns.

'I need you to befriend a Libyan diplomat in Botswana and to foster a relationship that will give us continued access to him', I explained bluntly.

'How close a relationship?'

'Close enough for him to answer your questions and share his secrets with you.'

Her dark eyes shone with a strange light. She appeared to be rehearsing the proposed part in her mind.

'What does he look like? Is he white?' she asked after a few moments.

I handed her a photograph taken with a telephoto lens from a distance.

She studied Jaghbub's picture with deep concentration. He was of average build and had raven black hair and a thin moustache. His typical Middle Eastern skin tone set off his gleaming white teeth. He looked younger than his 42 years.

'At least he's not fat — I hate a pot belly', she giggled. 'I think he's got hair on his back.'

We watched as she became drawn into the act.

120

She accepted the role.

*　　　*　　　*

'Lima, Uniform, Hotel', the call sign crackled in the headset of the pilot of the South African-registered Cessna 210. The six-seater approached the private landing strip from the east.

'You're cleared to land, runway 270, QNH 1019, wind 8 knots 259. Please report to immigration next to the tower.'

'Lima Uniform Hotel, finals 270 full stop.'

The pilot touched down at the Chobe Game Reserve in the north of Botswana. The blue and white plane rolled down the runway in a cloud of gravel and dust, the extended flaps slowing the aircraft sufficiently for the pilot to exit the runway halfway down its run and taxi towards the tower.

The growing international popularity of Chobe and the Okavango Delta brought many well-heeled visitors who flew directly there in private aircraft. It had necessitated the government providing a degree of infrastructure at the small airport, including customs and immigration officials.

The two-man camera and sound crew followed the slender figure of the female anchor into the immigration office. An apron attendant waited with a trolley loaded with luggage, cameras and sound equipment.

Liz Bowe, Steve and I cleared immigration within minutes. The tools of the photographer's trade were convincing evidence of our intentions and our reasons for being in Botswana. Like many other visitors, it was obvious we were there to film the abundant wildlife.

A Land-Rover collected us and took us to the main complex of the prestigious lodge. The kitchen, dining room and administrative facilities were in an open-plan complex built from gigantic logs and capped with a thatched roof.

We checked into one of the four-bed cottages amongst the surrounding trees. With the gear stowed away, we joined the other guests on the large patio with its view across a tributary of the Okavango River. We mingled with the other tourists, laughing and chatting and adding credibility to our cover as a film crew.

It had taken more than a month to set the stage for the operation. The Watchers had spent weeks in Gaborone monitoring Al Jaghbub's movements and behaviour. At Counter-Intelligence headquarters in Pretoria a team of experts had spent days sifting and evaluating reports and recordings of his telephone conversations, systematically building a profile of his personality and likely intelligence value.

An expert from Psychological Warfare had advised Liz on the way she should approach the target. They had changed her perfume and her wardrobe to cater for his perceived likes and dislikes, even taking his colour preferences into consideration. It was a total strategy focussed on her attracting him and keeping him interested.

Liz's meeting with him had to be fortuitous and in an environment far removed from suspicious eyes. The safety of the South African operatives, who would be operating illegally in a hostile black state, was another consideration.

I suggested the Chobe Game Reserve for several reasons. Luring him to South Africa might well put him at risk from his own intelligence service and from a paranoid Botswana government. Making a trip to the stronghold of the hated racist regime would be inexplicable. Keeping him on home soil would add to his sense of control and security. It had been discovered that the Libyan loved the reserve and had often said so after previous visits. The remoteness of the chosen place also effectively removed it from the reach of the Botswana Police and Botswana Intelligence. If something went sour, we could be airborne and across the border into friendly neighbouring SWA/Namibia within minutes.

Securing the unsuspecting Al Jaghbub's presence at the lodge had required skilful manipulation and an elaborate scheme constructed by other agents-in-place in Gaborone. Just a week earlier Al Jaghbub had been about to leave his wood-panelled office in the Libyan Embassy when his eyes were drawn to an envelope bearing the logo of the Chobe Game Lodge amongst the pile of new mail strewn on his desk. His curiosity got the better of him and he opened the envelope. To his pleasant surprise it contained promotional material and a complimentary invitation for two to visit the Lodge over the weekend of the 27th. He checked his dairy and finding no pressing engagements, he dialled the number of the Soviet Embassy.

'Come on Bupka, it's only for two days and it's free. No, I don't want to take her. I'll leave her at home and tell her it is work.'

'Why were you invited?'

'Probably because I've been there before. Wait . . .' He read the accompanying letter. 'Because of the heat at this time of the year the park is not as popular as in the cooler weather. So we have promoted this weekend to several businessmen in the city.'

'Okay, I'll come. I know you're only going to add another conquest to your unofficial harem.'

A recording of this conversation landed on the task team's desk within 12 hours. It confirmed that the Libyan's life had reached manipulation stage.

The snare had been designed and executed by Jimmy Jones, a long-standing agent of National Intelligence. This former British SAS officer had served with distinction in the Rhodesian Selous Scouts during the Bush War there. After Zimbabwe's independence he had left the country and taken up a position as senior game ranger in the Chobe Reserve. He had maintained links with many of the Rhodesian Special Forces personnel who had fled Zimbabwe and joined the South African military. His service background and specialist experience made him an appealing choice for the Service which was always seeking agents-in-place in neighbouring countries.

With the help of his wife, who worked in the reserve's marketing and administration section, the plan was easy to implement and the management approved the promotion as the lodge was indeed quiet at that time of the year.

With Chobe Lodge brought unwittingly into play by South African intelligence, the only thing left for the operatives to do was wait for Al Jaghbub to walk onto the stage for the brilliantly choreographed act and start performing.

Tom-tom, tom-tom, tom-tom.

The distinctive beat of African drums signalled that it was the end of the working day for most of the African labourers at the lodge. For the guests it signalled time for sundowners and then supper at the *lapa*.

We were amongst the first arrivals and accepted the exotic rum and pinacolada cocktails from the waiters. The group of businessmen who had been targeted for the promotion had grown to six, but there was no sign of Al Jaghbub and his Russian friend.

The cackling of hyenas and other sounds of the African bush floated in from the river on the evening breeze. I had the discomforting feeling that the Libyan had somehow escaped the noose. My eyes were suddenly drawn to the headlights of a vehicle approaching the main complex.

'It's him', an excited Liz said, nudging me in the ribs. 'Trust me, I know.'

A flamboyant Al Jaghbub and his Soviet colleague entered the circle of light. They were guided to the knot of other businessmen by one of the reception staff. Both men, still in their office suits, were relieved of their jackets and ties and served drinks.

I smiled as the Libyan openly started to assess his prospects for the weekend. It took only a few minutes before his roving eye rested approvingly on Liz who was sitting on a camp chair by the fire. She played the part of seductress to perfection, inwardly approving her own performance and her choice of a short, orange-coloured summer dress — her costume for this scene. From the corner of her eye she saw him staring, mentally disrobing her. Warming to her role, she crossed and re-crossed her legs, apparently unconsciously. Sensing that he was still looking she reached down for the glass at her feet, allowing him an unimpeded view of her braless breasts.

To increase the illusion of Liz's availability, Steve and I had drifted away from her. We watched her professional display of sensuality from a distance. She obviously had the Libyan's single-minded attention.

Steve took a sip of beer straight from the bottle.

'Ouch, he's caught.'

We gave it another ten minutes before we returned with plates of food from the buffet. Al Jaghbub had already joined her and Liz introduced us as her colleagues. We remained aloof, though, and concentrated on our food to allow the Libyan space to continue his pitch.

He beckoned to his companion to join them.

'This is Yuri, my Russian friend.'

It was a welcome bonus indeed. Control of Al Jaghbub might also give us free access to the Soviet diplomat.

Liz ate her dinner and entertained both men with her charm and humorous anecdotes of her career as an actress. We listened gleefully as the two foreigners reciprocated with revelations about their lives as career diplomats.

Intent on keeping the target's sexual appetite whetted, she glanced at her watch and fluttered her fingers along his upper arm.

'Al, you must excuse us. I'm afraid we have to prepare for tomorrow's shoot. Come on boys.'

She got up and began walking away before he could protest.

'Cheers, nice meeting you', we said cheerfully and hurried after her.

Once in the cottage we bubbled with enthusiasm over Liz's achievements so far. It was obvious that the fish had been hooked.

'He's tasted the honey, that's for sure', Steve remarked dryly. 'Now for the trap.'

We got down to plan the next phase of sealing his fate. We had to get him to disclose information that would be of such significant importance that it would well and truly compromise him.

'Don't go for him, let him chase after you. His hormones will soon make him take greater risks to impress you,' we advised Liz. 'He doesn't suspect anything and he's bound to get careless. Tomorrow we'll wire you for sound.'

124

In our guise as a South African film crew, we had been out since sunrise filming a herd of elephant at a waterhole. We returned to the lodge at midday feeling hot and dusty.

'Liz, Steve! I'm here at the bar', Al Jaghbub called, waving at us.

'Here it comes. Kill him girl!' Steve murmured.

We accepted our vodka-drinking host's offer of a drink.

Jaghbub was showing open adoration for Liz.

'Please, can I buy you lunch?'

'Thanks Al, but I normally don't eat during the day. Besides, I'm filthy and tired and I need a bath.'

'How about tonight then?'

She let him wonder for a few seconds.

'Okay, I'll meet you here at seven. If that's all right with Yuri?'

'Don't worry about him, he's a big boy', the Libyan said, slapping his Russian friend affectionately on the back.

That evening her outfit again reflected the role of seductive temptress that she was playing. The flowing lines of black silk hugged every contour of her shapely body. Liz's poised and confident entrance attracted the instant attention of every man there.

Al Jaghbub was instantly besotted.

'I'm going to have this woman no matter what', he vowed to Yuri.

'You look lovely', he said and she saw that he meant it.

Throughout the evening he tried every trick in his repertoire to impress and win her affection and approval — good food, expensive wine, flattery and even hints that he was part of some sort of aristocracy in Libya.

She appeared radiant and was obviously enjoying his company, but he sensed that he had not made the final conquest.

He would never be able to explain why he made his next remark.

'Yuri is going to Angola on Monday.'

Having exhausted all angles in his attempts to penetrate her invisible defences, he automatically changed his conversation to the subjects he knew best — which was work — and that meant politics and secrets.

'Why?'

She knew immediately that she had steered him down the right path.

'He's a military advisor to the Angolan Government. The Soviets are planning an offensive in Angola.'

'Really? How interesting.'

Pleased to impress her at last, he ploughed on.

'Oh yes, my dear, some 15 000 Cubans and 20 000 FAPLA soldiers are assembling in Angola.'

'We've got him', I said to Steve.

We were in our cottage listening to the conversation being transmitted from a concealed device in Liz's purse.

'Ssh, I can't hear. She had better play this right', I said, showing the nervousness I was feeling.

'You know so much! You must be a very connected man. Are you a spy or something?' she asked teasingly.

Steve almost had a hernia.

'Oh shit, she's blown it.'

'Wait, wait.'

'Well, as a matter of fact, I am.'

He seemed proud and sad at the same time.

Al Jaghbub's startling admissions had changed the script in a flash. The evening unpredictably unfolded into a sharing of intimacies.

'Now she's discussing the enemy's emotions and feelings, playing the air-headed actress as well!' Steve said venting his frustration.

The two of them seemed oblivious to everything. Perhaps for the first time in his life the Libyan felt truly accepted and appreciated by a woman. It showed as he talked about his life in shadowy places.

Liz seemed to develop real compassion for the guy, despite being only too well aware that she was setting him up.

'I mainly work with freedom fighters based in Botswana.'

He'd caught the team unprepared by his willingness to talk. He was on a roll and Liz lacked the knowledge to probe deeper into what he was saying.

'ANC guerrillas are sent to Angola to work with SWAPO in tracking UNITA's movements, but they don't like it because they want to fight in South Africa and not there.'

She didn't say anything and just stroked his outstretched hand.

'We're also trying to improve the poor relations between the Angolan Government and the ANC and SWAPO. The Americans are always poking their noses into other people's affairs. The US wants the Cubans and South Africans out of Angola so they can persuade certain African States like Gabon, Zaïre and Ivory Coast to recognise UNITA. They'll continue to supply the rebels from their base in Kamina and encourage Zaïre [now DRC] to continue operations against Luanda. By those means UNITA will ultimately be in a better position to force its way into a pro-US coalition government.'

Steve and I listened in amazement, unable to understand the Libyan's sudden disregard for professional conduct as he blurted out secrets to a woman who was a stranger. We marvelled at what hormones could do.

'It seems to me there's a lot of underhand politics', Liz said, unwittingly provoking more information.

He poured the dregs of the wine into their glasses.

'My beauty, you don't know the half of it. As always, US policies are always ambiguous. While Crocker and Reagan might disapprove of South Africa in some ways, the Pentagon and the CIA are less than critical. This issue was discussed at a secret meeting in November between CIA agents based in Zaïre and two South African Special Forces officers, Bert Sachs and Herman van Niekerk. They mutually agreed that America's Africa policy is a disaster and that the best thing to do would be to leave the South Africans to sort out their own problems. I think the intelligence and military worlds are all benefiting from the war in Angola. Even my own government is consistently undercutting diplomatic initiatives. That's the world I live in.'

'Can't you get into trouble for telling me all of this?'

'No, no. I decide who I trust and who not. It would be impossible to distrust somebody as lovely as you? I want to continue seeing you and I don't want you to have any future surprises.'

She smiled. 'Will you walk me to my room?'

'She might invite him inside', Steve said in a panic and swept the bugging receiver off the table and into a built-in cupboard. Like two mischievous children we pretended to be working on a film script.

'You're beautiful', we heard him say at the door. There was a pause and he kissed her goodnight.

Our mood was ambivalent when she came in. We tried to conceal our concern about her loyalty and future ability to remain objective. We were intelligence professionals and we could not take chances.

Liz in turn suspected that we might have noticed that she had become somewhat carried away.

She retired to bed almost immediately, which put a damper on the team spirit. The customary success of a mission was not celebrated, so there was no party and no promise of a hangover the next morning.

With the intention of consolidating her conquest, Liz spent most of the following day and the next evening in Al Jaghbub's company. At one point they disappeared into his condo and surfaced two hours later.

Steve and I monitored her every move from a distance.

'Spoiled bitch, I wonder if she fucked him for herself or for us', Steve said. 'Anyway, we still have a whole deck of cards to play.'

The three of us left the lodge before sunrise the next morning. Al Jaghbub, normally a late riser, was there to see us off as we boarded the Land-Rover for the airport.

'Bon voyage, guys, I hope we meet again.'

You can bet your life on it, I thought as I watched the Libyan kiss Liz on the lips.

'See you soon baby.'

His words sounded alarm bells in my head.

We had been airborne for about an hour when I decided to have it out with Liz.

'So what's he like?'

I knew I had to tread carefully.

'He's such a gentle and honest guy. He was so unconcerned of what he did.'

'Are you falling in love with him?' I asked bluntly, fearing that my plans could crumble because of my choice of agent provocateur.

'I don't know, Riaan', she answered honestly.

'He's still the enemy, Liz', I said. 'Our troops are fighting and dying in Angola and there are terrorist attacks at home. We need information. That's why you're here, remember?'

'I realise that but I can't help having feelings for the man. But I'm sure he'll tell me anything that I ask for.'

'How can you be so sure?'

'Because', she said, 'I think he loves me.'

That's possible Miss Actress, I thought, but what will you give away in return if you also find yourself in love.

We landed at Wonderboom Airport, ten kilometres north of Pretoria. Steve said he would take Liz home. I understood by then how Steve operated. He would sleep with her to dirty the water between her and the Libyan.

'Okay, see you later. Cheers Liz', I said, realising that she understood what the next move would be.

The information from my unwitting Libyan source was more than well received by the Service's Foreign Desk. As usual the analysts screamed for more information of the same quality. Also, as a matter of urgency, they wanted additional insight into the Libyan's knowledge of US policy. My operational report to Counter-Intelligence HQ conveniently omitted the nagging thought that my female provocateur might become an embarrassing security risk. It was an operational issue that Steve and I would have to handle.

To protect the security of the operation, Steve had Liz placed under full- time surveillance, including the monitoring of her phone calls and faxes and the interception of her mail. A black agent disguised as a hobo recorded the registration numbers of every vehicle that came to her premises. Withholding our suspicions of Liz from senior management, Steve and I took on the job of personally processing all the material gleaned from the surveillance effort. The magnitude of this

1. The tourists fly in.

2. The Reef Hotel, Mahé.

3. The diving group.

4. Covert collection for the [...] Service's information ba[...] The harbour, Mahé.

5. More covert collection: The Seychelles' 'navy' in harbour.

6. And more covert collection in Mahé: Ent[...] to the army base.

...uring the island in a Mini ... In reality they were ...ing the US satellite ...ng station.

8. Jacques Lavign: Seychelles Resistance Movement.

...Author interviewing a member ...ychelles Resistance Movement.

10. Soviet embassy in M
Rented to them by Jacky
Hunt's father.

11. Allan, the author and Jacques.

12. After the coup attempt.
The tourists escape the
effects of the failed coup b
going for a sail around the
islands on the yacht,
Southwind.

After the coup attempt. Seychelles' soldiers search boats in the harbour

After the coup attempt. US Navy destroyer visits Mahé

15. Langebaan Road Air Force Base. Para training for two Angolan 4-Recce operators. Jumping into the sea. Author centre.

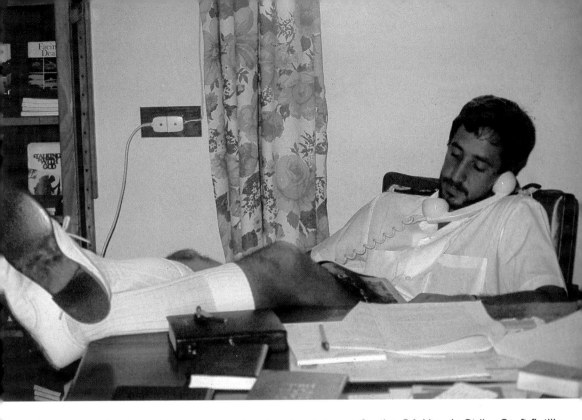

The author when chaplain at the command and support centre for the SA Navy's Strike Craft flotilla, ʋn as *SAS Scorpion*. Naval Base Durban.

Strike craft in harbour at the naval base.

18. Freetown, Sierra Leone.

19. Housing of local population in Freetown, Sierra Leone.

20. Covert offices of National Intelligence Service in Freetown.

The Soviet military attaché in Gaborone, Botswana, Colonel Anatoly Polozok, provided information of a Soviet-backed build-up of FAPLA forces in the Cuito Cuanavale region of Angola. The warning allowed the SADF to preempt it and inflict a major defeat on FAPLA.

(Above) 32-Battalion lays down a night barrage at Cuito Cuanavale.

(Right) South African artillery on the offensive in Angola.

23. (Left) FAPLA supply convoy devastated by South African air strikes while en route to Cuito Cuanvale.

24. The ANC's National Consultati[on] Conference, Kabwe, Zambia, June 1985. ANC president Oliver Tamb[o] standing right. Photograph taken b[y] NIS agent.

25. (Left) Photograph of Oliver Tambo ta[ken] by an NIS agent in the Lusaka flat of the president of South Africa, Thabo Mbeki.

26. (Right) SWAPO's Advocate Anton Lubowski was assassinated by the CCB. He was indeed a NIS deep penetration mole and an agent of influence.

South African, Angolan and Cuban
ᴴotiators in Cairo, June 1988. Minister of
ᵉnce Gen Magnus Malan and Foreign
ᴵister Pik Botha left and second left. The
ᵈ to Cairo had been smoothed by the
ᴴor's contacts with an Egyptian
ᴵlligence agent in Harare.

28. The negotiations led to
UN supervised elections in
Namibia in 1989. UNTAG's
military commander,
General Prem Chand
(centre) with South African
and UN personnel on a
familiarisation tour of
Namibia.

ᴰ. This resulted in a
ᴬDF withdrawal from
ᴬmibia. Train loaded
ᴵth South African
ᴵmoured vehicles pulls
ᴵt of Windhoek station.

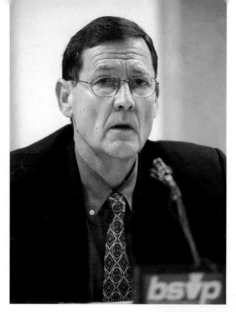

30. Niel Barnard, former Director General National Intelligence Service — from the assertive to the uncertain.

31. Phillip Swart, Deputy Head of Counter-Intelligence Division 061, his son and the author on holiday in Plettenberg Bay.

32. MK soldier Heinz Grösskopff headed TREWITS' wanted list.

The ANC's former offices at 130 [Fiel]d Street, Durban. A NIS team with a [por]table photo copier used to break in [and] search them weekly. All documents [fou]nd were copied.

34. Author (right) with a member of NIS' regional office, Durban at a braai in the bush. Briefings and debriefings of undercover agents were conducted at such places to avoid compromise.

[The] Author (left) getting [the] Director General's [Me]rit Award for [Ex]cellence from [Div]isional Director Phil [Ter]loo at the Royal [Ho]tel, Durban. It was [giv]en to Director Neville [du]l for safekeeping and [se]curity reasons.

36. The NIS searches of Jacob Zuma's desk at 130 Field Street, to the team's surprise, yielded virtually no intelligence. Zuma was then the ANC's head of intelligence and is now the South African Deputy President.

37. The desk of Alec Erwen (left) in COSATU's Durban offices was also subjecte to regular searches by the author's NIS tean It was usually in disarray and the searches produced a wealth of intelligence. He is now the Minister of Trade and Industry. The author infiltrated the ANC's senior circles by establishing a friendly relationship with the unwitting Mosiuoa 'Terror' Lekota — now Minister of Defence (right). Posing as a liber Afrikaner the author worked with him in an unsuccessful attempt to establish an ANC branch comprising Afrikaners in Durban.

39. The new NIS offices on 5th Floor, 66, Ring R Greenacres, Port Elizabeth.

38. The old NIS offices on 8th Floor, Brister House, Main Street, Port Elizabeth.

AZANLA laid four explosive
[cha]rges at Torego Flats, Uitenhage.
[The] unknown-to-them desensitised
[SM]X explosive charges were probably
[sup]plied by the NIS' Directorate K. The
[pur]pose was to stir up the wrath of the
[Afri]kaner right wing.

41. The Easigas storage facility in Port
Elizabeth harbour. It was also targeted
by AZANLA using Directorate K's
desensitised SMX explosive charges.

[42]. One of the
[de]sensitised SMX
[ch]arges that failed to
[de]tonate.

43. The AWB planned to blow up the water reservoir overlooking the Gelvendale coloured township, Port Elizabeth, before the 1994 election.

44. The AWB planned to park a car on the overlooking freeway and rain phosphorous grenades down onto commuters at the black taxi rank at the end of Russel Road, Port Elizabeth.

45. Despite the lavish MK-style military funeral for NIA's field offi Lulamile Shakes Mkalip, many suspect that he was shot by one his own.

task forced us to work a 12 to 18 hour day.

It was well past 20:00 and we had been at the office since 06:00.

'Steve, we've got a serious problem. Al Jaghbub has been calling her four or five times a day.' I said. 'If you care to listen, they are jerking off, making love over the telephone.

'What's wrong with this woman, has she lost her mind?' Steve asked in disgust.

That night just after I had retired I heard the beep of my pager at 23:00.

Expecting the worst I checked the message: 'Urgent message, phone Steve at home.'

Liz had just told Steve that she was booked on the midday flight to Gaborone the next day to see Al Jaghbub. Steve had played it cool, not letting her guess that an operation involving her would soon swing into action. He gave her the impression that because she was going to Gaborone at such short notice, she should continue without backup and report whatever she discovered on her return. He pretended to share her excitement and congratulated her on her breakthrough in arranging another meeting with Al Jaghbub. In the pretence that he believed she was acting on their behalf, he insisted on the Service arranging and paying for her accommodation at the Southern Sun Hotel in Gaborone. Her reservation, he said, would be confirmed by the hotel first thing the next morning.

It was a cross-border operation so Steve had no option but to advise Phillip of developments. In turn Phillip had to obtain authorisation from the divisional head to send a surveillance and technical team into a neighbouring state. A four-man team was nominated that night and told to be at the border post ready to cross into Botswana when it opened first thing in the morning.

By the time Liz booked in at the hotel, eavesdropping equipment and surveillance cameras would have already been installed in her love-nest. The beverage manager, who had been recruited by Phillip two years before, assisted, allowing the operators access to her room and getting them the room next door to it.

As the case officer I would control the operation from a hotel room two blocks away. To avoid the possibility of accidentally bumping into Liz, Al Jaghbub or Yuri accidentally, I had to settle in by 10:00 at the latest and stay off the streets until she left the country.

*   *   *

It was my first experience of commanding a team on foreign soil.

Steve's words still rang in my ears.

'For God's sake don't let them find you in town. You've no diplomatic immunity. If she crosses over to the other side and you are spotted . . . Well, you know what happens to spies caught in African States.'

When the South African Airways plane from Johannesburg touched down at Gaborone International Airport with Liz aboard, I was eating brunch on the balcony of my hotel room. A compact two-way radio that I had smuggled into the country in the false bottom of my holdall lay close by.

'Both subjects have just arrived and they are going into the hotel', a female voice said on the ultra high frequency radio. The rest of the surveillance team also noted it.

Capitalising on his wife's departure for Libya to attend an unexpected family funeral, Al Jaghbub had seized the opportunity to spend a weekend with his new actress friend. Confident and feeling in control, he personally collected Liz from the airport and took her to the hotel. He was disappointed that he couldn't take her to his mansion with its romantic luxuries like a bar and swimming pool. But his full time Libyan maid who might well be spying on them made it out of the question.

The Libyan hugged her close in the arrival hall of the airport. She was overjoyed that she could meet him without the controlling presence of Steve and myself. She smiled, pleased that she had only told Steve about her trip virtually at the last moment. That had made it impossible for us to accompany her. She dreaded what she had to tell Al, but she knew there was no option.

They made love the whole afternoon in the hotel room. That evening, as they settled down for a romantic dinner that had been prepared for them by room service, she knew she could no longer postpone the inevitable.

*   *   *

I was staring out at the moonlit night. My two-way radio had stayed silent the whole afternoon. My impatience got the better of me and I broke radio silence.

'Team leader this is Crow, what's happening down there?'

'They're still in the room. We can see candles burning through the window. I guess it's a dinner for two.'

'Anything from the men upstairs?'

I was referring to the two operators running the recording equipment in the room adjacent to the target.

'Nothing significant, just idle chit chat and lots of fucking.'

*　　*　　*

Liz withdrew from the Libyan's passionate grasp.

'Al, I have to tell you something.'

'Is this where you're going to tell me there's someone else?' he smiled.

'No it's not that. You know I like you very much, but there's something you must know. It might change the way you feel about me.'

Unable to contain her secret any longer, she blurted it out: 'You were set up.'

He dreaded her answer even before he asked the question.

'By whom?'

She confessed everything, National Intelligence's involvement and how Steve and I had used her to get a hold on him.

'Are they with you now?' His voice was hoarse with tension.

My radio crackled into life. 'Crow, she's gone over, it's a definite. Your name has been mentioned.'

I knew that I would have to act fast.

'No Al, I promise, I came alone. They trust me. I'm really sorry, I meant you no harm', she said beginning to cry. She was suddenly very frightened by the hardness in his eyes.

'What are we going to do?' she pleaded.

Al Jaghbub's mind was reeling. I should have known, he thought. He cursed for allowing himself to be drawn into such an obvious trap. He pulled himself together and realised it was important that he did not scare the woman off. If he played his cards right, he could turn her to spy for him.

'Don't worry, my girl.'

He held her close and gently kissed her.

'Calm down, everything is going to be all right. Trust me, I've got a plan.'

The Libyan's trained instinct as an intelligence officer resumed control.

*　　*　　*

It was 21:30 when I reached for my radio.

'Team leader, meet me in fifteen.'

'Qgh . . . Qgh.'

Pete hit the transmitter button twice to acknowledge the instruction. Using static instead of risking unnecessary talk on an unsecured transmission was standard procedure.

I refrained from using Afrikaans and scribbled my message in English on hotel stationery. I folded the note, placed it in my pocket and went downstairs to have a drink at the bar while I waited for Pete to arrive.

I ignored Pete as he entered the crowded bar and ordered a beer a mere five paces away from me. Twenty minutes later he brushed past me on his way to the men's room and unobtrusively took the note from me. He read it then burnt it, flushed the ashes down the toilet and left the hotel. Pete supported my decision to return to South Africa. His task now was to get the evidence of Liz's betrayal.

I finished my drink and returned to my room.

Pete slipped into the control room next to the target at 24:00. He dictated a detailed status report on his Perle micro-recorder and unnoticed by the sleeping bellboy in the foyer, left the hotel an hour later.

At precisely 03:30 I turned the corner into the darkness of the service lane behind the hotel. I vaguely made out the drunken hobo shuffling along the pavement towards my vehicle. He faltered as I drew alongside and with a drunken sway of arms flipped a cigarette packet through the open passenger window. I turned on the headlights as I exited the narrow lane and accelerated through the quiet streets of Gaborone. I intended to cross back into South Africa when the border post opened.

I had left early despite having been ordered to remain in Botswana until Liz left. I felt, however, that it was critical to begin the damage control as soon as possible. I was particularly concerned about Jim in the Chobe, whose cover she might blow. I decided to arrange to get the recordings out as soon as possible by diplomatic courier.

Pete dumped his disguise into a refuse bin and got in a waiting panel van. He had bought a dirty old coat from a homeless old man to use as a disguise for his rendezvous with me.

*   *   *

When Liz woke up the next morning Al Jaghbub had gone. There was a note on the bedside table: 'Will be back in time for breakfast, love, Al.'

148

Using his own keys, the Libyan slipped into the embassy through the front door, ignoring the register in the foyer for noting after hours visits. He entered the communications room and got to work copying 'top-secret' crypto codes on to a disk.

He returned to the hotel at 07:15 to explain his strategy to Liz.

'On your return to Johannesburg you must give this to your controller.'

She took the disk and placed it her bag.

'What is it?'

'It contains algorithmic codes that will allow the South Africans to decipher Libyan communications traffic. Trust me, when they get this they'll be convinced you've complete control over me. You can tell them that I want to buy my way into defecting to South Africa.'

For the next hour he briefed her on her new role, which would transform her from a South African agent provocateur into a Libyan field agent. He also detailed their future channels of communication and areas of professional interest.

His final instructions frightened her because she had heard the same line before.

'Do everything to win their confidence, even if it means sleeping with Riaan.'

*   *   *

Phillip and Steve were in deep discussions when I walked into the office.

'What the hell are you doing here?'

Both Steve and the deputy head were astonished.

'Are we missing something? Aren't you supposed to be in Botswana? And what about the rest of your team?' Phillip asked.

'We've got a serious problem. Liz is now working for the Libyan.'

I tossed the cassette on the desk.

'Put it on speaker.'

Pete's summary of what had transpired between the two left no doubt in their minds. We were stuck with a double agent.

'Shit, there's always a crisis on a Friday', Phillip said.

He dialled the head of Division 062 on the secure phone and arranged for a courier.

'We'll have to nip this in the bud', he said pensively, running his fingers through his slightly thinning hair. 'Still, let's not panic, at least not yet. Let's wait until Sunday when we have the evidence before we act.'

*   *   *

An operative from National Intelligence arrived in Gaborone on the late Friday evening flight travelling under diplomatic passport D7001. On Sunday morning at 11:00, travelling as a diplomatic courier from the South African Trade Mission, he boarded flight SA311 for Johannesburg. He was carrying an attaché case that was immune to customs inspection because of his diplomatic status. In the attaché case were the audio and video recordings from Pete's surveillance team.

A well-known South African television actress shared the same flight. Liz was going home.

11

The death trap

When I arrived at the office, Phillip and Steve were studying the audiovisual recordings of Liz and the Libyan that had arrived by courier from Botswana. The miniature camera must have been installed in the ceiling as it provided an aerial view of Liz straddling the enemy.

'What do we do now?'

'Continue the game until it dies a natural death', Phillip said adamantly.

Steve was toying with a lethal-looking letter opener. I suspected they had been arguing about future courses of action before my arrival and it seemed that the deputy head's decision had prevailed.

Phillip phoned Neil Fourie, head of the Cryptographic Department based at The Farm.

'I'll be with you in about half an hour', he said, putting down the phone.

'What's that all about?' I asked.

'The Libyan gave Liz a computer disk containing codes that will crack their encrypted communication traffic. I want our crypto guys to have a look at it.'

'Why would he have done that?'

'To throw us off the trail of having turned her. She says he wants to come over to us, in exchange for being allowed to see her in South Africa.'

'How did you get this disk?'

'She paged Steve this morning and he fetched it from her home.'

What utter bullshit, I thought, finding the level of pretence in the game almost unbelievable.

Phillip looked at his two subordinates with concern.

'Steve, forget it, as I told you vengeance is not the solution. As long as they remain unaware of what we know, we'll use her as a channel for deception and disinformation. We'll use Jaghbub to sow suspicion in the ranks of the enemy and its agents.'

Phillip opportunistically proposed a course of action.

'Riaan, there's a freelance German journalist, Wolfgang Muller, working in Johannesburg.'

I began to take notes.

'For the past three years sensitive military information and details of NATO's strategy for the southern African region have been leaked to the Eastern Bloc by a high-ranking South African official right under our noses. The Americans and British believe that East German Intelligence, the STASI, are linked to the operation. Information suggests that Muller is the local controller. If he is, that would make him an operative of the HVA (*Haupt Verwaltung Aufklarung*) — the foreign intelligence arm.'

He looked thoughtful for a few moments.

'We have been unable to break this network and discover the identity of the traitor in our own ranks. Leak the suggestion that Muller has betrayed his East German masters through the Libyan channel. Maybe the rats will eat their own and rid us of our problem.'

I was aware that National Intelligence had also suffered from the presence of a mole in its midst in 1983/1984. A graduate by the name of McKinnon from the University of the Witwatersrand in Johannesburg joined the Service. He was an English speaker and a known leftist. I personally found it strange that he had been accepted.

McKinnon worked as a desk officer in the research department at NIS headquarters, which gave him access to intelligence product from certain operations in Europe. For some unknown reason he had skipped the country for Britain, taking with him sensitive documentation. He had approached British Intelligence in London and offered to sell his information. They, however, closed the door on him saying they were not interested. It's uncertain why his overtures were rejected. It might have been because of MI6's good relations with NIS, or maybe because they thought he was a plant.

Phillip picked up his buffalo skin moonbag from the desk to leave.

'I have to go. Just remember when the Libyans eventually catch on to what we are doing, they'll drop Liz and the operation will die a natural death. That's what the game is all about.'

I walked into the office on the Monday morning to find that Steve, Phillip and Ron had been in session since 06:00.

'Grab a chair.'

At 05:00 the Cryptography Department had finished decoding a mass of routine low-level traffic between the Libyan Embassy in Botswana and Tripoli.

Phillip tapped the top-secret evaluation.

'Riaan, I hope you haven't planned to spend too much time at home in the next couple of weeks, because we have a major task for you. We'll support you wherever we can.'

In short I would remain Liz's controller. This meant that I would not only be responsible for the daily decoded Libyan traffic, but would also run the planned deception and disinformation project against the Libyans that was designed to set up the German, Muller. I would be relieved of all other duties and not be bound by normal office hours. I could come and go as I pleased.

'Let me have the outline of what you're planning, let's say 24 hours from now', Phillip told me.

I took my briefcase and went to find a quiet place where I could put together my plan of action. I drove past Sinoville, the northernmost suburb of Pretoria, and parked beneath the Jacaranda trees that surrounded the small terminal building at the Wonderboom private airport. I selected a table in the café that overlooked the runway to use as my office for the day. I had always enjoyed watching aircraft traffic as it came and went. I was known by the staff as a regular aircraft enthusiast and no one minded my presence at the virtually empty facility.

After ordering breakfast I started my first draft of the deception which I planned would lead to the German's downfall. I spent most of the day polishing it.

At 22:00 I phoned Phillip and asked for an early appointment to see him at his home the next morning to get his approval. My approach hinged on two important aspects. The first would need to be provided by the Watchers. They would have to establish which watering hole Muller used and when he frequented it. He was both a journalist and a suspected spy, so I could be certain he hung out at a local. He would need somewhere like that where he could pick up on gossip and recruit a casual net of low-level informers.

The most difficult part of the operation would be to introduce the information to Liz in such a way that it did not cause suspicion. I felt satisfied that I would be able to lure Muller into the net without compromising any sources, agencies or assets.

Phillip thought it was a well-worked proposal and promised to get the Watchers onto Muller right away.

My pager beeped and I checked the message.

'I have to go. It's the actress.'

Phillip stressed that I should stay close to her and stressed Steve's vindictive nature.

'What do you mean?'

'He wants to sink her. She's hurt his professional pride by turning against us. He wants to force Al Jaghbub's hand without using her. Look, I agree we have enough on the Libyan to blow him out of the water, but let's keep the whole farce intact until we have finished Muller. While you're on this assignment, stay away from the office and particularly from Steve. He's an excellent operator, but is also ruthless and sometimes reckless.'

I remembered the doctrine that Steve had voiced with confidence one night.

'If you can't manipulate the bosses and your own system, then you haven't got a snowball's hope in hell of manipulating the opposition.'

The spying game impacted on all dimensions of human interaction and even cut into deep-founded friendships. You learn that no one is ever completely on your side. Phillip's judgmental suspicions and Steve's no restraint attitude epitomised the trade's twisted morality of manipulation, deceit, opportunism and self-righteousness. It was evident in all of us — myself included.

*　　*　　*

'I'm sorry. I haven't even dressed yet.' It seemed that Liz had just got out of bed.

'I was up the whole night rehearsing and only came in at three this morning.'

The oversized man's shirt she was wearing as a nightie did little to cover her nakedness.

'Why did you want to see me?' I sounded brusquely official, ignoring the intended intimacy of the situation.

'Al Jaghbub wants to visit me and has asked if I could arrange for a looseleaf visa.'

'I don't know about that. When does he want to come?'

'The end of the month.'

'That's in two week's time and I have to get approval. Give me a couple of days, say till Friday.'

She accepted my assessment in silence.

'Can I make you some coffee?'

'No thanks, I have to go, maybe next time.'

I could not help but get an eyeful of her breasts through the gaping shirt as she got up to see me out. I wasn't fooled — my seduction was supposed to have been the order of the day. I pretended not to notice.

154

The personal favour she supposedly needed for Al Jaghbub convinced me that she was working for him.

The Libyans are after sanctioned access to South Africa by one of their operatives, I decided as I left her house.

On the Thursday morning Phillip relieved me of further handling of the intercepted Libyan traffic. I was amazed to learn that he had turned the codes over to the CIA station chief in Pretoria.

'In a week's time the codes will be useless to us. They will have been routinely changed as happens the world over. The Yanks have the technology to decipher future communications from what we've passed to them. They also have the ability to monitor all Libyan stations abroad. Anyway, most of the current product is about the US air raid on Tripoli and Gaddafi's palace. We'll get our value in return at some stage.'

I told Phillip about the latest developments regarding Liz Bowe. I knew he would take my revelations to the Director General. Niel Barnard, in turn, would sound the alarm at the President's office.

'The Watchers have made an early breakthrough', Phillip told me. 'Most afternoons between 17:00 and 18:00 Muller goes to a place called Tarantinos. It's a small Portuguese bar in Hillbrow. All you need to do now is let Liz 'find out' about the new East German agent you've recruited.'

'Phillip, there's a new twist in this saga around Liz. She's asked me off the record if I know anyone who works in Pelindaba.'

'What!' Phillip jumped to his feet, intensely agitated.

'Yes, that Pelindaba', I said. 'Pelindaba is the major nuclear facility west of Pretoria. She says a journalist friend is doing a story on South Africa's enriched uranium for an overseas publication.'

'Fuck, this stupid bitch is really pissing me off. I can't keep this quiet. I'll have to go and tell the DG that someone we recruited is seeking information on the most sensitive installation in the country. I'm going to be shat on all over. It's a key national installation. If the whole bloody world wants to find out what's cooking up there, they'll have to re-evaluate the plant's security and re-check the security clearances of everyone linked to it.'

I said a girl I had gone to school with was a scientist there. Maybe I could obtain some harmless information from her.

This infuriated him even more.

'Are you out of your mind? It would never be approved. For disinformation to be credible you've to give away something valuable and they'll never agree to that.'

'So what do we do?'

'Stall her. Let's just get Muller out of the way first because the division is under extreme pressure to plug this damned leak.'

'I think we should try to identify this journalist she has mentioned.'

'Journalist my arse, it's one of Al Jaghbub's front men for sure. But it is vital we check it. It is important you compromise Muller, so just screw the bitch if you can think of no other way.'

I pitched up at Liz's apartment unannounced. It was a few minutes before she opened the front door.

She wore no make-up and was dressed in old denims and a floppy short bearing the dirty paw marks of her dogs. She seemed pensive as we both evaded the reason for my unexpected arrival.

I sat down and she brought a bottle of champagne and two glass. I opened it and poured two drinks. I didn't mention anything about work or Al Jaghbub, but led the conversation into the sphere of the arts, literature and travel — topics on which I could easily hold my own.

It soon became apparent to her that I was not planning to leave. She eyed the half empty Champagne bottle on the coffee table between us.

'Why don't you stay for supper?'

I pretended indecision, but we both knew I would stay.

'Aren't you going out tonight?'

'No, I had nothing planned.'

I knew she was lying because I had noticed her glancing at her watch.

'Go on, stay for supper. I'll get us some pizzas from Antonio's around the corner. Can you open another bottle.'

She went to her bedroom to freshen up.

I selected a wine and poured it. I listened attentively. I could hear her talking on the phone, probably cancelling her date for the evening.

It's ironic, I thought. We are going to screw each other and probably enjoy it, but in the end sex would be just a friendly way of gaining control — for both of us.

Much later, in the aftermath of lovemaking, I casually mentioned — as if to a trusted and accepted colleague — that I had managed to recruit a top East German agent. My heedless disregard for secrecy opened a window of opportunity for the vigilant if inexperienced double agent.

Liz tried to lull my senses with alcohol to erode my resolve not to reveal the agent's identity. With practised skill I divulged snippets of detail about the recruitment, labouring sufficiently for her not to suspect that I was setting her up.

When she became particularly persuasive I told her that he worked in Johannesburg as a foreign correspondent. She continued probing for the name of the traitor. Afraid that she was losing the moment, she changed her tactics.

'Why don't you stay the night? You can't drive in this condition.'

'I'm afraid I can't stay, sexy', I said, 'I have got to meet Wolfgang at six o' clock.' I glanced at my watch. 'That's in four hour's time.'

Jubilant at beating an intelligence professional at his own game, she let me leave.

As she watched me get into the car I knew what was going through her mind. Tomorrow, she was thinking, I'll find out who this Wolfgang character is. Somebody in the SABC's news department will be sure to know. Al will be so proud of me.

*   *   *

On Saturday afternoon I phoned Phillip and told the outcome of my evening with Liz. A personal meeting with him had to wait until Monday. Phillip and myself, as the inner circle of the operation, normally met daily. Al Jaghbub was still the target of the multiple-pronged disinformation campaign that was being driven through the unaware Liz Bowe.

Phillip voiced his doubts the following Thursday morning.

'It's been almost a week since your heart-to-heart with Liz and there's still nothing to show for it. Are you sure she is capable of piecing everything together and coming up with Muller as the answer?'

'Yes, I'm convinced of it.'

'Let's give it another week. We can't drag this out any longer than that. Her interest in Pelindaba poses a critical threat. I'll have to get sanction from the top before we can even attempt to feed her any form of nuclear secrets, even if they're incomplete or distorted. The subject is far too technical for us anyway. Surveillance on Liz, by the way, has come up a lemon. We also have no leads as to who the so-called journalist might be. She's so deep in with the media clique that it's impossible to single out a suspect. We'll have to try to get her to pinpoint this phantom journalist — if he exists.'

'And in the meantime?' I asked impatiently.

'Just wait . . . avoid contact with her for at least a week. Tell her you'll be out of town and can only see her next Sunday. That will give us enough time to prepare.' He ended on a sombre note: 'Our careers are on the line — right on the line.'

*   *   *

The 'top secret' priority communiqué from Moscow addressed to

Colonel Herman Gunter was short but forcefully to the point. It sought the full co-operation of STASI in investigating a presumed East German agent in South Africa. The signal said further that a KGB major from the local embassy would be reporting at 22 Normannenstrasse in East Berlin at 09:15 for personal consultations with the *Herr* Colonel — Chief of *Abteilung II Spionage Abwehr*.

Colonel Gunter's inexpressibly bleak corner office, with its dingy brown colours, lace curtains and bulky furniture, was on the sixth floor of the eight storey office block. The hideous redbrick edifice represented the centre of an apparatus from which STASI's 86 000 full-time agents reinforced by 100 000 unofficial ones and countless informers, held communist East Germany in its thrall.

East Berlin was a dismal city. Unbroken Nazi and then Soviet dictatorial rule had squeezed life there into a static grey paste. Communal housing, exhaust fumes from the tinbox Trabant cars that were East Germany's pride, the thick smog and pollution from industrial plants and coal burning power stations, unrestored war damage, ill-lit streets and the dead end of the Berlin Wall created a physical and spiritual claustrophobia.

The fact that the signal had arrived at only 08:00 that morning had infuriated Gunter. The short notice was in total disregard for his senior position — an unthoughtful gesture typical of his Soviet counterparts.

Colonel Gunter paced his office in annoyance and frustration at the delay because the KGB emissary was already ten minutes late and he was not used to being kept waiting.

Finally, at 09:30 Major Gregor Sverdlovsk was shown in. The Soviet officer took a seat in front of the desk as his host ordered coffee.

'What can I do for you, Comrade Major?', Gunter asked when his secretary had left.

'You're handling an agent in South Africa, a West German', said Sverdlovsk. Without waiting for an answer the Russian supplied details not contained in the signal.

'Our station chief in Botswana is convinced of the authenticity of a report he has received from a Libyan intelligence officer stationed in the same country.'

The KGB exerted firm control over its satellite intelligence services within the Eastern Bloc, a fact well known although resented by Gunter.

'According to the Libyan agent', Sverdlovsk continued, 'one of your agents, a West German by the name of Wolfgang Muller, was recruited by South African intelligence a few weeks ago.'

He refrained from identifying the source as a woman in the fear that the chauvinistic inclinations of his older comrade might cloud his judgement.

Gunter's initial feelings of amused disinclination changed firstly into despair, then escalated into full-blown panic. Muller was not only an agent of long standing he was also a personal friend. The Soviet officer's assumptions seemed preposterous.'

'Is he one of yours, comrade colonel?'

The East German officer swallowed hard and braced himself for the question he knew would come.

'Haven't we used him a few times on your recommendation — I think to lift dead letter boxes on the Cape Peninsula?' Sverdlovsk asked.

The East German had his career and imminent retirement to consider.

'I believe it's the same man, Comrade Major.'

Sverdlovsk rose to his feet with a formal finality.

'We cannot allow our assets in South Africa to be blown. Either you deal with it, *Herr* Gunter, or we will.'

Herman Gunter's day was ruined. I'm far too old for this, he thought. He weighed his options. In the circumstances he knew that Muller would not respond to a sudden recall from behind the Iron Curtain.

He reluctantly reached for the black telephone on his desk.

*　　*　　*

I was waiting for something to happen.

It came in the guise of a Swiss businessman flying from Zurich on a scheduled British Airways flight.

When the aircraft touched down at Jan Smuts Airport (Johannesburg International) I was having coffee with Phillip at a Hatfield, Pretoria, coffee shop. Phillip found it difficult to write off the disinformation attempt as a failure.

The German-speaking Swiss, Karl Bidermann, passed through customs without a hitch. He found accommodation in an obscure boarding house in Hillbrow, a ten-minute walk from Tarantino's bar and restaurant.

Bidermann waited until 17:00 before he joined the Friday crowd at the popular Portuguese establishment. Tarantinos was packed with its regular Friday evening crowd taking advantage of the discounted liquor served during happy hour from 17:00 to 19:00.

Mediterranean-looking girls, probably the daughters or relations of the Portuguese owner, served the rowdy business types who had spent a week working up their thirsts. Muller, sitting with his back to the wall and facing the door, attracted no attention. He was obviously well known to the other regulars.

By 19:00 most of Tarantinos' customers had gone home to their waiting wives and children. Muller decided on one more drink before he left. When that was finished he would go for a steak at the restaurant across the road.

He ordered another beer and went to the toilet.

On his return to his table he failed to notice a man at the bar counter who was watching his every move.

He reminded himself of the words of his boss, *Herr* Herman Gunter, that he had heard on another continent 36 days ago: 'Muller has signed his own execution order by not declaring his links with South African Intelligence.'

Two hours later Bidermann stood in a darkened doorway waiting for Muller to return to his car parked half a block from Ponte City, Johannesburg's tallest apartment block. Earlier in the day he had purchased a poor quality Chinese manufactured dagger from a street vendor for ten rand. He waited patiently, not moving or smoking, just staring calmly at the cylindrical building's only exit.

Muller turned in surprise as he was shoved from behind while trying to open the door of his Mercedes. He felt no pain as the tapered blade entered below his rib cage. Nor did he recognise the smiling man who effectively and professionally smothered his mouth with a cloth and stifled his screams.

The second penetrating stab went in three centimetres below the sternum, slicing through his lungs and piercing his heart. A gloved hand ripped the watch and wallet from the body that lay in the gutter next to the luxury German sedan.

Bidermann walked slowly away. He pushed the knife into an overflowing dumpster on the pavement. A drunk asleep in a shop doorway would wake up to the mystery of finding a Rolex watch and a wallet with a wad of rand notes in his jacket pocket.

The KLM flight to Amsterdam was already clear of South African airspace when the bloodied body was discovered in Hillbrow. The press card found on him identified him as Wolfgang Muller, a freelance political correspondent based in Johannesburg.

That evening, for no particular reason, I switched on the SATV's late news broadcast.

It took me a few seconds to comprehend the female news anchor's words '. . . journalist slain in Hillbrow . . .'

'Coming up next . . . the news headlines.'

She got my complete attention as she continued.

'In an apparent robbery, a free-lance journalist was killed in Hillbrow on Friday night. Mr Wolfgang Muller, a foreign correspondent, was stabbed and killed earlier this evening after leaving a popular nightspot. Robbery appeared to be the motive as his watch and wallet were not found at the scene.'

12

Quest for agents

By January 1986 I was being pressured by Division 061 to settle in an African state and adopt a suitable cover. I had travelled to Mauritius in July 1985 to investigate the possibility of running an undercover project from there. My cover as a diving instructor was good enough and the country posed no particular problem except that it was too far away from most countries in Africa. Many intelligence services used the island as a meeting place, but it was out of the loop of my target which was ANC intelligence.

I eventually decided, after lengthy discussions with Phillip, that Zambia might be the answer. The only credible cover I could come up with was based on my theology studies. The Dutch Reformed Church always retained a minister in Lusaka to cater for the many Afrikaners who farm in Zambia. Professor Johan Heynes, the head of the Theological Seminary in Pretoria who was assassinated in 1994 by a person or persons unknown, had commenced his career as a minister in Lusaka.

In one of my secret unauthorised meetings with Anatoly Polozok the month before I was due to go to Lusaka to investigate my options, I mentioned to him that I needed to recruit a member of the ANC's intelligence wing. He just smiled and mentioned that he had someone in mind, but refused to elaborate.

I continued my preparations and made contact with a Rev Pieter de Wet who ran the Dutch Reformed Church's mission to the communist world. He was en route to Moscow and he couldn't help me personally, but he told me about a Reformed seminary in Lusaka that had positions available. An interview in Lusaka was arranged.

Just after this, Polozok phoned and suggested we meet. Not wishing to attract attention I sneaked away from Pretoria on a Saturday and met him in Mafikeng. He suggested that I rendezvous with him in Zambia in ten day's time when he would introduce me to an MK agent whom

I could take over.

His suggestion happened to coincide with my planned visit to Lusaka and I jetted in via Harare. After spending a day in Lusaka I decided it was not the place for me. Why settle in a backward hell hole like that. Mauritius suddenly seemed a far more attractive option. I did not even bother to go to the seminary for the interview.

After meeting Polozok the next evening in the foyer of his hotel, we went up to his room. This time we drank cheap vodka instead of brandy as he explained his plan. He would introduce me to his agent as Riaan, an Afrikaner communist who worked for him. I would become a sort of alternative handler to Polozok. If the MK person was sent to South Africa I would become his contact person.

Later in the evening there was a discreet knock on the door and Guy Ndhlovu, a short and small man, entered. He accepted the Soviet officer's reasons for introducing me into the relationship without raising any objections. He understood the difficulties he would have keeping contact with Polozok if he was sent to the Republic. I seemed a good alternative. There were plenty of other white Afrikaners within the ranks of the ANC and SACP, so he had no reason to doubt me.

It took most of the night for Guy to relate his story.

*   *   *

Born to farm labourers on a white-owned sugar estate, Guy Ndhlovu's education prospects were limited. A primitive farm school catered only for the first grades. To yank him out of the poverty cycle his parents had sent him to stay with his grandmother in Soweto at the end of 1975 to get a better education.

At the beginning of 1976 Guy joined Soweto's Young Lions Football Club. Frazer Mzwake, his best friend who was on the club's executive, paved the way for his assimilation into the fraternity. Unbeknown to Guy, the elitist and exclusive club subtly coaxed the brightest boys into joining a pool of candidates for recruitment into the ANC's military wing, *Umkontho we Sizwe* (MK). Guy became indoctrinated with black revolutionary politics. Until then his farm-boy upbringing had sheltered him from such influences.

On 16 June 1976 thousands of youths spilled onto the streets of Soweto in protest against the use of Afrikaans as a teaching medium. Confrontations with the police led to the death of 130 people and the wounding of more than a thousand. Guy and Frazer evaded arrest and two weeks later, together with four other youths, the ANC underground helped them to cross illegally into neighbouring Botswana. From there, transport to the ANC's headquarters in Lusaka was arranged.

From Zambia they were taken to Tanzania. Guy was sent to the Solomon Mhlangu Freedom College (SOMAFCO), in the interior south of Dar es Salaam to complete his high school education. In November 1981 he declined a three-year engineering scholarship in Melbourne, Australia, and joined the MK for military training.

In July 1982 he did his basic military training at the ANC's Bengu Camp in the heart of the Angolan bush.

In August 1983 Guy's platoon was ambushed by a joint South African/UNITA patrol. They also raided Bengu Camp and the political commissar was killed. The MK unit's PKM machine gun jammed and this led to the death of several comrades. The camp commander later ordered the execution of MK member Mthunzi Tsikila whom he found had sabotaged the machine gun.

Comrade Tsikila had indeed been a South African spy and saboteur who had been recruited by a man called Tom of the National Intelligence Service. When it became known that Tsikila would be going to Angola for MK training, he was introduced to his handler, Lieutenant Groenewald of Military Intelligence.

His orders were to promote tribalism and incite mutiny inside the Angolan camps. When passing through Johannesburg his group was issued with passports by Winnie Mandela and briefed on where they were going by Vuyisile Sefako.

He left for Botswana on 13 May in the company of Stelfox Godlo, Vela Qwamashe and somebody called Motlatsi. They then travelled via Lusaka and finally arrived in Angola in September. A month later they commenced their training at Bengu Camp.

On what became known as the 'night of the python', Tsikila was performing sentry duty at a anthill machine-gun post. It gave him the chance to conduct his first act of subversion against his comrades. Using pliers stolen from the maintenance unit he emptied the gunpowder from the first five and the last five cartridges on the ammunition belt for the PKM company machine gun that was later issued to Guy's patrol.

The ANC High Command was incensed about the attack. They felt the camp had been compromised and ordered that it be closed before a South African air raid inflicted more casualties there.

A month later Guy was selected for training as an officer in the Soviet Union.

He arrived in Moscow in November 1983 with some other

candidates. Guy was in Peter Shope's group and their course leaders were Colonel Shaliapin and a female KGB member, Major Valeska Vanavskaya. In September 1984, when in Moscow, Polozok recruited Guy as an agent.

Guy remained in the USSR for 12 months during which he received specialised training that concentrated mainly on political orientation, intelligence work and military combat work (MCW). From there he moved to Cuba where he spent three months at the Communist Party School in Havana. He returned to Angola in January 1986.

Although destined for a posting in Angola, he was diverted to Lusaka, Zambia, for debriefing by the ANC. They settled him in a bachelor flat in the centre of the capital. For two months he worked at ANC headquarters compiling a training manual based on his experiences and on what he had learned in Moscow. It was intended that he should implement the practical application of intelligence work in the field together with his MCW skills when he returned to Angola for a new posting. He remained in Lusaka until 7 March when he flew to Luanda.

When I met Guy, he seemed to enjoy speaking to someone from home — even a white Afrikaner like me. I immediately judged that he had the potential to be an excellent agent. The problem was maintaining contact with him. There was no chance of him communicating with me from Angola, nor could a covert channel of communication be established. Covert communication was a common problem within the Service. Many field officers were successful in recruiting agents-in-place within the ANC, but when they went to Tanzania or Angola for military training, it became impossible to handle them. Many a field officer lost his star agents that way. Wait for intelligence until they returned to South Africa somewhat defeated the object.

Guy agreed to resume contact with me if he returned to South Africa and I did something I have never done before or since. I gave him my parent's Pretoria phone number, because I was constantly on the move but I knew they would always be at the same address. There was a reason for my unorthodox behaviour. The Service had a complex ritual for recruitment. A form containing the target's background information had to be completed and sent to head office for approval. One question that I always found quite bizarre was about the potential agent's loyalty towards South Africa. It was outright stupid because black South Africans, particularly members of the ANC, held no loyalty for the white apartheid government and, in fact, regarded it as the enemy. We field officers normally just filled in a positive, so as not to jeopardise the recruitment.

Despite the procedures, I usually first recruited an agent before I sought official approval. The Service, as a norm, steered clear of agents known to work for other intelligence agencies. But when you are in the field and under pressure to produce information, instead of at at head office with your bum on a chair, you work with all sorts and types regardless of their desirability.

Polozok, for instance, was off limits because of his American connection. And because Guy came to notice through him, his recruitment would never have been approved if I had let on. However, I trusted the Russian as a fellow operator and I accepted that Guy would provide me with the information we needed and which head office was screaming for.

Polozok and I only parted company when I lost sight of him during the turmoil of change when communism fell and the Soviet Union reverted to being Russia. Guy lasted much longer.

*   *   *

I returned to Pretoria and told Phillip that I was not prepared to live in Zambia, that my cover for there was unsuitable and that I would seek a more suitable alternative.

When I arrived at the office on the Monday morning, Phillip and Steve were meeting behind closed doors. Every now and then their raised voices reached me in the adjacent office. It was clear they were having a major disagreement.

'Why the hell did you go behind my back?' I heard Steve say.

Phillip's answer was too muffled to decipher.

'What was that all about?' I asked Steve later.

Steve voiced his anger.

'I wanted to know personally from him about Liz and whether we are going to continue with the Libyan.'

'Why?' I asked, not understanding his anger.

'Mr Swart has taken personal control of Liz's handling', he said bitterly. 'This thing about her defecting to Libya is bullshit. It was a plot construed behind our backs weeks beforehand.'

'What was the point?'

'According to him, my sleeping with her clouded my judgement when dealing with her. But when she apparently sided with the enemy, I became alienated and stayed away from her.'

Listening to him I was already anticipating the next problem. With Phillip taking over the handling of Liz, I would have no agent left in the field. I knew that I would have no option but to go all out and make a spectacular recruitment as soon as I could.

The fact of the matter was that Phillip had got the hots for Liz.

Steve bitterly mentioned an unwritten law that was jokingly referred to by field officers: 'You are not allowed to sleep with your own sources . . . but you can sleep with your colleagues' sources.'

So despite official policy prohibiting personal relationship with sources and agents, it often happened in the field. In the end Phillip withdrew Liz from the field and from the operation involving the Libyan. She had become Phillip's girlfriend. This created a major rift between Phillip and Steve. Steve resented being reprimanded for sleeping with Liz while his superior officer was doing just that. He also lost an agent in the process.

13

Broederbond and Ruiterwag
Agents of influence and operators with influence

I witnessed the Service's co-operation with the Taiwanese during a spell at The Farm. A group of six technicians from Taiwan's intelligence service was assisting NIS staff with training and with the expansion of its satellite eavesdropping programme. The original technology including the satellite dishes had originated from West Germany, but the system was in need of a major upgrade. The UN arms embargo had closed the doors to the Germans and Taiwan filled the void. The visitors lived in a condo close to me at the training facility, hidden from the general traffic of people.

In the same year a group of National Intelligence officers was sent to Singapore for a course on psychology in the field of intelligence gathering. Such training was put to good use later during the constitutional negotiations between the South African Government and the liberation movements. Our psychologists, doubling as assistants to the government negotiators, attended the meetings to gather information on the characters of opposition members. Video and sound recordings were made. From this, psychological profiles were assembled for study by the government's team of negotiators.

Later on, to get up to speed on the region and to further preparations for a posting to Harare, I worked on the Zimbabwe desk at Division 031. This provided me with a broader perspective of what was happening in the Service. I was not acting in isolation as I had been when working undercover at Division 061.

I learned about a totally different style of operation. Divisions 031 and O32 were arms of government used to establish secret relationships with countries through their intelligence services. Many member states of the OAU found it impossible to have open ties with the Republic because of the general abhorrence of apartheid. This was the main reason why the departments of Foreign Affairs and Trade and

Industry had failed to establish relationships in Africa and in other sensitive parts of the world. National Intelligence filled the void by establishing covert links with the intelligence services of those countries and building on those relationships to establish and maintain communications with the respective governments.

Over the years the Service had established invaluable covert offices in hostile territories with the covert assistance of those local senior intelligence officers who had been recruited into our stable.

While a desk officer with Division 031 I confirmed that we had such an office in Zaïre as had been suggested by Jakes. There were also offices in the Ivory Coast and Togo. I personally assisted in the establishment of a similar project in Sierra Leone. The divisional head, Dr Daan Opperman, had recruited the president's tribal chief who was codenamed *oompie* (little uncle). Through him permission was obtained from the president for a NIS presence of one officer in the country. In exchange, the president was given money and foodstuffs to the value of R1.5 million, small arms including AK47s and a number of Buffel mine-protected infantry fighting vehicles.

The gifts were freighted to Freetown by SAFAIR — an air cargo transport company with links to the South African Air Force — at a cost of more than R100 000 per return flight. Another operative, Bennie Kotze, and I personally paid the money to SAFAIR in cash, having drawn it from the Service's pay office in the Concilium Building, Pretoria.

A large house on the outskirts of Freetown was provided by our hosts. There were no telephone links with South Africa so alternative communications had to be established. A technical team headed by Pierre Fourie visited Freetown but discovered that the enormous radio mast required to provide a direct link with Pretoria would cause too much attention. Instead, it was decided to route communications through the Service's London station.

The Freetown station chief, Chris van Koller, travelled to Freetown via London. Road conditions in the country were primitive, so Chris was given a Mitsubishi Pajero for transport.

At the beginning of 1990 he recruited a member of the intelligence service of adjacent Liberia. He often crossed the border to see his agent in the capital, Monrovia.

On one such visit he was almost arrested. Someone had leaked information to the Liberian authorities that a South African agent was in its territory. At the time Chris was debriefing his agent in Monrovia. Only ten minutes after he had crossed back into Sierra Leone he heard a police message on Liberian Radio. They were looking for a white man driving a Sierra Leone-registered Pajero. The description matched Chris and his vehicle. This put an end to his Liberian trips and after that he liaised with his agent in neighbouring Guinea.

The operation came to a sudden halt in 1990 when the opposition rebel movement toppled the Freetown government. Fortunately for Chris, his sources in Freetown warned him of the pending overthrow of the president. Abandoning everything, including the Pajero, he caught the next flight to London only hours before the insurrection started. The station was closed and National Intelligence lost a valuable foothold in West Africa.

The main purpose of having stations in West Africa was to focus on Nigeria and infiltrate their security services and government. The secondary objective was to create a pro-South African sentiment in the region that could positively influence the OAU's negative stance towards South Africa.

On certain projects, like the Freetown operation, close operational links existed between NIS and the SADF. Dr Opperman and SADF Chief, General Kat Liebenberg. Military Intelligence established a covert base in Malabo, the capital of Equatorial Guinea, which is on the island of Bioko (formerly Fernando Po) in the Gulf of Guinea off the coast of Cameroon. This helped to fill the gap left by the Freetown closure.

Certain southern African states traditionally opposed to the white South African government and acknowledged as staunch supporters of the ANC, still co-operated with it through intelligence channels.

One of the best examples of such a secret co-operation agreement was the one between National Intelligence and President Kenneth Kaunda of Zambia. He was recruited as an agent of influence and handled by Dr Daan Opperman. Kaunda also worked for the British MI6. At the same time he was giving ANC president, Oliver Tambo, a safe haven at State House in Lusaka and providing rear bases for MK.

Daan regularly chartered an aircraft to visit President Kaunda in Lusaka. I was often sent out shopping to buy large quantities of groceries for the president's household that Daan would present on his arrival. Always on the list were several five-litre boxes of 'Fruit Tree' fruit juice which Kaunda, a committed teetotaller, called the nectar of the gods. He was never shy about asking for a resupply. Most consumer goods were in short supply in Zambia because of the president's economic misrule. The visits always included lavish lunches or dinners for which South Africa provided the wherewithal. Chicken, a favourite of Kaunda, was invariably on the menu.

On one occasion Daan phoned me from State House in Lusaka. The Service's eavesdropping satellite station at Rietvlei outside Pretoria routinely recorded our conversation. On Daan's return to Pretoria the divisional director rebuked us both for compromising the operation.

These liaisons, with President Kaunda's co-operation, provided National Intelligence with technical data that allowed it to eavesdrop on local telephone conversations in Zambia. A wealth of information about the ANC and its leaders was obtained in this way. The money on fruit juice was well spent.

*   *   *

The pervasive influence of the National Intelligence Service within every South African government department can be illustrated by a covert project that was launched in 1987/88. Because the ANC was using the Kingdom of Lesotho as a springboard for its activities, the Service decided it needed to establish an intelligence gathering structure there. Because NIS had no official representation in the country, Division 031 decided to place an undercover officer in a structure based in Lesotho.

South Africa's Department of Water Affairs was working in partnership with the Lesotho government on the development of Lesotho's Highland Waters Scheme which was designed to provide water for the often drought-stricken Witwatersrand. A member of Division 031 was appointed as a project manager with Water Affairs and sent to Lesotho. This was called *Operation Gordon*.

Operation Gordon targeted the ANC in Lesotho until the first stages of the water scheme were completed. Substantial quantities of tactical information regarding cadres of the ANC and other liberation movements in the kingdom were forwarded to TREWITS (Counter Revolutionary Target Centre) in South Africa. South African agents also abducted a MK member, Joseph Nduli, from Lesotho. Later, in 1989, I recruited him as an agent while he was involved as a member of the ex-MK combatants in Durban.

On the strength of intelligence gained through *Operation Gordon*, the SADF mounted several armed raids against ANC houses and personnel in Lesotho. The officer who ran *Operation Gordon* in Lesotho, is still serving with the new National Intelligence Agency (NIA).

In a concerted effort under the able leadership of Dr Niel Barnard, National Intelligence gained access to and co-operation with the intelligence services of most African states — often without the knowledge of their heads of states. A senior Nigerian intelligence officer frequently paid secret visits to South Africa. Members of Division 031 would whisk him through customs and immigration without checks at Jan Smuts (Johannesburg International) Airport. He even had an eye operation performed in South Africa that was paid for by National Intelligence.

These inter-service relations were not only used for the gathering of information but also as channels for negotiation and influence. Much of this occurred without the official knowledge of South Africa's Department of Foreign Affairs, although Foreign Minister Pik Botha — because of his position with the State Security Council — would probably have known. The SADF with its huge budget, infrastructure and technical support, like air transport, was the Service's greatest ally.

Japan is another classic example of intelligence co-operation. The country openly opposed the South African government and initially vetoed diplomatic links, but through the influence of its intelligence service, NIS was allowed to open a covert liaison office in Tokyo.

Division 032's sole function was liaison with foreign intelligence bodies. It produced intelligence products that were sent to NIS stations abroad for sharing with the host services. The material was usually of a political or economic nature, but often included intelligence about the opposition in the host's country.

Many services reciprocated by furnishing NIS with regular intelligence products. Included were the intelligence services of Malawi, Lesotho, Mozambique, Swaziland and even Zimbabwe. Ironically, although these countries supported the ANC, their intelligence services had been subtly ensnared in a web that had been carefully laid by the Service. This soft handed approach often resulted in the receipt of intelligence that was detrimental to the ANC.

The low level of professionalism evident in the compilation of such reports often provided insights which enabled the Service to determine the sources of information. This facilitated the recruitment of sources and agents who were already working for other countries' intelligence organs under 'false flag operations'. Through its contacts with other intelligence organs, NIS obtained extensive examples of travel documents, entry stamps, inks and passports from most African countries. This facilitated the production of forged passports and other documentation that was issued to field officers on the ground for use in false flag operations.

The liaisons between National Intelligence officers and their opposite numbers, provided many opportunities for recruitment. Field officers of Division 032 always attempted to recruit their opposition and often succeeded. Agents recruited by this means had perfect covers as they had been sanctioned by their own organisations to maintain contacts with National Intelligence officers.

When information was exchanged officially through liaison, money never played a role. National Intelligence, however, always managed to subtly subvert the situation to ensure it obtained far more information than had been officially sanctioned.

Most black African states looked on National Intelligence as a superior service and co-operated, so liaison meetings became useful vehicles for disinformation. Reports for exchange were cleverly prepared to contain a large content of truth, but there was invariably a subtle undercurrent that played one neighbouring state off against another. This process was not difficult as the governments of most black states had some form of violent opposition or armed rebel group to deal with.

It was the classic case of divide and rule — so British, so diplomatic.

Money and personal favours were strategies used with great success in dealings with the intelligence officers of black-ruled states like Malawi, Lesotho, Swaziland, Zimbabwe and Mozambique. NIS enjoyed representation and intelligence co-operation with all those countries. The local intelligence officers there were never officially recruited — they were just paid handsomely for what they provided off the record.

As with their British counterparts, the French Counter-Intelligence Agency (*Service de documentation étrangère et de contre-espionage* — SDECE) was well aware that South African agents were operating on its soil. During my association with National Intelligence's Foreign Division, one member, Louis Steyn, was declared *persona non grata* and kicked out of Paris for activities unbefitting an accredited diplomat.

Due to an international arms embargo, South Africa was short of certain sophisticated military technology. With the aid of opportunistic businessmen and sympathetic bodies like the CIA and countries like Israel, the local arms industry was able to procure and develop most of the weaponry needed by the SADF.

The South African arms manufacturer, Armscor, progressed to become a world leader in many areas of military technology. The G5 and G6 155mm artillery pieces — masterpieces developed with the input of West German technology — won and are still winning military acclaim internationally. Continued military co-operation with Israel secured South Africa's nuclear capability which led to the testing of a device in the Indian Ocean in the early 1980s — vehemently denied at the time.

173

However, with Soviet MiGs dominating the airspace above the Angolan battleground, the South African military were in dire need of high tech surface-to-air missiles. Unable to obtain either the Soviet SAM7 or the US Stinger, and with mounting military pressures in Angola, other avenues had to be explored.

In the quest to obtain such elusive technology, Louis Steyn, protected by his diplomatic status as First Secretary at the South African embassy in Paris, frantically searched Europe for alternative hardware. He was compromised in a disastrous failed attempt to buy the British designed Blowpipe missile from arms dealers. The international media got wind of it and confirmed the compromise and his expulsion from France. On his return to South Africa, he was appointed deputy divisional head of Division 031.

Because of the lucrative financial and career benefits of a foreign posting, back stabbing and favouritism within Division 031 was rife. The situation reminded me of what Steve van Zyl had once said.

'Be careful of the *lang baadjies* [long jackets]. They are everywhere', he had warned. 'You are not a member, are you?'

He was referring to the *Broederbond* and its junior organisation, the *Ruiterwag*. The Afrikaner *Broederbond* (organisation of Afrikaner brothers) is an ultra-secret organisation designed to promote Afrikaner control and power on both the political and economic fronts. President PW Botha and his entire cabinet members with the exception of two, were members of the *Broederbond*. This sinister organisation controlled the National Party, the cabinet, the SADF, the South African Police and most certainly the National Intelligence Service.

While serving on the Zimbabwe and Mozambique desks, I received a memo from Director General Niel Barnard ordering an investigation into a tea exporter in Mozambique. Attached to his memo was one from Acting State President Chris Heunis, ordering Barnard to conduct it. I later discovered that Heunis' family was in the tea business. The investigation had nothing whatsoever to do with the security of the state — only with the furtherance of the Heunis family business.

'No, I'm not a member', I replied. 'Why?'

'Because this is a *Broeder* hothouse. Most of our senior and middle management officers belong to it. You'll be wise to avoid saying anything detrimental about it. If you keep quiet they'll think you're one of them, or maybe an active sympathiser. Your career, promotion and future postings probably depend on it. They always ensure that the best assignments go to their own.'

I did not really believe, at the time, that the Service could be so trivial. That was something I would come to learn later in my career.

Brian Campbell, the head of Division 031, a talented English-speaking operator and an ex-Rhodesian Selous Scout, was formally reprimanded by Niel Barnard for daring to criticise the *Broederbond*'s baleful influence over the Service. When Campbell was serving as station chief in Washington in the late 1980s, the FBI harassed him so much that he found it difficult to handle his agents. He sent an urgent message to the head office requesting the Director General talk to the CIA, since that service was allowed a much greater operational latitude in South Africa.

The request was denied and he was reprimanded for complaining.

National Intelligence, however, continued suffering at the hands of the FBI. An officer from Division 031 by the name of Els was compromised when he was caught in the act of handling an agent in the State Department.

Els had entered a record shop to collect documents from the agent who by arrangement, was browsing in the shop. The agent had placed the material in the cover of a particular record displayed on a shelf. As Els retrieved the documents the FBI moved in and arrested both handler and agent. The intelligence concerned had absolutely nothing to do with the security of the United States. Els was expelled forthwith from the country. He returned to Division 031 in Pretoria.

The collection of information about the Freemasons and the Illuminati was also prohibited at the NIS.

I considered that being a member of National Intelligence was an honour. The Service was undoubtedly the most elite of all government departments in regard to ambitions and financial rewards.

Within the organisation there were definite positions of advantage. Promotions and appointments in divisions like Directorate K, Division 06, Division 031 brought status, more personal liberty and greater financial benefits. In normal circumstances a field officer of similar seniority serving at a regional office would never get the exposure, the status, the promotion opportunities and the financial rewards of his counterpart in London, Paris or Washington. They also brought tremendous financial benefits. Such postings were much sought after by field officers. Most of those who made it had the right connections — membership of the *Broederbond* — regardless of their operational successes or lack of them. A four-year stint was sufficient to set an officer up financially and status wise for the rest of his career.

Such favouritism frustrated the majority of operatives who were not fortunate enough to be invited to join the *Broederbond*, or were willing to subject themselves to its credo. Transparently biassed decisions were frequent. I recall an officer fluent in German being posted to a backwater in South America while someone with absolutely no language skills got the senior post going in Germany.

A certain officer placed undercover in an African state and earning British pounds sterling instead of weak South African rands produced less than ten intelligence reports in 12 months. It was obvious incompetence failure that would have been frowned on in any National Intelligence office, but nothing happened to him. Other officers with proven competence in the field never seemed to get the nod for any lucrative positions that came up.

Certain privileged positions were reserved for certain individuals regardless and more often than not they belonged to the *Broederbond* or *Ruiterwag*.

Nepotism was rife. Johan van den Bergh, son of former BOSS Chief, General 'Lang Hendrik' van den Bergh, was a senior analyst. Dr Nico Barnard, younger brother of Director General Niel Barnard, was a divisional head analyst. Several members of Deputy-Director General Gert Rothmann's family were employed by the Service. This included Peter Whitehead who was married to Rothmann's daughter. And so it went on. Most of their careers rocketed to stardom. They all served in what can be termed privileged units and reaped the financial benefits. At least one such officer brought disgrace to the NIS while serving as a field officer, but it made no difference and he was retained in his position with little quibble.

Another case in point was a field officer with a reputation for incompetence, who was awarded the annual Director of Operations award while serving in a training capacity. Other operators were astounded to hear that he had been given such a prestigious award ahead of the many operators who had served in the field with distinction.

As a junior officer he had served in two fairly senior foreign stations but with little operational success. On his return to South Africa he held a private function for South African diplomats which was attended by many senior officers, including the then Director General of Foreign Affairs.

His sucking up to superiors and his membership of the secret Afrikaner clique were widely accepted as the reasons for his rise to stardom.

The Service became a vehicle used for bestowing long-term privilege and prosperity on the favoured few. The financial disparity today between former officers of identical rank with the same number of year's service is astounding. Many former officers known to me who found favour, can be found living in retirement in luxury homes along the magnificent Garden Route of the Eastern Cape. Other highly competent and successful former field officers, have been left to eke out an existence on their standard and ungenerous government pensions. They had not, of course, experienced the blessings brought about by plum foreign postings.

I again stress that this has nothing to do with former rank differences or experience. It was, to quote from George Orwell's *Animal Farm*, merely that 'all animals are equal, but some animals are more equal than others.'

Understandably, such a system of favouritism and nepotism in appointments prejudiced the Service's operational quest for quality intelligence. It was not necessarily the right man for the job, but rather the best job for the favoured man. Because of the long shadow cast by the *Broederbond* and the *Ruiterwag*, this tendency was undoubtedly multiplied in the stratospheric levels of the Security Forces, National Intelligence and in the National Party cabinet itself.

14

Directorate K

The most profound development within National Intelligence and the best kept intelligence secret of pre-democratic South Africa was the establishment in late 1986 of Directorate K. 'K' is the abbreviation used for the Afrikaans *koverte* (covert). The name said it all. Directorate K was tasked to conduct any covert action required by National Intelligence or the State Security Council. Its operational ambit extended far beyond that of any other arm of the South African security and intelligence forces — except probably the military's covert Civil Co-operation Bureau or CCB.

In contrast to other branches of National Intelligence, Directorate K initially had no specific organisational designations like foreign collection or counter-intelligence. Shortly after its formation, though, it was split into two divisions, K1 and K2, to separate internal and foreign operations. The base for foreign collection was Pretoria and the methods it used were fairly unorthodox. In contrast to the accepted norms in intelligence services, K's officers were never placed under diplomatic cover and were only rarely placed as illegals in foreign countries.

The key word was 'covert.' The directorate engaged in actions considered too sensitive for a normal intelligence service. Their functions included sensitive surveillance, intelligence gathering by *any* means — by implication, dirty tricks. The directorate was structured in such a manner that it always provided the Service and the national government with the right of denial. Its covert configuration was not restricted by any of the statutes that governed the greater South African intelligence community.

K was the personal fiefdom of Mike Kuhn, an over-assertive and arrogant man. The image he portrayed was one of uncompromising discipline. He was the Service's tough guy, the strong man who rode roughshod over literally anyone who got in his way. He personified his directorate and he frequently meddled in the affairs of other divisions. If a division had an agent that he wanted, he just took him. If a field officer from another division was working a case and Kuhn decided to take it over, he just did so. He assumed seniority over all other directors of the same rank in the Service.

Kuhn had a safe house in Kings Road, Chelsea, London, that was purchased for £274 000. What has happened to it is anyone's guess.

Initially, he worked directly under the Chief Director Operations and had offices on the same floor in Concilium Building, Pretoria. If I remember correctly, it was the fifth floor. He was later promoted to Chief Director which put him on equal footing with the Chief Director Operations who controlled the Service's total operational force, both foreign and internal.

An officer of the old school, Kuhn had started his career with the Service when it was still the Bureau of State Security (BOSS) commanded by General 'Lang Hendrik' van den Bergh. Kuhn became a member of the *Broederbond* in 1977.

Staffers required by K were removed from the National Intelligence mainstream countrywide. They resigned from the Service and re-joined under false identities. Many of them had salaries paid in cash. A select few field officers were recruited directly into the directorate.

K's resources, the composition of its manpower and its organisation gave the directorate executive capabilities. The National Intelligence Service, an intelligence service established under the law, had no executive powers nor were its members trained in functions. In other words it had no 007s with licences to kill. I am sure that K did, but it will be denied. Former members of the Security Branch and the SADF's Special Forces who possessed such skills, however, were recruited into Directorate K. This strengthened its abilities in areas not usually identified with intelligence services.

Its field officers worked individually or in small teams from their homes or from private offices. Their function was completely independent of regional National Intelligence offices within whose domains they operated. The regional representatives across the country had no knowledge about either the directorate's presence or the operations it was conducting in their regions. This allowed its operators great latitude in conducting false flag operations and in the infiltration of enemy targets.

Agents were recruited from all over Africa, Europe and the Americas and handled from Pretoria. To curb expenses, the case officers had to travel all over the world to manage their networks, instead of creating infrastructures in place. The field officers of K22, a division of the directorate, operated from a smallholding in Midrand between Pretoria and Johannesburg. From there they handled activities in Europe and Africa. This included surveillance on the SACP's Ronnie Kasrils at his residence in Golders Green, London and on Joe Slovo at his home in Lime Road, Camden.

Through Niel Barnard and Mike Kuhn, Directorate K became a mirror image of the National Intelligence Service and the private intelligence service of President P W Botha and his inner circle. An example was the surveillance ordered and executed on Minister of Foreign Affairs Pik Botha. Despite what might have been said to the contrary, there was no love lost between the two Bothas. Pik's heavy drinking habits, the perception that he behaved badly around women and his loyalty or lack of loyalty to PW's leadership, became suspect. Directorate K was ordered to monitor his activities. The bugging of his telephones was conducted by K22 from its Midrand listening post. All the minister's telephone conversations were recorded, transcribed and passed to Mike Kuhn. There seems little doubt that the end product ended up with President PW Botha.

PW Botha's unease about his foreign minister originated with a chain of events that occurred in the mid 1980s.

In the middle of 1985 Pik paid visits to Western leaders in Europe to pave the way for a speech that PW was planning to make on 15 August 1985. He was expected to announce startling political reforms to South Africa's apartheid policy and to order the release from prison of Nelson Mandela.

When delivering his address at the Natal Congress of the National Party, however, the president made no mention whatsoever of a future unitary state, common citizenship for black and white or the pending release of Mandela, let alone democratic elections. The speech was covered by the world's media and it was a huge let-down. It was said that PW had not crossed the Rubicon and the speech became known forever after as the 'Rubicon speech'.

There were immediate suspicions that someone had set out deliberately to create false expectations. All fingers pointed at Pik Botha.

The *Daily Telegraph* in London reported on the incident thus:

'Mr Pik Botha, Foreign Minister, spent the weekend defending himself against charges that he had caused a crisis of expectations worldwide by 'overselling' what Mr PW Botha was about to announce. He said he had told the American, British and West German governments nothing that had not been contained in the State President's speech.'

Suspicion against him, however, lingered because of things that had happened before the address.

US Congressman Stephan Solarz let it be known that in a meeting between himself and President PW Botha on 13 August 1985, he told the president that he had been informed by Pik Botha at the beginning of August that the government was thinking about abolishing the black homelands system and creating a unitary state.

PW denied Solarz's accusation and insisted that Pik was his friend and confidante.

A startling turn of events followed when on 6 February 1986 Pik told a press conference that he would be willing to serve under a black president.

Ministers Chris Heunis and FW de Klerk, then the leader of the Transvaal National Party, immediately asked the president to repudiate the foreign minister as his statement created doubt with the electorate over the party's policy directions.

PW took Pik to task during a parliamentary sitting, but added a rider saying he appreciated his minister's long standing support and achievements.

Later in the year Pik Botha began to contemplate the idea of forming a new political party that would be called the National Democratic Party. Pilot studies were conducted and promises of financial support were elicited from various quarters, but he finally dropped the idea.

National Intelligence had used a specific procedure for approving operations. The various levels of management — regional representatives, heads of divisions, deputy heads of divisions, directors of divisions, the Chief Director Operations, the Deputy Director General and the Director General himself — had ceiling levels in terms of what they could approve, including financial expenditure.

Activating an operation against a fellow officer had to be approved by the Chief Director Operations. The Director 06 could approve an operation against an officer or member of another government department. Investigating a government minister or even a member of parliament could not be embarked on by National Intelligence alone. It required presidential authorisation and such sensitive investigations would be handed over to Directorate K.

At this time, the SADF's Special Forces, despite worldwide condemnation, were continuing a programme of attacking ANC targets in neighbouring states.

In June 1986 President PW Botha wrote a letter to President Ronald

Reagan in which he explained South Africa's position on the attacks. The communication was routed through the National Intelligence Service and CIA channels. He explained that his reason for not despatching it through normal diplomatic channels was to avoid the hands of the US State Department.

> 'I'm concerned at the mind set concerning South Africa which is evolving in your State Department and certain other circles in the USA, which does not take account of the inevitable consequences of a handover of power to a communist dominated organisation.'

What he failed to spell out was that he not only distrusted the US State Department, but also his own foreign minister and his Department of Foreign Affairs.

President Reagan responded formally in a message to President PW Botha delivered via the usual diplomatic channels through the South African ambassador in Washington. Reagan, unlike Botha, had no desire to communicate via the intelligence services of the two countries.

Shortly after my transfer to Division 031, Steve van Zyl was transferred to the controversial Division K where he recruited and ran an aide to Britain's Prime Minister Margaret Thatcher as an agent. MI5 eventually caught on to his activities. In a top level communication to National Intelligence, MI6 expressed the Iron Lady's extreme displeasure at South Africa's spying spree in her own backyard. Steve was immediately instructed to break all ties with the agent, but I do not believe he did.

Directorate K had a military helicopter at its disposal and one of its officers was an ex-SAAF chopper pilot.

Prince Charles, in his capacity as Director of the Commonwealth Development Corporation, visited Swaziland, Malawi and Kenya over the period 22 March to 2 April 1987. After the completion of his official duties he moved to Botswana with his personal friend and guru, Sir Laurens van der Post, to spend time in the Kalahari Desert. He arrived in Botswana on 2 April 1987. They joined up with Botswana historian, Alec Campbell, and camped out in the desert at a saltpan, 275km north west of Gaborone.

In an amazing twist, the operator who acted as Directorate K's pilot turned up in Botswana and worked as Prince Charles' pilot during his private visit.

The Botswana Intelligence Service, to say nothing of Britain's MI6, must have slipped up badly during their screening processes. If by a remote chance, which seems highly unlikely, the Botswana government had asked the South Africans for a pilot, a member of Directorate K would have been the last person they would have provided because it might easily have blown his cover. If there were special reasons for his use we were unaware of, the matter remains open to conjecture.

15

Zimbabwe

In January 1987 Phillip took me to lunch in the affluent eastern suburbs of Pretoria. The setting was far removed from the office with its constant interruptions and pressurised atmosphere. The tranquil surroundings made it the ideal setting for Phillip to discuss my future career. Specifics were broached over Cognac after the meal.

'We need you in Zimbabwe', Phillip said, 'a new situation has developed in Harare . . . you'll be appointed as Assistant Trade Representative to the Trade Mission.'

For the next four months no one saw much of me. I spent most of my time between The Farm and Division 031 in Pretoria, getting to grips with Zimbabwe's politics, diplomatic protocol and cryptography. Most evenings I slept over in the bungalows provided for officers on course. I read through piles of intelligence reports on the country and discussed them with Phillip whom I met regularly in the evenings.

'At 05:00 yesterday our Zimbabwe agent codenamed *Menace* utilised his emergency channel of communication', said Phillip. 'He called Timothy, the Harare Station Chief, on his home telephone. He wants to meet one of us as soon as possible. I can't take the risk of using Timothy as he represents Division 031. *Menace* is a counter-intelligence matter and one of our division's sources. You'll have to get up there within the next couple of days. The order comes directly from the Director General.'

I reviewed the realities. I would be going to Harare to take control of an agent code-named *Menace*. He had been recruited two years before and handled from South Africa by Steve. Face-to-face meetings between the agent and his controller had been limited to quarterly ones. They had taken place in neighbouring countries like Malawi or Mauritius.

Until then most of *Menace*'s top secret material had been transported across the border into South Africa by diplomatic courier. The growing hostility between the two countries, aggravated by Robert Mugabe's own paranoia about spies, made that method

33 June 1987

Mr E MUTEWERA
Director-General
Central Intelligence Organization
Harare
ZIMBABWE

Dear Mr. Mutewera,

I would like to inform you that Mr J VAN ZYL, assistant to this Service's representative in Harare, will be returning to South Africa during August, 1987. He will be replaced by Mr A S LABUSCHAGNE. A curriculum vitae of Mr LABUSCHAGNE is attached.

I trust that you will find Mr LABUSCHAGNE a worthy successor and suitably co-operative.

Yours Sincerely,

L D Barnard

DIRECTOR-GENERAL:
NATIONAL INTELLIGENCE SERVICE
(L D BARNARD)

Author's letter of appointment to the Harare Trade Mission.

hazardous. Mugabe was completely unpredictable and it was felt there was an off chance that he might one day order a courier to be intercepted and his diplomatic bag checked. This precaution, in the

185

end, was not as far-fetched as it might seem — in March 1990 Mugabe actually did order the interception and opening of a British diplomatic bag causing a major international furore. To obviate this possibility the Service decided to place a member of the Counter-Intelligence Division in Harare under diplomatic cover to control *Menace*.

The intelligence product from this senior Zimbabwean intelligence officer was of inestimable value. He was in a key position which gave him access to the heart of Mugabe's cabinet as well as the Zimbabwe Central Intelligence Organisation's (ZCIO) Liberation Desk — responsible for liaison with and support of the South African liberation movements based in Zimbabwe.

My first nasty experience occurred when I was en route to Harare. About 100km south of Harare I was stopped at a combined army and police roadblock. My South African registered VW Jetta with its white driver attracted aggravated attention from the personnel there.

'Step out of the car and open the boot', a policeman ordered while a soldier stood with his AK47 cocked.

My diplomatic status, confirmed by my passport and courier's letter, stopped them from searching the boot and discovering the three firearms I had concealed under the luggage.

When I arrived at the South African Mission an hour later, an administrative official from the Department of Foreign Affairs took me to my official residence, 29 Beeston Avenue in Mandara, a northern suburb of Harare. The three acre property was beautifully set amongst large trees and it sported a tennis court and swimming pool. Two black servants, a maid and a gardener-cum-cook, were awaiting my arrival.

I wanted to make contact with *Menace* as soon as possible, but my first day at the mission didn't allow me any time to concentrate on my primary task. It was taken up with administrative red tape, a meeting with the head of the mission, meeting the rest of the staff and getting settled in.

An office had been set up for me in the west wing on the third floor. My official cover would be that I was there to promote trade links between the two countries, seek new opportunities for South African businessmen and advise Zimbabwean businessmen on trade prospects in the Republic.

The Mugabe government was well aware of a National Intelligence Service presence. Director General Mutewere of the Zimbabwe Central Intelligence Organisation (ZCIO) had personally cleared my appointment. He had been notified of my pending arrival by a letter from Niel Barnard on 28 June 1987.

I met the Service's station chief for the first time the next morning,

Timothy or Tim as he was universally known, was a slim man of almost frail build. His freckled face was crowned by a growth of flaming red hair. His blue eyes, partly concealed by thick rimmed glasses sparkled with enthusiasm and left me in no doubt about his alertness.

'I'll support you wherever I can. The Department of Foreign Affairs staff at the mission are paranoid about spooks. They look on us as rogues and worry that our actions might threaten their personal safety or jeopardise their exalted diplomatic status. If we offend Robert Mugabe it might end their soft life here.'

Brandt Brooks, a South African Air Force Colonel, who was Military Intelligence's representative at the mission, joined us for coffee. He ran his operation with his wife as his assistant from the fourth floor.

We never shared details about our sources, but we co-operated closely. Where possible we assisted him in his quest for military information about Zimbabwe and neighbouring states. Like us he primarily focussed on the ANC and MK in particular.

But *Menace* was my priority. I studied the clandestine communication alternatives I had been given by Steve in the privacy of my office. The list of ten meeting places, identification codes and safety signals had been agreed upon six months before. That was the last time Steve had met *Menace*, which was in the safety of a holiday resort on Mauritius.

After careful consideration I decided on meeting place number seven for our first face-to-face meeting. Before my departure from Pretoria I had been instructed not to use telephones when establishing contact as all our sensitive lines were routinely monitored by the ZCIO. The directive applied to all foreign missions, the homes of their staff and certain public phone booths. The phones of sensitively placed officials in the Zimbabwean security apparatus were also routinely tapped.

At 13:00 I left the building and joined the flow of lunch hour strollers on the pavement. I walked east along Samora Machel Avenue, turned south into Julius Nyerere and then into Angwa Street. A tail was clearly reflected in the shop window to my left. A tall African male wearing a brightly coloured floral shirt was shadowing me, and not very expertly, on the opposite side of the street.

I bought a wall calendar from a street vendor and crossed the street. I estimated that my tail was no more than 20 paces behind me.

'Happy Birthday', I said, passing the rolled up calendar to a visibly surprised passer by.

I rounded the corner and glanced back. My minder had ripped the calendar from the perplexed stranger's hands and was pushing him around and frantically questioning him. The ZCIO man had reacted instinctively, figuring he had caught my contact red handed.

By the time he realised his mistake I had disappeared into the crowd and was two blocks away in Samora Machel Avenue, circling back towards the mission. I paused at a yellow fire hydrant on the pavement for a short moment and without anyone noticing, I chalked a cross on the side facing the road. The South African flag was fluttering on its staff on the roof of the mission about 100 metres away.

MNR G H ROTHMANN

nooi u graag na 'n geselligheid
  in die Direkteur-generaal se
  privaat eetkamer, 5de Vloer,
    CONCILIUMGEBOU.

DATUM   :   11 Augustus 1987

TYD   :   12H00 – 14H00

  By geleentheid van lede se

  BUITELANDSE PLASING

Invitation by Deputy Director General G H Rothmann (the Arab) to the author to attend a function in the Director General's private dining room on the 5th Floor of Concilium Building. While on a visit to Pretoria from Harare.

I typed a cryptic code on a scrap of paper, folded it and slipped it into an empty 35mm film case. The note read: 'Seven, Friday 10:00.' Its meaning would be decrypted by *Menace* from pre-arranged codes. It meant that the meeting was scheduled for option seven (Lake Chivero — formerly Lake MacIlwaine), one day and two hours later than the message stipulated. I pondered on his next move and hoped he would notice my cross marked on the fire hydrant which he was supposed to check daily. It told him that the dead drop would be loaded that evening and would be ready for lifting.

The Anchor was a prestigious club/restaurant in the city centre owned by a flamboyant Italian businessman, Bruno Peagno. His establishment served as a watering hole and meeting place for the mainly white patronage of diplomats and foreign journalists. The membership fee of Z$500 was a little too much for most of the local blacks. One could be sure that the only blacks there were wealthy businessmen or privileged officials of the ZANU-PF government.

I showed my card at the door and entered the dimly lit interior.My membership had been arranged by the Mission before I arrived in the country.

'Would you like a table sir?' a waiter asked politely.

'No thanks, I'm having a drink at the bar.'

The heavy mahogany counter really didn't blend with the overpowering black and red decor. It reminded me of sushi bars in Hong Kong.

I ordered a Scotch and prayed silently that *Menace* would arrive.

He entered the bar at 16:30, neatly dressed in dark suit and tie. I heard him speak for the first time as he ordered a Castle beer. He took his beer and sat on a stool just down the bar from me.

Menace had fought in the liberation struggle as a senior and trusted officer of ZANLA (Zimbabwe African National Liberation Army), ZANU-PF's military wing. He had been close to the ZANLA commander, Josiah Tongogara. Tongogara was assassinated in Mozambique in December 1979 and his death was covered up to make it look like a road accident. It's believed that the killing was done at the behest of Robert Mugabe who believed Tongogara posed a threat to his position.

Menace was later appointed to a senior position in the ZCIO. In the early 1980s he was on the periphery of a plot to assassinate Robert Mugabe. Someone, however, tipped of the authorities. Although others in ZANU-PF were arrested, *Menace* was not implicated and he continued to enjoy party favours.

The former ZANLA officer was a calculated professional and he used his top-level access to become a professional spy. He sold his country's secrets not only to the South Africans, but also to the British, the Germans and the French, earning large sums of US dollars. I learned about *Menace*'s quadruple role from a French intelligence officer who very generously co-operated with us and passed on intelligence without the knowledge of his head office.

With *Menace* in position to collect the drop, I didn't waste any more time. I went into a cubicle in the men's toilet and locked the door behind me. I inserted the small plastic cylinder into a hidden cavity behind the grill of the air vent. I flushed the toilet and left without returning to the bar. Our meeting was scheduled for two days hence.

I left for Lake Chivero early on Saturday morning with my fishing gear. My meeting with *Menace* was set for midday. To foil any effort by the opposition to follow me, I drove around the centre of town, checking my rearview mirror for signs of surveillance. When I was certain I was clean, I drove out on the Bulawayo road to the lake which is a short distance outside the capital.

I parked under a clump of Msasa trees about 800 metres from a run-down boathouse and restaurant complex. After ensuring that no one was watching, I gathered my gear and walked to a secluded bay on the lake.

With my hook baited and cast in the water I scanned the lake with my binoculars. There was nobody to be seen, but I had almost an hour in hand until our 12:00 meeting.

Eventually my powerful Pentax binoculars picked up a small hired boat chugging in my direction from the east. It was *Menace*.

'Jump aboard.'

I sloshed through the shallow water and pulled myself aboard.

Menace killed the motor in a quiet creek and lowered his tackle into the water.

'Pleased to meet you Mr Labuschagne, I've seen your accreditation papers submitted to our Foreign Office.'

He was a no-nonsense unpretentious individual.

'You gave one of ours the slip the other day', he laughed, then became serious. 'You must be careful not to be too professional. It focusses attention on you and that's the last thing we want.'

Menace knew what he wanted and he dictated the pace. His life was in my hands and in those of the other controllers he dealt with.

He struck me as being extremely fly and every inch a true professional.

Just in case our meeting was prematurely interrupted, we immediately got down to arranging new clandestine communication signals, meeting places and dead letterboxes. The longer the time we spent together, the greater the risk of discovery.

Without unnecessary elaboration *Menace* divulged his latest information.

'The ANC have embarked on a mission to destroy military aircraft at your South African bases. A MK task team arrived in Harare about three weeks ago with a request for expert military assistance. They were taken to Thornhill Air Force Base in Gweru where they stayed for three days. They made a close study of military aircraft and were instructed in the most effective ways of blowing them up. They were also interested in how to calculate the range, speed and height of a moving aircraft and when it would be most vulnerable to a missile strike.'

'How far have they gone towards implementing this plan?' I interrupted.

'I'm not sure, but I think that their operatives will have been infiltrated into position by now. I do know that the weapons allocated for the attack are still in Botswana. Some members of the high command are hesitant to use missiles. They are afraid the men at the sharp end might be captured and they don't want sophisticated hardware falling into South African hands. Until two days ago the ANC were still arguing about whether the infiltration should be done through Botswana or Zimbabwe.'

'Can we get the names and timings soon?' I asked.

'I can't ask directly as it's not within the direct sphere of my responsibilities . Aid to the ANC is dealt with by the Liberation Desk, but I'll try.'

We parted company. It would be a long time before we met again. Our future communications would be via unwitting intermediaries and dead letterboxes.

A few days later after a signal from *Menace*, I lifted a message from the secret cavity at The Anchor. I read the note in the toilet cubicle, burned the scrap of paper and flushed the charred remains.

I despatched an urgent signal to headquarters. It read: 'Follow-up to initial report. MK attack Swartkops Air Force Base. Infiltrated by black civilian doctor who apparently treats air force personnel at base. Name unknown. More to follow.'

My initial report created an enormous stir with National Intelligence's management. There had been attacks on SADF installations before. In 1981 MK had taken a decision to coincide an attack with nationwide anti-Republic Day demonstrations. On 9 August one of their Special Operations teams attacked a military complex at Voortrekkerhoogte outside Pretoria. At 20:30 five 122mm rockets were fired from an open space between plot 240 Mooiplaas and Laudium. Some buildings were hit, but a large fuel depot was missed. The attack had no serious military implications, but its psychological impact was great.

In May 1983 MK detonated a massive car bomb in front of SAAF headquarters in Church Street, Pretoria. Nineteen people, including SADF and SAP members, were killed and another 200 injured. The two MK operatives conducting the mission also died in the blast.

So warning of another strike against a military target had to be taken very seriously. The long-standing credibility of the source made his information a priority.

Menace was the most senior and productive spy recruited by the Service in Zimbabwe in the 1980s. In fact, I rate him the best I ever came across during my entire career in intelligence. He was never caught and must rate as one of the most successful spies in the annals of espionage.

There was always a flair in his information. During the 1980s the ZCIO Counter-Intelligence executed a regular joint annual operation with British MI6. A week before the end of the Muslim Ramadan festival, a British MI6 team would arrive in Harare to prepare for an operation with ZCIO. On the night of the full moon at the height of the religious festivities, a joint team would break into the Libyan embassy, crack open all the safes and copy every document.

For good measure *Menace* used to make copies for us. National Intelligence traded most of this haul with the Americans for stuff that we needed. Handling *Menace* was a full-time job. He produced about a hundred or more top secret documents each month. We obtained most of the intelligence reports generated by the ZCIO as well as cabinet briefs. His level of production created logistical problems. It was difficult to process the large volume of material in a manner that disguised its origin. Another complicating factor was that a large portion of the intelligence generated by him had to be shared with Military Intelligence and the Security Branch for action.

This explains why National Intelligence emerged clean at the end of the Truth and Reconciliation Commission hearings in the late 1990s. The fact was that it had no executive powers. The organisations executing the actions were the SADF and the SAP, which left National Intelligence in the clear.

*   *   *

Towards the end of 1987 *Menace*'s cover was almost blown by an aspirant South African spy.

Major Andre Pienaar had worked in the security department of the Special Forces HQ at Speskop, Pretoria under Colonel Johan Theron and Commandant Eric Kennelly. The other staff in the section were Citizen Force corporals Danie Phaal and Paul Heyns.

Pienaar was transferred from Speskop to the Zimbabwe Desk of Military Intelligence's Department of Covert Collection (DCC) where he was responsible for intelligence material sourced in Zimbabwe. Tactical information generated by *Menace* also crossed his desk. Most of those documents still bore the seal of the ZCIO and it appears he managed to piece together the likely identity of the Service's star Zimbabwean agent.

Major Pienaar had large debts, problems with alcohol and with his marriage. The convoluted state of his personal life arose from his involvement with another woman. He fell in love with the sister of one of DCC's Zimbabwean agents and she became his mistress. She turned out to be a wastrel and spendthrift who continually demanded fine clothes, other luxury items and an expensive lifestyle. Completely besotted by her, Pienaar sought ways of making extra money so that he would not lose her. He came to regard intelligence documents as saleable commodities.

He was a highly trusted DCC officer. He surreptitiously had duplicate keys cut for the office safe and one night he stole a file containing reports from *Menace* and other stuff from the Mozambique Desk run by Major John Birch.

His first approach was to CIA officers at the US Embassy in Pretoria. The Yanks, however, told him to piss off. They only recruited agents with the rank of colonel or above. This selectivity indicated that it was unlikely they were short of such agents!

Devastated by the rejection he next approached the Zimbabwe Trade Mission in Johannesburg. He told the ZCIO officers there that he had proof there was a high-level spy in their midst in Harare. He promised to name the spy and provide documentary evidence. The ZCIO officers passed the report to Harare with a request for instructions. Fortunately for *Menace*, he intercepted the report when it crossed his desk. Consequently, the men in Johannesburg were told that under no circumstances should they take possession of the material. They should instead make arrangements for the walk-in to personally bring the files to Harare.

Menace advised me of the new developments immediately and provided me with the traitor's name. The defector, during his negotiations with the Zimbabweans, had said he was a Special Forces officer but the name he used turned out to be false. Our head office went into a panic at the thought of losing their most valuable asset. The Service and its opposite numbers in Military Intelligence rushed around in ever decreasing small circles but they failed to identify the traitor. Meanwhile, arrangements were made for an air force helicopter to be placed on standby to extract *Menace* and his family from Zimbabwe if they failed to locate the spy and his cover was blown.

I kept *Menace* informed and warned him to get his family ready to move just in case. Although almost frantic with worry, he retained his composure and continued his daily routine.

When the time came for the walk-in's departure to Harare, he had still not been identified. The departure area of Jan Smuts (now Johannesburg International) Airport was swarming with National Intelligence and Security Police officers, but they couldn't identify their man. They even delayed the flight to Harare. Eventually though, by sheer luck, they approached an apparently innocent young man with short hair on spec. A search of his hand luggage brought to light a stack of top secret ZCIO documents. It was Major Andre Pienaar. He was promptly arrested, charged, convicted of espionage and gaoled. *Menace* could breathe again and live to spy some more — which he did for several years to come.

Pienaar was released from prison after serving eight years. While inside he befriended Dieter Gerhardt, a former South African Naval commodore who had spied for the Soviet Union until his arrest in 1982. Gerhardt had supplied secret South African defence information and also sensitive details relating to Israel's military with which South Africa had strong ties. He also leaked details of co-operation between South Africa and Israel on biological, chemical and nuclear weapons. The CIA arrested him in Washington in 1983 and returned him to Pretoria. He was granted a presidential pardon in 1992 at the request of the Russian president. He currently lives in Switzerland.

*   *   *

I arrived at my office in the Mission at 07:00. I started to run the deciphering programme on my computer and noticed that I had three routine and one priority signals from Pretoria.

I poured a strong coffee and made myself comfortable. I eyed the stack of paperwork and decided to focus my attention on the priority signal first.

'Subject: MK, subversive activities. Your report dated the 12th

194

<u>L E T T R E De C O U R I E R</u>

<u>TO WHOM IT MAY CONCERN</u>

This is to certify that the bearer of this letter,
MR. A.S.LABUSCHAGNE , has been appointed as an ad hoc diplomatic
courier and will be travelling on diplomatic passport
number D00U06853 .

MR. LABUSCHAGNE will be carrying one attache case containing
diplomatic material only , between the SOUTH AFRICAN TRADE
MISSION in HARARE and the DEPARTMENT OF FOREIGN AFFAIRS in
PRETORIA on 18 April 1988 .

In terms of agreement the said attache case is immune to
inspection.

T.E. CLAASEN

<u>ASSISTANT TRADE REPRESENTATIVE</u>
SOUTH AFRICAN TRADE MISSION

HARARE

Author's *Lettre De Courier* used to protect 'diplomatic material' (intelligence from *Menace*) being taken to Pretoria.

in this regard refers. Two Soviet trained MK cadres and three collaborators, including a Dr Bafana, were arrested yesterday. They're currently being held for questioning. A large amount of explosives and firearms found in their possession were confiscated.'

Bloody hell, *Menace* has been right all along, I thought.

I scanned the rest of the document. The word 'Zimbabwe' in a paragraph at the bottom of the page caught my eye. ' . . . a third suspect and a member of MK's special operations, Guy Ndhlovu alias Joe Phiri is also being sought. There's a strong possibility he might have crossed into Zimbabwe.' I turned the page. 'Confirm Ndhlovu's entry into Zimbabwe and determine whereabouts', the signal ended.

I would have to brief *Menace* as soon as possible.

I locked my office and rushed down the passage to attend the heads of departments meeting at 08:30. It was 08:31 and I was late. Ndhlovu, it somehow seemed familiar. There had been so many names of black terrorists that had recently come up in *Menace*'s reports so maybe I had seen it in one of those.

During the meeting I suddenly remembered. Ndhlovu, Guy Ndhlovu. It had to be him, the agent introduced to me by Polozok in Zambia more than a year before. He must have returned from Angola.

'Mr Labuschagne.'

I jolted in my seat. I had missed the Head of Mission's last remark.

'Excuse me, could you repeat that, please?'

Viljoen was clearly irritated with the junior diplomat for not paying attention.

'As I said before, I've received a circular from Pretoria that details emergency evacuation procedures. In terms of arrangements between the Department of Foreign Affairs and the SADF, in case of an emergency everyone will evacuate to a designated point north of the city. The stipulated place is the open ground adjacent to Mr Labuschagne's residence. I think you're all familiar with it?'

Everyone nodded in acknowledgment.

'In such an event all staff and their families will assemble at that point. We'll be evacuated to safety by SAAF helicopters. Any questions?'

There were none.

'Please bring it to the attention of your staff.'

I decided not to remain for the customary post-meeting coffee. It was important that I get hold of *Menace*.

'Mr Viljoen, please excuse me. I've an urgent matter to attend to.'

South Africa's most senior diplomat in Zimbabwe was an impressive figure of a man whose English accent and features belied his Afrikaner origins.

As I closed the door behind me, I met his enquiring stare. I pretended not to notice. My business was of no concern to the Head of Mission or the Department of Foreign Affairs. Ndhlovu was an exclusive intelligence issue.

I drafted an urgent signal to Pretoria asking for more information on Guy Ndhlovu. I had to be sure. The priority now was to get a request through to *Menace*. I checked the schedule for the location of the next dead drop. It was the Harare Club. I cleared my desk and put my diary and all documents in the safe. I locked my office and left the building.

I got to the Harare Club just after 15:00. *Menace* and I were both members. Using the public phone in the bar I dialled his direct office number. I had to let him know about a drop.

'Hello?' I recognised his voice.

'Sorry wrong number', I broke the connection, satisfied that *Menace* had recognised my voice and would lift the message on his way home.

I ordered a scotch and sat waiting for half an hour. I reckoned that *Menace* would arrive any minute. I glanced at my watch and got up. On my way out I went into the men's locker room. I made sure no one was watching and opened *Menace*'s locker with a duplicate key. I slipped a note into the false heel of a boot at the bottom of the locker. It read: 'Guy Ndhlovu alias Joe Phiri, expected to cross into Zimbabwe from South Africa. Require details urgently.'

*   *   *

The commander of the rural police station at Bubye River on the Beit Bridge-Harare road, immediately phoned ZCIO headquarters in Harare, advising them of the arrest of a suspected South African spy.

ZCIO headquarters reacted swiftly. The station was instructed to hold the prisoner until further notice. An urgent message giving details of the arrest was delivered by hand to the Counter-Intelligence Division.

At 12:35 *Menace* happened to see a memo of the Bubye incident by his Chief of Operations, David Muchiniripi.

'A South African using the name Guy Ndhlovu has been detained for questioning at Bubye police station. He entered the country illegally during the night. He carries no identification but claims to be a member of MK. He's possibly a South African spy attempting to infiltrate the local ANC. Please advise.'

Menace shook his head at the twist of fate. The man I was seeking had been delivered. He picked up the phone and discovered that two men had already been despatched to Bubye to escort the prisoner to Harare.

He scribbled the details of Ndhlovu's whereabouts on a piece of paper.

I returned to the office to find a response from Pretoria to my urgent signal.

The report confirmed my suspicions. The man sought was indeed the agent I had recruited under the false flag of the Soviets. He had now led a failed MK operation to sabotage South Africa's military aircraft. But how could I find him?

I thought about the invitation to attend a cocktail party at the Polish embassy. It was the official launch of some sort of Polish aid programme to Zimbabwe.

I arrived at the embassy in Angwa Street at 18:00. Judging by the large number of cars outside, the function was well attended. Numerous black Mercedes, the standard government issue car for officials, were parked at the entrance.

I accepted a martini from a waiter as I entered and drifted through the crowd. I noticed my head of mission in the far corner, but apart from him there were no familiar faces to be seen. The diplomatic circuit was a circus. The real diplomats had more in common with their professional peers from various countries than with their own countrymen in the intelligence profession.

In the covert world there's almost a club-like atmosphere. Intelligence professionals respect each other, even across the barriers of opposition and hostility. So at a function like that, the true diplomats would huddle in one corner adhering to every form of etiquette while the spies would probably be huddling in another.

It was not uncommon to find the resident KGB officer conversing with his British, South African or American counterparts.

'Hallo, Riaan.'

It was Jennifer, an equestrian instructor at the Avondale Riding School. Horse riding was a popular pastime amongst the diplomatic community and I often enjoyed an outride over weekends.

We stood, drinks in hand, making small talk.

I suddenly spotted *Menace* across the room and our eyes met. Seconds later he came walking over to us.

He wouldn't, I thought. But I was wrong.

'Good evening, Jennifer', Menace greeted her. He looked at me.

'You are Mr . . . '

'I'm sorry, we haven't met. I'm Riaan Labuschagne.'

'You must be South African.'

'Yes, I'm with the trade mission.'

A waiter diverted Jennifer's attention and *Menace* pressed a note into my hand. It would have been difficult for anyone to notice in the crowded room.

'Not tomorrow, but the day after I would like to take an early ride before work', he said to Jennifer. I would like to take a gallop on the golf course. If it suits you. Could you make it at 06:00?'

'I'll have a horse ready for you', Jennifer confirmed.

'I learned to ride in China some years ago', he said looking at me.

He wants to meet at the sixth hole on the Avondale golf course at 06:00 the day after tomorrow, I interpreted.

'I must go. It was nice meeting you Mr Labuschagne.'

He strolled across the room and joined a group of government ministers. I recognised one as Emmerson Munangagwa, Zimbabwe's Minister of State for Security.

I went to the toilet and read the few sentences on the note in disbelief. I memorised the detail, burnt the note and as usual flushed the ashes down the toilet.

Guy was in Zimbabwe and he was being brought to Harare. *Menace*, my agent in place, would have access to him. It was a surprising turn of events. After more than a year I was about to cross paths again with my Soviet agent, this time in another country.

Two days later, wearing my jogging kit, I stood amongst the trees towards the back of the green on the sixth hole. It was drizzling and the sky was overcast. I wondered if the meeting would take place. My Seiko indicated it was 06:15. I decided to wait for another five minutes. It's always the waiting that gets to you.'

Menace's horse snorted as it cantered up the embankment. He reined in, dismounted and joined me amongst the trees. My agent related what he had found out about Guy.

'He was taken to an ANC safe house in Bulawayo last night — 16A Jungle Road. It's guarded by the police and the ZCIO keeps a list of all such places used by the liberation movements. He handed me a copy of the list.

'There are eight ANC guys staying there. As I said, it's guarded, so whatever you guys do, please don't create an international incident.'

The meeting lasted exactly 12 minutes.

I contemplated my latest orders from headquarters.

'Proceed with target analysis on Bulawayo safe house and ascertain identities of residents.'

I read the message for a second time before shredding it. That meant that an attack on the facility was being planned. I wondered how I could contact Guy before the strike.

I told the Head of Mission's secretary that I would be out of town for a couple of days. I had decided to go to Bulawayo to check the safe house for myself. I knew that once my report got to Pretoria they would make their decision and whatever it was I wouldn't be able to alter it.

My father had phoned to tell me that a black man had phoned for me. He had no idea who he was so he merely said I was out of town. Unfortunately, the caller did not leave a number or a forwarding address but he said he would phone again. It could only have been Guy. I was frustrated at not being able to speak to my long lost source.

Guy phoned again about two weeks after that. My father said he sounded distressed. Unfortunately, the line went dead before Guy could give the number of the call box. I arranged that, should he phone again, my father would immediately call me with a contact number and I would phone him back. I had no wish for Guy to discover my true allegiance. That was something I could only tell him in person.

But he never phoned again.

At 08:00 I was enjoying breakfast on the hotel veranda, having arrived in Bulawayo less than an hour before. I wanted to ensure that my trip remained a secret and had left home in Harare just after midnight.

I knew that my sudden disappearance would cause my watchers some embarrassment with their superiors. Having established my daily routine over the last few months, the ZCIO's surveillance team had relaxed their vigilance. Not suspecting that I would give them the slip, they waited for me at a static position near the Trade Mission. They would be sadly disappointed when I didn't turn up.

I used a false Australian passport in the name of Clive Johnson when I checked into the hotel. I had to make sure that I could not be connected to any incident that might occur in Bulawayo.

I felt confident about my decision. I would try to establish contact with Guy before I sent in my final report. If I was successful in warning him about the impending attack it would buy me credibility. Guy was far more useful alive than he would be dead. The problem was I had no idea how to contact him. I was hoping that I might just bump into him on the off chance.

I ran through my plan of action once again.

A road map enabled me to find the address in the suburban area of Trenance, but I did not drive into the entrance to Jungle Road. It was a cul-de-sac and I might have attracted the attention of neighbours and the police guards. I would only get one chance to drive past the house and I decided to leave that until I had formulated my plan. I turned around and headed out of the area.

My strategy, I decided, would be to cruise around the immediate vicinity and see if I could spot Guy. I would go to 16A Jungle Road itself only if all else failed. I familiarised myself with the area as I drove around, noting police stations, escape routes and so on. That night I checked the traffic flow in the neighbourhood area and noted the amount of light available from the lampposts. I also photographed features in the area.

The next day, having seen no sign of Guy, I decided it was time to have a close look at the house. I turned into Jungle Road and cruised past 16A. The house was behind a high brick wall and a green metal gate obstructed the view. I ignored the two policemen at the gate and turned into the drive of number 18.

Fortunately, no one answered when I rang the front doorbell at number 18. My excuse — that I was looking for a Mrs. Smith — was superficial in the extreme. After ensuring that no one was watching me, I photographed number 16A's front yard over the wall between the two properties. I noted a third policeman sitting on a chair under a tree by the front door.

Ten minutes later I exited Jungle Road and headed back to the hotel. I was confident that my vehicle couldn't be traced back to me as I had taken the precaution of fitting it with false number plates before I left Harare.

The next morning at 09:00 I positioned myself in a side street opposite Jungle Road, but my view of the safe house's entrance was extremely limited. I felt irritated as I still had no idea how to contact Guy. All I could do was keep watch from a distance and hope that an opportunity would arise.

At 10:30 I broke my vigil and drove to a café two blocks away to get a drink. The weather was sweltering hot. I was standing outside drinking a can of Coke when I saw two men approaching from the direction of Jungle Road. One was a policeman, but the other — even though he was a lot fatter than when I last saw him — was unmistakably Guy Ndhlovu.

They both entered the café and I got back in my car which I had fortunately parked right in front of the shop. Anyone coming out had to notice me.

My nervousness increased tenfold. I was confident that Guy had recognised me already, but I was unsure of his possible reaction. I scribbled my private telephone number on a corner of newspaper and kept the note in my hand.

Guy dawdled out of the shop while the policeman was still looking around inside. He was carrying a bag containing what looked like a loaf of bread and some tinned food. I got out of the car and approached him. Did he know where I could find a petrol station in the area? He shook his head negatively. For a moment I thought I noticed a flicker of recognition in his eyes and I decided to take a chance. I pressed the bit of folded newspaper into his hand which closed around it.

I immediately turned around, got back in my car and drove off without a backward glance. The encounter posed an enormous risk but it was the only course of action I could think of at the time. I was shaken by the encounter, but I returned to my observation post. I assumed that Guy had recognised me and I hoped that he might leave the safe house alone to look for me at the café. He didn't and I eventually returned to the hotel at 20:00.

Daybreak found me parked opposite Jungle Road again. I waited for some time, but there were no further signs of Guy. Details of my recce of the safe house and the accompanying photographs had to be in Pretoria by the following morning in accordance with Pretoria's instructions. The diplomatic bag containing the material had to be at Harare Airport by 15:30. and there was still a seven-hour drive ahead of me.

By 08:10 I could wait no longer and left for Harare. I made my deadline with half an hour to spare. Jammed under my office door at the Trade Mission were several messages and a sealed envelope marked urgent. One of the message slips was a dinner invitation from a journalist friend of mine. The envelope had Tim's handwriting on it and I tore it open.

'A black male with a South African accent phoned the mission earlier and had said he wanted to speak to Riaan urgently. He said he'll phone again at noon tomorrow. PS: You know the lines are bugged so be careful. Your agents should not phone you at this number.'

I shredded the piece of paper hoping that it was not the ZCIO trying to lure me into compromising myself.

I picked up the phone after the first ring. It was unmistakably Guy, but I listened giving nothing away.

'I'm sorry', I said knowing full well that the conversation was being recorded by the ZCIO, 'this is Riaan Labuschagne. Who is speaking?'

'It's Oscar Dlamini', he said, using the fictitious name we had agreed on more than a year before. 'I need to speak to you in person urgently. I've only got two hours.'

Oh, God, I thought, if head office found out about this they would freak.

'Where are you, Oscar?'

'In a phone booth in town.'

'Okay, Oscar. Go to the movie house above the Avondale Centre. It's about a 15 minutes drive. I'll see you there.'

I was uncertain what to do next as nothing like this had happened to me before. Field operatives were all lectured and warned to be aware of the constant possibility of a 'walk-in'. But then, but most of us spent our entire careers without ever having to deal with such an eventuality. When it does happen, the walk-in simply appears on your doorstep and offers his services for some or other personal reason.

Now I had one, but he still thought I was working for the Soviets. I would have to tell who I really was. However, if he did not co-operate he would know that I could compromise him with the Russians. There were rules in the instruction book about walk-ins, but I had no time to play things by the book. I had no doubt that the ZCIO's monitoring service had recorded our conversation. But it was impossible to listen to everything at once, so there was a good chance they would only listen to the tape later, perhaps the following day. By then it would be too late.

I parked my car outside the Avondale shopping centre at 12:15. It was school holidays and the centre was crowded with mothers, children and college students. I walked through the mall to the movie house and bought two tickets for a show that had started 15 minutes before. Guy, who had been standing at the sweet counter, followed me into the darkened theatre. Without a word we took our seats at the back. Richard Attenborough's political movie *Cry Freedom* didn't seem too popular and except for a few rows in the centre, the place was virtually empty.

'It's good to see you, Guy.'

In less than an hour he related everything that had happened since we last met.

*   *   *

Six weeks after our meeting in Zambia, Guy was sent to Cacaluma camp in Angola as a platoon commander. He arrived on 14 February 1986 and fought through many battles alongside FAPLA and the Cubans against the SADF. The MK cadres suffered heavy casualties.

About 18 months later he returned to the ANC's headquarters in Lusaka where he was personally interviewed by ANC president, Oliver Tambo. Afterwards he was given orders by Rashid (Abubakar Ismail) and Obadi (Montso Mokgabadi) who were with Tambo on the command council of MK's special operations unit. The task was to infiltrate South Africa and attack two Air Force bases near Pretoria. For two weeks the team — comprising himself, Bobo and Lux — were thoroughly briefed in Lusaka with the aid of drawings and photographs of Swartkops and Waterkloof Air Force bases. Both were used as launching pads for airlifting logistics to the Angolan front. The team was also tasked to reconnoitre the civil airports of D F Malan (Cape Town International), Louis Botha (Durban International) and Jan Smuts (Johannesburg International) with a view to future attacks.

'Destroying the South African military transport planes on the ground could hasten the end of the war and deal the enemy's morale a devastating blow', Joe Slovo the MK commander had said.

In August 1987 they were driven from Lusaka through Botswana and infiltrated into South Africa close to the Ramotswa Border Post. The military hardware, plastic explosives and SAM-7 ground-to-air missiles required for the operation were being smuggled into South Africa by another MK team using a different route.

Their first contact inside South Africa was Sibusiso Mtembo, a Soweto businessman. He met them after they crossed the border, drove them to Pretoria and supplied them with pass books and drivers' licences. In South Africa blacks were effectively second class citizens. They were not issued with the same identity cards as whites, but were given 'pass books' instead. These had to be produced if the police stopped them in a white area. Guy was also given a letter indicating that he was working for Martin Jonker Motors in Pretoria.

The three-man team was housed in the Winterveld, a black township just outside Pretoria. Their host, Dr Bafana, a doctor and an Indian, despite his African name, had access to the targets because he treated patients at both bases.

From the outset the operation ran into difficulties. A problem arose in trying to smuggle the weapons across the border from Botswana. It was resolved by Mtembo travelling to Botswana in a closed vanette and fetching the stuff. But this created an unforseen delay which increased the risk of compromise.

By the time Mtembo returned with the weapons a week later, a South African surveillance team of Watchers was waiting for him at the Lobatse Border post. They followed his vehicle to a parking lot in Krugersdorp. A two-man team remained to keep an eye on the van, while the others followed Mtembo on foot as he walked away on foot. He stopped at a public telephone booth, placed his travel bag between his feet and called the cutout to announce his arrival and tell him where the vehicle was parked. He walked to a taxi rank and boarded a taxi. He was safe. It cut the connection between himself and the bakkie's deadly cargo.

Watchers maintained their surveillance in three vehicles alternating with one another to ensure they were not tumbled. They followed as the taxi headed east towards Johannesburg. When it turned onto the Soweto Highway, the Watchers could be reasonably certain that the quarry was heading for home.

As he reached his house and was about to enter the front door, Mtembo got the shock of his life. Security policemen appeared as if from nowhere and arrested him. They took him to the notorious John Vorster Square Police Station for interrogation.

The pursuit vehicles broke off and headed for Krugersdorp after being alerted by the two Watchers in the parking lot that someone had pitched up and was driving off in the van. The two set off in pursuit in their vehicle, but back up was needed. They called for assistance.

Fifteen minutes later a police helicopter was overhead, flying high and following the target a few kilometres to the east. A military reaction force at Wonderboom Army Base north of Pretoria was alerted to the unfolding drama and ordered to prepare for a possible shootout with a group of terrorists somewhere in the Pretoria region. Three Buffel armoured personnel carriers laden with crack paratroopers left the base in a hurry and assembled in the bush alongside the road leading to the black townships north of Pretoria.

When the bakkie with its load of arms drove into the Winterveld Township, the whites only surveillance team following veered off to avoid possible compromise as they would have been only too obvious. The helicopter was ordered into position to pinpoint the van's destination so that the paratroopers could move in.

Thirty minutes later a combined National Intelligence, Security Branch and Army task force converged on the identified house and surrounded it. They arrested Bobo, Lux and the vehicle driver who surrendered without resistance.

The police found the arms in a shed next to the house. The fresh tracks made by dragging the heavy wooden cases through the sand made the search elementary.

Guy had been en route to the safe house to inspect the weapons but, fortunately for him, he was in time to see the Security Forces surround the place and he realised the operation had been bust. He fled the scene, boarded a taxi outside the township and headed for Messina close to the Zimbabwe border. He knew that by then the scheduled escape route through Botswana would also have been compromised.

The following night, 21 August, he crossed the border into Zimbabwe illegally and was arrested by soldiers of the Zimbabwe Defence Force on suspicion of being a South African spy.

Shortly afterwards he was released into ANC custody and taken to the safe house in Jungle Road.

*   *   *

I had many more questions to ask, but Guy said he had run out of time. He also explained that as a commander with MK's Special Operations, his superiors wanted him to return to Angola. He had managed to stall them for a while because he wanted to go back to South Africa.

'Riaan', he said, 'I've a vast amount of information that will be of great value to whoever you are working for. Who is that anyway?' I think he knew the answer even before he asked the question. 'It's not the Russians is it?'

'No, the South African National Intelligence Service.'

'Oh, I see.'

To my astonishment he made no protest.

'I'll give you everything', he continued, 'but I want a pardon from the government.'

'It's not for me to decide, Guy, and definitely not here and now. Give me a couple of days.'

'Okay', he said, 'I'm staying in an ANC safe house at number 33 Highfield Road. I'll make a point of going for a run each morning at 04:00. You can pick me in two days time and I shall want an answer then.'

He detailed a general rendezvous area.

'How do I know that you're for real?'

'Don't give me that bullshit, Riaan.'

'But you work for the Russians.'

Guy didn't respond to the accusation — there was insufficient time.

'What information can I get you that will prove I'm on the level?'

'I need the floor plan and names of the people in the Jungle Road house you stayed in.'

Guy nodded, got up and left the darkened cinema without another word. Ten minutes later I followed.

Back at my office I locked the door and drafted a signal for the attention of the Chief of Operations in Pretoria. Files on all National Intelligence registered sources and those under recruitment were held in a centralised registry that he controlled. Regulations on recruiting sources were clear. The full background and biographical details of the

206

candidate had to be submitted to head office, together with an operational plan for the intended recruitment. Only once approval had been granted could an operator continue with the process. I chose to ignore the regulations.

However, I knew it was essential that I register a source to explain the influx of fresh information on the ANC that I could expect from Guy in the future. With this in mind I completed the prescribed forms using the details of Peter Ndhlovu, a known ANC operative in Harare. I would keep Guy's recruitment to myself — it would be difficult to explain because of his involvement in the attempted attacks in the Pretoria area.

I checked the transcript of my message and transmitted it. It was not the first time I had taken things into my own hands and done it my way. I had broken the circle of blind adherence to the rules of the game. I had lied to my masters and registered a fictitious source to protect Guy's identity. I felt good about it.

It had become obvious to me over the past few months that the State Security Council had adopted a strategy of not only eliminating the ANC's foreign-based MK cadres, but also those engaged in non-military activities such as providing intellectual, financial and moral support to the movement. I had been receiving requests for tactical information on certain prominent ANC officials resident in or visiting Zimbabwe almost on a weekly basis.

I caught up with Guy on his morning run at 04:15. I slowed down and briefly cruised alongside him as he jogged steadily along the Highfield Road. In one swift movement he tossed a cigarette packet through the rolled down passenger window.

'The map and the names are inside.'

He kept looking ahead.

'So what did your bosses say? Do I have a deal?'

'I haven't had an answer yet', I lied.

I could never allow him to defect and I never intended to suggest it. The Service's *raison d'être* reason was to run agents-in-place. What Guy knew currently belonged mostly to the past. I needed him in place within MK structures in South Africa once the banning on the ANC was lifted and all the exiles had returned home. I was certain, from my information, that it would not be long before that happened.

Guy had no inkling of this but it was important that he played along with me for whatever the reasons.

'Goddam it Riaan, don't play games with me.'

'We have to meet first, there's a lot to discuss', I said playing my man.

'Okay', he responded after a moments silence, 'meet me at 08:00 next Sunday. You'll find me on the Mazoe Road just outside of town. He gave me details of the exact rendezvous point.

At the next corner I turned right and sped towards the city. Guy continued running.

I despatched the encrypted floor plan of Jungle Road and the list of names to 031's divisional head. I also shared the information with Military Intelligence's Colonel Brandt Brooks at tea later that morning and came to the realisation that an attack on the house was imminent.

'I already sent a floor plan of the house to Pretoria some months ago,' he told me.

I honestly thought for the moment that he was just bragging.

Having no idea what was really happening, I went back to my office to catch up on paper work. It was January 1988 and unknown to me the military already had full details of the facility.

I worked late but awoke again at 04:00. Realising that further sleep would be impossible, I dressed and left for the Trade Mission. Spurred by my restlessness, I decided to drive along Highfield Road where I expected to find Guy on his morning jog,

There was no sign of him but I noticed a broken branch by the side of the road. I recognised it as a signal that Guy had loaded the dead drop. I pulled off and checked the hollow in a tree that Guy had pointed out. I retrieved a crumpled brown paper bag, kicked the branch onto the verge and continued along Highfield Road.

I read the note inside and discovered to my horror that the ANC had sent him back to the Jungle Road facility in Bulawayo for some reason. His note assured me, though, that the date time and place of our next meeting in three days time remained unchanged. He would be returning to Harare in a couple of days.

Guy you fool, I thought. They are going to attack the house.

*   *   *

A visibly shocked secretary was quick to inform me about the bomb blast as I left the lift on the fifth floor of the Mission.

'Mr Labuschagne, have you heard what happened?'

'What, Penny?'

'It's just been on the news. They say the South Africans have bombed a refugee house in Bulawayo.'

Penny, who was married to one of the admin clerks, was close to hysteria.

'Do you think they'll retaliate against us?'

'No, Penny, relax. We don't even know what has happened. Who can say that it was the South Africans.'

I couldn't stand around discussing things with her. I had better things to do.

'Will you please excuse me?'

I disappeared down the passage and into my office. I struggled to keep my composure amidst the seeming normality of the day. When I left the office that afternoon there had been no word from Guy. I had no idea whether he was dead or alive. I knew it was pointless but I drove along the Highfield Road on my way home, but there was no sign of him.

The late night news gave no further details of the Bulawayo bomb blast. There was no mention of the number of people killed or injured and no names were given out. The announcer, however, made a scathing attack on the racist South African regime for bombing innocent refugees.

I only learned afterwards what had happened on that day in January 1988. An agent of the SADF's top secret CCB organisation, Henry Thompson, had handed Z$8 000 in notes to a black man Philip Conjwayo, an ex-member of the British South Africa Police of Rhodesia, in a room at Bulawayo's Holiday Inn. He left the room with the money tucked into his hip pocket.

'See you later', Conjwayo said.

With the money he bought a car from a secondhand dealer. Thompson, who had been para-dropped with three consignments of arms at Carlson's farm several weeks before, had ordered him to take the vehicle and park it at Bulawayo's Sun Hotel. Two operators, Kit Bawden and Michael Smith, would collect the vehicle and pack it with explosives.

Conjwayo went to the government employment exchange and picked up Obed Mwanza, a Zambian national, whom he had hired as a driver the previous day. Obed, unaware of the explosives he would be carrying, was instructed to collect the vehicle from in front of the cinemas in Grey Street the next day. He was to go to 16A Jungle Road, turn into the drive and hoot three times. The occupants, who were dealers in foreign currency, he was told, would come out to the car.

The South African agents watched the house from the corner of Jungle and Hydrang roads. They watched Obed as he turned into the drive and hooted. They triggered the remote control device. Orange flames, black smoke and flying debris billowed 20 metres into the air. The car and the innocent Obed were blown to kingdom come.

It later appeared that there were six people in the house of whom four were injured. The blast damaged houses 200 metres away.

Conjwayo, Kevin Woods, Rory Maguire, Mike Smith and his wife Eileen, Barry and Guy Bawden were arrested. Kit Bawden evaded arrest and skipped the country for South Africa.

At the time of writing Phillip Conjwayo, Kevin Woods, and Michael Smith are still imprisoned under awful circumstances at Chikurubi Maximum Security Prison. Their continued incarceration is a terrible disgrace to the former South African military elite who gave the orders and who are now living in luxurious retirement.

For the next three days I left home at 04:00 and drove along the Highfield Road in a quest for my missing source. I even risked stopping at our agreed dead-drop to check the hollow in the tree trunk for a message. By Saturday evening I had accepted that Guy was dead and struggled to come to grips with the harsh reality of the secret war we were waging.

On the Sunday morning I decided, despite everything that had happened, to drive to the rendezvous point I had agreed with Guy. I put some beers and meat in the car — I would go on to the Mazoe Dam regardless and spend the day at a cabin I had rented.

I was ten minutes late at the rendezvous, but I did not for a moment expect Guy to pitch up. I turned onto the Mazoe Road and headed out of town. I could scarcely believe it when I saw a man wearing a broad brimmed hat and an overcoat waiting at the agreed meeting place. I could see at a glance that it was Guy. He walked to the car as I came to a halt.

I opened the passenger door.

'Ndhlovu, my God, I thought you were dead.'

Guy removed his hat and climbed inside.

'Riaan, you bastard.'

I pulled back onto the road, exasperated. We headed for the dam.

'What's wrong with you?' I said later after we had arrived at the dam.

'You knew they were going to blow up that place', he accused.

'Bullshit, I had no idea. It wasn't us.'

'Who do you mean by us?'

'It wasn't done by National Intelligence agents.'

'Maybe, but who provided the intelligence?'

'When you gave me the floor plan of the house, you knew what it was for', I answered coldly. 'You're in the game yourself, so just look at it as unfortunate.'

Both of us calmed down after a couple of beers. We had a lot to do and we only had one day. We spent most of the morning relating our relevant pasts. I used a micro-recorder to record a detailed portrait of the ANC and MK leadership and their structures in exile.

In my recruitment of 'Oscar Dlamini' I had found another star informer, just like Al Jaghbub so many moons before. I was proud of my latest acquisition. But this time I was not playing things by the book and I would keep my cards close to the chest. *Stealth*, I decided, would be the code name for Guy Ndhlovu, alias Oscar Dlamini.

Guy's detailed product was objective, well interpreted and covered a wide range of subject matter. The NIS researchers would definitely sit up and take notice when they got it.

'One day in the not too distant future, the ANC will become the ruling government in South Africa and Nelson Mandela will be the president,' Guy said.

I had made peace with the political realities. I knew that change was in the offing, but I also knew that in Africa those who hold power never relinquish it freely. And the existing government and its entrenched Securocrats still had a lot of fight left in them. There was still a lot of blood left to flow.

I shrugged and avoided discussing politics.

'So why are you here? Why are you betraying them?'

Guy's response showed no remorse.

'Control.'

I did not want to shatter the moment, so I left him continue.

'Control of my life and future, just in case liberation doesn't happen in time for me.' He seemed as if he was talking to himself. 'Many of the top guys in the movement are lining their pockets with money from the enemy. Whether it's from the National Intelligence Service, Military Intelligence or the Security Branch, everyone is on the take. Some of them also work for the Germans, the French, the British or the Americans. They sell each other out, but in the main they sell out the ordinary rank-and-file. Hardly any of our missions are successful. Once cadres cross into South Africa they're invariably shot or arrested.'

I didn't want to confirm or deny the truth of what he was saying, but I knew from my own position within the South African Intelligence community that it was true.

'For me it's not just the money. Am I getting paid, by the way?'

'Yes, you are.'

Unusually, for an informer, he made no further mention of payment.

'I want my life back', he continued. 'I want to be able to go home freely without being arrested. I've lost my home and my family. I don't even know if my father is still alive. To get that back I'm willing to trade all I know.'

We contemplated our positions silently.

It was clear that Guy had experienced a change of heart. Defecting to the opposition, in its truest sense, had to be an impulsive decision. But for me, burning his bridges with the ANC would be a wrong move. If they made it into power, he would be ruined. It would be more beneficial for both him and me if he continued to play both sides.

'It will be better if you remain in place in the MK. Deserting and switching sides at this stage will mean that you'll lose your value to us', I answered honestly.

They returned to Harare as the sun was setting. Bound by similar professions and our own secret pact, we would live our lives on opposing sides of the fence that divided our country and its people.

Two days later I was instructed to return to South Africa for urgent consultations.

The night before my departure I loaded two separate dead-drops to communicate my absence to *Menace* and to the newly registered *Stealth*.

*   *   *

I met Louis, a section head with Division 031, at the House of Coffees in Pretoria.

'You've done a great job with *Stealth*'s recruitment.'

I expected their appreciation and was relieved they hadn't discovered my ploy to hide the source's true identity.

Louis appeared to have aged drastically over the last 12 months.

'Things in the country are not going as well as we had expected', he told me

'Why?'

'All measures, including the national state of emergency, have not blunted the ANC/SACP's thrust. It seems inevitable that the government will be forced into negotiating a political settlement. That will mean an end to armed hostilities and the unbanning of the liberation movements. Political prisoners, Mandela and the rest, will be released and exiles will be allowed to return.'

This news didn't come as a complete surprise, but I was still shocked. I wasn't expecting it to happen so soon and I was worried about how it would affect my career. In every country the intelligence apparatus is the organ closest to the head of state. If the ANC took power it would cleanse National Intelligence of the likes of me. Of that I was sure.

'So what now?'

'We can't stop the momentum of what's already secretly happening at the top level of government. That's why you've been recalled. We need to rid the ANC of its communist allies and the hawkish elements that pose a danger to us. We want to deal with moderates whom we can control at the negotiation table. It is the only way to ensure that we continue to have a place in the sun. Without that ascendency over them we'll be overrun.'

What has that got to me with me?' I asked. 'You surely didn't get me to come all this way just to tell me about South Africa's changing political climate, did you?'

'No, we didn't. A committee code-named 'TREWITS' (*Teen-Rewolusionêre Inligtings Teiken Sentrum* — Counter-Revolutionary Target Centre) has been formed. It's comprised of specially appointed representatives of National Intelligence, Military Intelligence, the SAP's counter-terrorist unit C1, the Security Branch and Special Forces and is commanded by a senior police officer.'

National Intelligence, he explained, was on the committee because it collected a great deal of intelligence beyond South Africa's borders. It had representatives in every South African mission or embassy abroad and in many African states where South Africa had no formal representation.

TREWITS's mandate was two-fold, he continued. It was to gather and update tactical intelligence on individuals who posed a major threat to the security of the state — like SACP leader Joe Slovo and ANC president Oliver Tambo. It went beyond them, though, and included certain intellectuals and other individuals who, it was considered, were supporting the liberation movements. All these names were on a 'priority list.' It was a directory for the elimination of those on it.

I asked what happened to the information and who was the end-user. He explained that when the committee decided to act against one of the listed targets, tactical information would be forwarded to the relevant 'executive body.' This was a fancy way of describing an organisation that had 'executive powers' — a euphemism for having the authority to kill. Such 'licences' were held by Special Forces for external targets and C1 plus the relevant regional Security Branch headquarters for internal ones.

Monthly meetings were held in the various Security Branch regions to update the priority lists. If a target had moved, for instance, from Botswana to Angola, which put him further out of reach and made him less of an immediate threat, his name would be shunted further down the list.

I was appointed as the National Intelligence representative who would be the co-ordinator for Zimbabwe, Mozambique and Malawi. I would not be transferred back to South Africa, but would remain in Zimbabwe and return once a month for committee meetings. I was warned not to share any information about my sources with the committee.

The first meeting I attended was held at the General de Witt Police Resort at Nylstroom where facilities were available for the committee to stay overnight. I arrived a few minutes after 10:00 and the meeting had already started. The men were seated amongst the trees with clipboards on their laps. I was introduced as the National Intelligence representative by the lanky and blue-eyed Brigadier Schoon.

There was an assertive aura of finality and death radiating from the small group as they watched me make myself comfortable. They seemed to look down on me as the only non-executioner on the team.

Director General Dr Niel Barnard, in evidence to the TRC, would later plead ignorance about the purpose of TREWITS.

'TREWITS', he said, 'was established to co-ordinate security intelligence and to establish an information data base. I am not going to say the information collected by TREWITS led to the death of people. I could not ask the line function departments what they did with the information.'

Anyone who believes that will believe anything.

I assessed the men on the committee as the meeting progressed. Leon Nel of Special Forces was a quiet man, a true soldier and more of a follower than a thinker. Colonel Eugene de Kock, the officer from C1 who headed Vlakplaas — the police facility that turned and used ex-terrorists against their former comrades — impressed me with his calm and knowledge of the ANC. Hiding behind old-fashioned thick-lensed glasses, De Kock didn't appear to be the master strategist that he was. He carried with ease the responsibility and prestige of his appointment as the country's number one anti-terrorist expert.

Most of the discussion centred on individuals unknown to me. It became apparent that until then the committee had mainly concentrated on activities within South Africa's borders. They had mountains of intelligence on local activists like the Rev Frank Chikane, Peter Mokaba, head of the ANC Youth League and Bishop Desmond Tutu. It took an hour before Brigadier Schoon focussed his attention on neighbouring states.

'Riaan, we need a more comprehensive picture of activists in Zimbabwe and Mozambique. You can start with Stanley Mabizela, Kallie and Derek Hanekom who are all in Zimbabwe and Albie Sachs in Mozambique.'

I explained my position along the lines instructed by Louis. The Service was worried that it was entering unchartered waters. It feared that uncontrolled liaison between members of the different branches of the intelligence community could compromise information. Therefore reports of a sensitive nature still had to be channelled through head office. This included all target analysis together with everything captured on film and video.

'We need your product urgently', was De Kock's only contribution.

It was midday when the meeting broke up. In true Afrikaner tradition, we helped ourselves to beers amply provided by courtesy of the state and a fire was started for a braai. Discussions continued on an informal level while we socialised. More policemen on De Kock's staff arrived later in the afternoon and joined the festivities.

By 16:00 I decided that I had enough and would not stay over. I felt something of an outsider. I only provided intelligence while the rest were fighting men.

De Kock pulled me to one side as I was leaving.

'Do you remember the car bomb planted by MK in front of the Krugersdorp magistrates' courts in 1987?'

I had a clear recollection of the incident. It struck terror in the hearts of the general public because of the brutal killing and injuring of innocent people. It was also a slap in the face for the Security Forces as it challenged their abilities to protect the ordinary man in the street. Added to that was the embarrassment that the main perpetrator was believed to be the son of a staunch and respected Afrikaner family. Heinz Gröskopff's alleged act of war as a member of MK shocked his white compatriots.

'I'm familiar with the incident, yes.'

'Heinz Gröskopff appears to have vanished off the face of the earth. He's definitely not in South Africa or we would have found him a long time ago. I believe he might be hiding in London, but he might also be in Zimbabwe or Lusaka. Please keep an eye out for him. He's at the top of my list.'

He gave me a black and white photograph of the target. The eyes behind metal-rimmed glasses appeared strikingly cold. The oval face was framed with long hair and a full beard.

I had early meetings with both *Menace* and *Stealth* at separate venues. I briefed them on the change of focus. In future they should concentrate more on tactical than strategic information. I provided each with a verbal list of targets together with a copy of Gröskopff's photograph.

Menace and especially *Stealth* both appreciated the gravity of the change. Gathering information on people targeted for assassination was dangerous and repercussions could easily haunt them afterwards.

*   *   *

One Saturday morning a powerful bomb blast in Maputo almost killed Albie Sachs. Sachs, a prominent ANC activist, was considered an enemy of the state. Of Lithuanian Jewish descent, he had been a civil rights advocate at the Cape Town Bar in the 1950s and 1960s. He had been detained twice by the Security Branch under the so-called 90 day law which made provision for the detention of suspects for 90 days without trial. During his two terms of detention, 168 days was spent in solitary confinement. He went into exile in 1966 and settled in London. In 1977 he returned to Africa and became professor of law at the university in Maputo, Mozambique.

From his base there he continued to champion civil rights and the ANC's cause. TREWIT's decision to target the academic and intellectual support icons of the ANC brought Sachs to the attention of the Civil Co-operation Bureau (CCB).

He was a keen jogger. On 7 April 1988 he left his Maputo apartment and drove to the beach where he intended to have a run followed up by a cold beer. When he unlocked the boot of his car to get something, there was an explosion. The blast ripped off his right arm and blinded him in one eye. In the 1990s he became part of the ANC's negotiating team at the constitutional talks. President Nelson Mandela later appointed him as a judge of the Constitutional Court.

An ex-Special Forces Major, 'EJ', who headed a CCB team in Durban, explained what had happened. The characteristics of the explosive device used against Sachs were similar to the one used in an earlier attack on Jeremy Brickhill. Its base was some form of liquid nitroglycerin derivative. The Security Forces had experimented with it for a long time and it was held to be very effective. The operators on the ground, however, found it unstable and not particularly effective and many refused to use it.

Stealth responded quickly and in a dead-drop I found a detailed account of Stanley Mabizela's movements. The information was passed up the line but no attack was carried out against him.

During my tour of duty in Zimbabwe several attacks were executed against targets within the country. On 13 October 1987 an attempt was made on the life of Jeremy Brickhill. He survived a car bomb at the Avondale Shopping Centre where he went for coffee each morning.

Brickhill had fought for Joshua Nkomo's ZIPRA during the Rhodesian Bush War and had worked as assistant to Dumiso Dabengwa at ZAPU's Lusaka-based Department of Analysis and Research. He was also a dedicated supporter of the South African liberation movements.

I happened to be in the vicinity of the shopping centre at the time of Brickhill's attack. I heard the blast and rushed to the scene. Using a miniature camera concealed in an attaché case, I photographed the scene without knowing the identity of the victim. I sent in my report with the photographs and found myself severely reprimanded by Pretoria for my trouble. They said they had no wish to be linked to the incident in any way and my presence at the scene could have compromised the Service.

In the same year the wife of an ANC activist died in an explosion meant for another ANC official. A bomb placed inside a television set exploded in her first floor flat in Harare central and killed her. The incident had its origins in Maputo. Leslie Lesia, an art dealer from Bloemfontein, was recruited by the CCB to eliminate ANC terrorists. He was instructed to donate three cases of poisoned beer, a case of poisoned brandy and one of poisoned vodka to the ANC in Maputo. He gave some of the beer to an ANC official, Gibson Ncubo, who later died from the effects of the toxins.

In June 1987 Lesia's CCB handlers gave him a TV set that had been booby-trapped with explosives. His instructions were to give it to the ANC's chief representative in Maputo. Instead he passed it to a Mr Mhlope. Mhlope gave it to a minor ANC official, Frank Chilisi, who took it to Harare. It was Mrs Chilisi who set off the explosion and killed herself.

Lesia was arrested in Maputo and flown to Lusaka for interrogation by the ANC. He firmly maintained his innocence. From there he was taken to Harare and handed over to the ZCIO who eventually broke him and he confessed. Charged with the murder of Chilisi, Lesia was taken to Chikurubi Maximum Security Prison.

He was released on 26 July 1990 at the expiration of Zimbabwe's State of Emergency. The CCB flew him back to South Africa by private aircraft, but as soon as he arrived he instituted legal proceedings against the SADF.

It took me two weeks of personal surveillance to complete the target analysis on the Hanekom brothers who lived in the centre of Harare. I followed their zebra-striped Combi on many occasions, logging their destinations. Although the study had been forwarded, no action was taken against them. Both were draft-dodgers who had fled to Zimbabwe some years before. Derek later became the Minister of

Agriculture in Nelson Mandela's government.

After my return to Zimbabwe, President Mugabe's contempt for South Africa and its leadership turned to open hatred. Because of attacks on the ANC in what was effectively Mugabe's own backyard, I feared reprisal attacks on South African installations or personnel. At night I slept with my bedroom door locked and a loaded hunting rifle by my bed. I installed a wire mesh screen over the main bedroom's front window to counter the possibility of a hand grenade being thrown through the window while I was asleep.

Surveillance on me increased. ZCIO watchers virtually camped outside my home and followed me openly wherever I went. This complicated my communications with *Menace* and *Stealth*. Face-to-face meetings became out of the question and I mostly had to rely on dead-drops.

Menace continued his usual flow of high-level information. This included cabinet briefings, intelligence reports to Mugabe and progress reports on ongoing ZCIO investigations. With his help, double agents run by the ZCIO were identified, fed disinformation, arrested or killed by their South African opposite numbers.

While I was absent from Zimbabwe, the local ANC appointed *Stealth* to assist cadres about to infiltrate South Africa with their preparations. By leaking names, dates and entry points, he blew the covers of virtually every MK member who passed through Zimbabwe. Most were either shot or arrested when they entered South Africa.

To ensure that *Stealth*'s position was not compromised and to cloud the source of information, a few terrorists were allowed to operate in South Africa for a while. Only when it was felt that sufficient time had elapsed since their entry were they arrested or killed.

I worked 18 hours a day, servicing dead-drops, processing information and typing reports. Much of *Menace*'s information was captured on film. This necessitated me developing and printing films in my garage which I had converted into a darkroom. I did this mostly at night as I had no time during the day. The majority of documents photographed by *Menace* were original ZCIO or cabinet papers bearing official seals, so I had to rewrite them to conceal the origin of the information. Despite this, some were so bulky that I had no alternative but to despatch them in their original form.

The toll of my increased workload and the stress of fulfilling duties accompanied by the ever-present danger of arrest soon caught up with me. I lost eight kilograms over three months, I slept poorly, lived on junk food and drank far too much. My social life became non-existent.

Then the Chief Director Operations informed me that I was being transferred back to South Africa and outlined my future duties. I was leaving Division 031 to head a covert project in Durban. Division 051, my new division, was responsible for intelligence gathering within South Africa. The infrastructure had already been set up. A senior officer from the Durban regional office had been appointed liaison officer for the project. Premises had been leased in Durban-Westville to house the team that I could select from operators assigned to the local office.

I began my preparations to leave Zimbabwe in June 1988. A major hurdle I had to cross was advising *Stealth* and *Menace* that I was going. It demanded personal meetings. Not wanting to break the news to them at the last moment, I arranged for two days in the first week of November when I could see them individually.

Menace took the news in his stride. The comings and goings of spymasters didn't worry him. He had been in the business for many years and had become used to being handed over to new handlers. It was part of the game. I felt relieved. I had managed to outsmart the opposition by getting volumes of top-level intelligence from a highly placed spy for two years without him being compromised. And he was still in place. *Menace*'s safety would become the responsibility of my replacement.

For my meeting with *Stealth*, I chose a picnic spot out in the bush north of Harare. Having a more personal relationship with him as a fellow South African, I decided to make our meeting more of a social occasion. I set out with a bag of firewood, a coolbox packed with beers and meat for a braai.

I picked him up five kilometres outside the capital. He was posing as a hitchhiker. We drove north for about 20 minutes and then left the national road. A neglected signboard indicated a picnic spot about 50 metres into the bush. I had discovered the spot several months before. A spy was always on the lookout for innovative dead-drops and venues for covert meetings.

We each took a beer and *Stealth* started a fire.

I handed him Z$850 in notes. For the past two months he had been getting a monthly retainer supplemented by an occasional bonus.

'You didn't get me here just to pay me.'

He signed a receipt in the name of Oscar Dlamini and handed it to me.

'I've been transferred back home.'

I was surprised by the look of shock on his face.

'When?'

'The end of the month.'

Stealth angrily tossed the empty beer can into the fire and opened another.

'What about me? What about your promise to me? I've taken blood money from you. I've betrayed my own people because I've trusted you.'

'I paid you for the information, didn't I?' I said. 'You never refused the money.

'I agreed to work for you because you promised to get me a pardon from your bloody racist government and I want to go home. That was the deal and I've paid my side with the blood of my comrades.'

'You're not a child who got lured into this', I said. 'You've been in the game for more than ten years. Like me, you know how it works. I haven't got the power to get you a pardon. Besides, what about your own people? If you just walk away they'll look for you and kill you. Think of all the leaks you were responsible for. If you remain in the ANC fold and continue producing, I can protect you.'

I fumbled in my pocket for a scrap of paper and scribbled on it.

'This will be my telephone number in Durban. If the ANC decides to send you back to South Africa out of their choice, phone me.'

Embittered by the turn of events, *Stealth* stared at the white snippet of paper and memorised the area code and number — 581-7777 which was easy to remember. He crumpled the paper and threw it in the fire.

'Fuck you, Riaan, and your bloody white government. I'll be back in South Africa but it will be without your help. And do you know what? We are going to take power and then you won't matter any more. You may not have realised it, but you are finished.'

Before I could react he turned and walked off towards the road. I had no intention of running after him. I decided to wait a few minutes to give him time to cool down before I followed him. When I did, I found he had flagged down a passing motorist and was gone.

Before leaving Zimbabwe I netted another recruit. I was dining at the residence of a University of Zimbabwe lecturer, a Pole by the name of Aleksandra Bujakiewicz, who introduced me to an Egyptian diplomat. It did not take us long to sum each other up and privately decide that we shared the same profession. We took a liking to one another and he seemed to appreciate South Africa's political situation. I invited him to my residence which he visited a week later.

Through this I succeeded in recruiting the Egyptian intelligence chief in Harare. It resulted in the development of close co-operation between National Intelligence and the Egyptian Intelligence Service. This co-operation eventually moved beyond the intelligence services to the Egyptian government itself.

16

Durban

I returned to South Africa in late July 1988. My debriefing and preparations to move to Durban took three months, during which time I was able to catch up on a lot of the internal politics within the Service and South Africa in general. In the meantime I continued at Division 031 in my position as desk officer for Zimbabwe and Mozambique. The Jungle Road incident in Bulawayo a few months before, and the subsequent arrest of the Bawden brothers, Woods and Smith had left a general atmosphere of unease and disappointment. Although not necessarily National Intelligence agents, the field officers felt very sorry for them and hoped that the government would intervene to secure their release.

On my return from Zimbabwe I was surprised to learn that ZCIO's representative in Johannesburg was Olaf Reed, a Scandinavian. His presence angered everyone as he was one of the ZCIO officials who had brutally tortured and interrogated the South African agents. Division 031 was responsible for liaison with and the general well-being of foreign declared intelligence representatives within South Africa. As the desk officer for Zimbabwe, Reed became my baby. Despite my hatred and resentment of the man, I set out to recruit him.

I had several official liaisons with him in Johannesburg. At the time, an arrangement was still in place that allowed information to be officially exchanged between National Intelligence and the ZCIO. It was low grade stuff and consisted mostly of intelligence relating to economic issues and neighbouring states. I tried very hard to corrupt him but my recruitment efforts were unsuccessful.

Having failed to recruit him, I decided it was time he understood the peculiar position he was in. I sought the unofficial co-operation of a Special Forces operator whom I had met while serving on TREWITS.

As one of the few remaining white officers in the ZCIO, Reed was in an enemy country that was littered with ex-Rhodesians who would dearly have liked to take him apart.

I asked my Special Forces friend not to harm him physically, but to push him over the edge mentally. A few nights later there was a mysterious burglary at his home. Silent intruders wearing balaclavas first damaged his car and then broke into his house. He awakened to find them trying to smash down his locked bedroom door. His wife went into hysterics and the terrified Reed jumped naked through the bedroom window, scaled the garden wall and shouted for help from his neighbour.

As his liaison officer, he reported it to me the next day. The police were called but they failed to solve the case and could find no fingerprints or other evidence.

He was visibly shaken and not nearly so cocksure as he usually was.

Another attack was laid on the next night. Around 20:00 his wife answered a knock on the door. She found a pool of blood on the porch with a note saying they were both going to be killed. Reed phoned me in a state of panic. I rushed to Johannesburg, picked them up and booked them into a hotel in Pretoria.

The next morning the Zimbabwean Government lodged an official complaint with the Department of Foreign Affairs. National Intelligence was notified and I was called in. I denied all knowledge and said the culprits were obviously ex-Rhodesians.

I thanked my Special Forces friend and asked him to cease the harassment. By then, though, knowledge of Reed's presence in the country had spread amongst the ex-Rhodesian members of our Security Forces — and they genuinely wanted to kill him.

Reed's wife fled the country for Zimbabwe, but he had to remain behind. He became the perfect target to jitter. He was terrified and never left his office. This made it impossible for him to function as an intelligence officer in South Africa. I closed in for the final push and a week later took him for lunch at a strip bar. The Service's technical team was in covert attendance.

The dancer-cum-stripper-cum-hooker and the establishment's management had agreed to co-operate. It was not long before the naked and very attractive woman had Reed on stage, had taken off his clothes and had very publicly screwed him.

The event was neatly captured on film.

A week later I broke the news to him that I had set him up with the hooker and that a copy of the very explicit film was about to be sent to his wife in Zimbabwe. With his marriage already on shaky ground and fearful for his own safety, Reed decided to co-operate.

It turned out that the level of South African sources run by the ZCIO through their Johannesburg Trade Mission was of small significance. The only value we could find in Reed was his knowledge of the ZCIO, its structures, operatives and intelligence needs. He returned to Zimbabwe a few months later. Perhaps he still works for the ZCIO.

*   *   *

I returned to active duty on 7 November1988. I had a breakfast meeting scheduled for 08:00 at The Deck, an elevated, circular single storey pub and restaurant on Durban's north beach. I was in the habit of always being early and I ordered a filter coffee as I waited for the National Intelligence delegation to arrive. I took a sip and noticed that I still had another half an hour to wait. I didn't mind.

Even though it was a normal working day, many people were strolling or jogging on the esplanade. Bronzed bodies lay spread out on colourful towels on the white sand.

The move to Durban provided a new lease on life for me. I was back in the safety of my own country and away from the brooding animosities, surveillance and inherent dangers that went with spying on enemy soil. Besides, I had always liked living at the coast. My two-year stint at the Durban Naval Base all those years ago made it feel like a homecoming.

A middle-aged man, with balding blond hair and wearing a suit, led a smartly dressed young woman in her early 30s up the landing and into The Deck.

It must be them, I thought as the couple approached. They were clearly the regional representative and my case officer.

I got up to meet them.

'Mr Labuschagne?'

'Yes, hi . . . I'm Riaan.' I shook my new boss' proffered hand.

'Neville Höll, I'm head of station.'

Their formality and correctness in dress, speech and manner amused me. The management staff of the overt structures of National Intelligence presented an image of innocence, morality and Christian Nationalist values. I had come to realise it was nothing but bullshit, a facade inherited from the British — like so many other colonial habits that had been absorbed into National Party government structures. The truth was we were much the same as the demonised KGB, the CIA and everybody else in the game. We corrupted, extorted, lied, stole and murdered — or rather we got someone else to murder for us — just like the others did.

The officers assigned to undercover structures operated at arm's length from the formal environment. For us life was about handling sources, our tradecraft, getting the product and remaining inconspicuous. Office politics, status and protocol hardly featured in our interaction.

'This is Sonja Alberts, your case officer. She will meet you regularly and act as logistical support and liaison between yourself and the regional office.'

Her handshake was surprisingly firm for a woman.

'Pleased to meet you Riaan, I've heard a lot about you.'

Such a conventional thing to say, but yes, maybe it was true. She had come prepared. We sat down, she produced a flip file and presented the outline of my project, code named *Operation Jaguar* .

'Our client, the government of the day, has entered a phase where we have been tasked to provide as much up-to-date strategic information as possible. The target is clearly the alliance of the ANC, the South African Communist Party (SACP) and the Congress of South African Trade Unions (COSATU). We need to know everything about their strategies. And you must dig up as much dirt as you can — anything that will aid our client in its negotiations.'

'You understand that this might take some time', I interrupted. 'I've just arrived and I have no sources in place and no idea who the players on the field are.'

'We know that, but we can assist. The office has a database showing the political players in the region. We have excellent co-operation with the Security Branch and share data bases. We are also given a lot of information sourced from their interrogations. Most of the top personalities are under ongoing electronic surveillance and that will assist you in building profiles. You can look at the material as soon as you're ready.

'Since the political unrest of the early 1980s the local National Intelligence office and the local Security Branch have pooled their resources and knowledge about MK. Scores of activists and suspected terrorists arrested by the Security Branch have been interrogated jointly. The Durban station seconded two officers to assist the Security Branch with interrogations and the recording of extracted information. All internal tactical information is passed to the Security Branch. Knowledge of this intimate co-operation between the two branches has been kept from low level field officers.'

This co-operation had not been restricted only to Durban. It had also occurred on a national level as I had discovered while with Division 031.

Neville made his first contribution to the discussion.

'We've decided to go with a variation of your cover — you'll be a sort of researcher-cum-journalist on an assignment to cover the political changes in South Africa — as you perfected in your previous division. You can work out the finer details. When you've finalised your cover let me know. We will then assist with supporting documents and whatever else you might need.'

I was impressed by their thoroughness. It was the first time I had worked in the Service's domestic arm.

'Your name is not Labuschagne any more either. We've altered your records at Personnel. They now show you as Riaan Marlow, married with two children. Copies of IDs and birth certificates for the children have been placed on your file to support your new identity.'

I nodded in acknowledgement. There was nothing I could do to change the way the system worked. Employing me under a fictitious name was just another ploy used to cover their arses. If I was compromised or became an embarrassment, the Service would simply deny that a Riaan Labuschagne had ever been in its employ.

If there was a slip-up because of the use of my real name in the field and Riaan Labuschagne was plastered across the front pages of the tabloids, I would be left to carry the can myself.

Sonja handed me a pager, my business address in Westville and a set of keys to my new office. When the three of us left The Deck two hours later, Neville handed me an envelope.

'It's a shortlist of operational officers at the Durban office whom you might want to incorporate into your project.'

'I'll liaise with you once I've been through it. For the moment I just want to find my feet. Give me time to get up and running, then I'll decide about involving more people.'

I walked to my car and decided to go and inspect my new offices.

I pondered the future and wondered how things would work out. I would be operating with a woman I had only just met who would be my sole lifeline. And I had not the slightest idea of her skills as an operator.

17

Politics and negotiations

Rumours about disunity amongst South African politicians began coming to the notice of field officers. We took little notice, though, as internal politics were far from our minds and we never thought it would have a serious bearing on our reality.

Unknown to us, factions had begun to form within the ruling National Party. It began with the establishment of Club 22 as early as May 1987. It was rumoured that this was a supporter group for Pik Botha. Members denied such rumours and insisted it was a social club for new parliamentary members. There were many leaks to the media about internal discussions within the National Party caucus. Then a bug was discovered in the National Party caucus chambers. This was of great concern to President PW Botha and he called in Director General Niel Barnard.

The president's distrust of those close to him, excluding the National Intelligence chief, became evident as early as 1986. At a closed meeting in the October of that year, PW warned South African ambassadors gathered in Pretoria against the dangers of being recruited by foreign and ANC intelligence agencies. Two years later he repeated the same warning to South African diplomats in Zurich.

Although PW favoured reform, he did not agree with the party's left-leaning members like Wynand Malan and Denis Worral. He believed the policies they advocated, without insisting the ANC first renounce violence, would lead to unqualified dialogue with the ANC, the release of Nelson Mandela, a government with a black majority and the disappearance of Afrikaner culture and community life,

In the light of the changing times the secret formation of Directorate K, was not a surprise. The president felt he needed a covert force around him that he could trust.

The rift between PW Botha and other senior members of his cabinet would come to a head in 1989.

In June 1988 Foreign Minister Pik Botha; Minister of Defence Magnus Malan; the Director General Foreign Affairs, Neil van Heerden; Derek Auret, Director Foreign Affairs; SADF Chief General Jannie Geldenhuys, Major-General Neels van Tonder of Military Intelligence; National Intelligence Service Director General, Niel Barnard; Joe Boshoff of National Intelligence; and a delegation of about 50 other officials attended what became known as the Cairo Conference. Its aim was to establish a regional peace settlement, end the 13-year Angolan war and bring independence to SWA/Namibia.

The meeting, chaired and mediated by US Assistant Secretary of State Chester Crocker was held at the stately Hyatt El Salaam Hotel in Cairo. The Egyptian government kept a low profile, only providing security services at the hotel. Egypt was chosen because of the secret links forged between National Intelligence and Egyptian Intelligence by myself in 1987.

Through Egypt's influence with various African states, the national carrier, South African Airways, had been allowed to use their airspace when flying delegates to Cairo. This had been forbidden for many years.

As Pik was boarding the South African Airways flight to Cairo before the conference, operatives from Directorate K who were keeping him under surveillance saw another well-known member of the directorate discreetly hand him an envelope. Its contents, slanderous material and a hidden warning, were only learned later. It elaborately described alleged heavy drinking bouts by Botha and other matters concerning his personal life. Pik, was understandably furious. He was unable to identify the person who had handed him the letter because he had not taken much notice and had only opened it after take off. He created a major furore on his return to South Africa. To no one's surprise, National Intelligence never identified the culprit.

There are two possibilities. The officer who handed the letter to Pik, or someone senior in Directorate K, disapproved of the minister's lifestyle and wanted to use his inside knowledge to warn him. It was significant that he had been handed the letter personally just before his departure for Egypt. There was a fairly widespread suspicion amongst intelligence and military personnel that Botha might have had links with the ANC and could not be trusted. Perhaps that belief was vindicated when he later became a member of that organisation. If that was the case, then it could have been a personal concern for many officers.

The other option is that it was delivered on orders from the top, but I doubt it. I personally believe that it was done by someone with a

227

grudge who was involved in the investigation into his activities.

There was a joint Angolan-Cuban delegation. Foreign Minister Alfonso Van Dunem led the Angolans while Jorge Risquet led the Cubans. A Soviet presence in the form of Vladilen Vasev, head of the Soviet Foreign Ministry's Directorate for Africa, also attended. It is believed he was there by arrangement with the Americans to arm-wrestle the Angolans into agreeing to a settlement. The Soviet Union's evil empire, as President Reagan of America had called it, was crumbling, despite the Berlin Wall still being in place. But it had had enough of Angola and wanted out. On the first day the crucial tripartite talks adjourned after just two hours after 'sharp exchanges' between the South African and Cuban delegations. The major point of difference centred on the timetable for Cuban withdrawal from Angola. The Cuban-Angolan contingent were willing to make concessions on earlier proposals for a staged withdrawal over four years. They resisted South Africa's rapid exit option for Cuban troops as long as Pretoria had forces in Angola and continued to back UNITA.

The delegations broke off for separate consultations. The Angolans and their Cuban allies stayed together and the Americans met with the South Africans. These separate meetings to discuss tactics were held in the open air because the delegates were concerned about being bugged.

Owing to Soviet and American influence, the talks continued into the next day and ended with reasonable success. Both parties agreed to hold further talks in Washington or New York in two weeks time. On his arrival back in South Africa, Pik Botha announced that a framework for a regional peace settlement had been established.

In 1988 Directorate K initiated *Operation Spaghetti*. K22 operatives installed eavesdropping equipment into a house where prominent members of the SACP were living in London. The persons concerned and the specific address is unknown to me, but senior members of the ANC and SACP visited the house frequently. Extremely valuable information on the ANC/SACP underground and its leadership was obtained in this way.

Once when confronted by British agents about the presence of the recording device, the South Africans explained that the Church Street bomb explosion in Pretoria was planned from the house in question. The explanation was that the surveillance was needed to protect the South African public. Given the problem that the British had with IRA bomb blasts in and around London, they allowed the South African agents to continue and co-operated with them.

The tapes needed to be changed daily. Because of the risks involved, the task was given to British agents with MI5 or MI6 links. To avoid embarrassing the British government, routine arrangements were made for British agents to hand over the recordings to NIS agents in Portugal.

Negotiations between Directorate K and British MI5 took place in Estoril, Portugal. Mike Kuhn, using his *nom de guerre*, Mike Killian, arranged the deal personally. The operators from Directorate K who met Kuhn in Europe regularly were uncomfortable with his alias — it was too close to his real name.

Bugging equipment is usually linked to telephone lines and the recording equipment set up in the nearest telephone exchange. In this case, though, using the exchange would have attracted attention and indicated official British involvement. So the signal emanating from the bugs was intercepted at the nearest telephone cable and the recording device was buried in the ground close to the house.

MI5 was usually aware of South African intelligence-gathering operations in London. In the late 1980s, Directorate K sent a team to London to photograph and follow Joe Slovo. It was known that he was travelling on an Antiguan passport and would land at Heathrow Airport. On the agents' return to their hotel, they found a fire engine parked out front and they were barred from entering. They were told there was a fire in the building, but that was patently untrue. When they entered their rooms an hour later, it was to find that their belongings had been searched. As a consequence they moved to another hotel. The general feeling was that MI5 tolerated the presence of South African agents in London as long as they stuck to intelligence gathering and did not bring arms into the country.

Dulcie September, the ANC's representative for France and Switzerland, was based in Paris. On the morning of 29 March 1988 she was found dead at the entrance to her fourth floor apartment in the Rue des Petites Ecuries near the Gare du Nord. She had been shot five times with a silenced pistol. The apartment served as the ANC's office in the French capital.

September, a former teacher from Cape Town, became a member of the National Liberation Front, an ANC front organisation. After serving five years in prison for treason and sabotage she left South Africa in 1972.

The claim by certain Western Intelligence sources that the deed was done by a Z-squad team from National Intelligence is incorrect. The author's information suggests the assassination was carried out by the CCB. A former member of Special Forces who became an operational team leader in the CCB, was in Paris at the time of the incident. He was accompanied by members of his team. His wife, a CCB staffer responsible for administration and logistics, was arrested while en route to South Africa, on suspicion of being a foreign agent connected to the murder of September. She was released due to a lack of evidence.

Members of Directorate K were also in Paris at the time. On their return to South Africa they expressed dismay at the timing of September's murder as it had endangered them and complicated their future actions in Europe. Explanations were never given but agents often conducted operations without a background briefing or ever knowing the end result.

In 1988, after Namibia's independence, a team from K22 was sent to a farm there where they retrieved cases of small arms, RPG7 launchers and rockets. These were transported into South Africa without the vehicles being searched on either side of the border. The weapons were taken to Pretoria. In Pretoria other agents took over the stuff for its final disposal. No one involved knew what the weapons were for or who got them in the end.

Activities of the directorate were performed on a strictly need-to-know basis with field officers, in the main, having no idea what their colleagues were involved in. In the immediate aftermath of the Dr David Webster killing by the CCB in Johannesburg on 1 May 1989, the police issued identikits of two men but they later withdrew them. The identikits bore close resemblance to two field officers of Directorate K. My personal belief is that these operators were seen in the vicinity a day or two before the murder happened. They were probably conducting a surveillance mission targeting either Webster or the members of the CCB involved in the operation.

By the early 1990s Directorate K had become a microcosm of NIS and had virtually duplicated its services and functions. It had its own admin people, field officers, technical staff, analysts and budget. It became the elite unit for the privileged few. Mike Kuhn, a senior *Broederbonder*, was its driving force in Niel Barnard's empire.

With the National Party government's demise in sight at the beginning of 1990, many officers believed the directorate would continue its covert struggle against an ANC government and possibly even lead a counter-revolution. Such was the belief of those who found the inevitable change of power unacceptable.

My short stay with Division 031 before leaving for Durban revealed much of the progress the Service had made during 1988/89 in establishing covert links with its former enemies. The person responsible for this was Niel Barnard.

Accepting an invitation by the Soviets in 1988, Barnard and a senior research analyst, Dr Nel Marais, paid a secret visit to Moscow. In 2000 Marais would be contracted to the intelligence unit that Barnard was running within the Western Cape Government.

Relations between South African and Soviet intelligence may have originated from contacts made during Pik Botha's earlier visit to Cairo to negotiate the SWA/Angolan peace deal. Either Victor Chebrika, who headed the KGB between 1982-1988, or his successor, Vladimir Krjutjkov, approved co-operation between National Intelligence and the KGB. Krjutjkov was the KGB boss until it was disbanded in 1991. It is not known to me if the Soviet head of state was aware of the arrangement between National Intelligence and the KGB.

Michail Gorbachev became the Soviet president in October 1988.

Dr Barnard's trip was cut short because of the death of a parent. The Russians were very sympathetic — because there were no direct flights between Moscow and South Africa, they provided a plane to fly him to the nearest connecting airport for a direct flight home.

Barnard's brilliance resulted in the establishment of a covert NIS office in Moscow, long before the Department of Foreign Affairs was able to establish a presence in Russia. Again the Service had fulfilled its dual role of gathering intelligence and equally important, using the Soviet intelligence services to build links between the two countries.

The point of using intelligence services rather than diplomatic channels, was to avoid public and media attention and to save the two former enemies any embarrassment over the new co-operative relationship. National Intelligence's Moscow station was run by a single member from Division 031.

President Kenneth Kaunda of Zambia, Division 031's agent of influence, was central to the 1989 National Party row that led to the resignation of President PW Botha.

In 1987, as mentioned earlier, President PW Botha ordered National Intelligence to double as an intelligence service and as a secret government negotiator with Nelson Mandela and the ANC.

In May 1988 a NIS task force was established to enter into discussions with Nelson Mandela. It comprised the DG Niel Barnard, his deputy, Mike Louw, the Commissioner of Prisons, Willie Willemse and the Minister of Constitutional Development, Fanie van der Merwe.

National Intelligence had bugged Mandela's cell on Robben Island, at Pollsmoor and Victor Verster prisons. Every section of the garden and the surrounds of the house he stayed in at Victor Verster had been fitted with electronic devices.

In mid-1989, Barnard told President Botha that Nelson Mandela had requested a private audience with him. This secret meeting took place on 5 July 1989 at the president's Tuynhuys office. The conversation was electronically recorded, but shortly afterwards the tapes mysteriously went missing.

In response to presidential orders, National Intelligence also initiated secret talks with the ANC leaders in exile. Barnard and Louw made the first contact at an undisclosed venue in Europe. Mandela voiced concern about this approach. He suggested that only one channel of communication between the government and the ANC be used and offered to facilitate contact the moment he was set free.

Despite this, there were two further meetings before Mandela's release.

National Intelligence, at this point, favoured negotiations for a political settlement with the ANC. Niel Barnard voiced his support to President Botha for the release of Mandela. PW, however, had staked his career on modernising apartheid. He was a cold war warrior who refused to negotiate with communists or the ANC.

Niel Barnard and National Intelligence struggled for two years to budge PW from this position, but he turned it down.

Fate stepped in on 18 January 1989 when PW suffered a debilitating stroke. In February while recovering from his illness at home, he sent a letter to the National Party caucus in which he resigned as the leader of the National Party. He emphasised, though, that he would continue holding his position as State President. He deliberately separated the offices of National Party leader and State President, not only to downgrade his responsibilities, but also in the belief that his new apolitical stance would make him acceptable to the ANC. This autocratic decision was met with a mixed reaction by his peers in the National Party.

FW de Klerk suggested the election of a new party leader. Chris Heunis, the acting State President, opted for an attitude of 'wait and see.' Foreign Minister Pik Botha openly propagated the appointment of a new president.

De Klerk's suggestion was accepted and the party caucus went ahead with the election of a new leader. There were four candidates in the running — Barend du Plessis, FW de Klerk, Pik Botha and Chris Heunis. Three rounds of voting took place before a majority decision could be reached. FW de Klerk became the new leader of the National Party with 69 votes against the 61 cast for Du Plessis.

The dilemma was, however: who was ruling the country? Was it the leader of the majority party in Parliament or was it PW Botha, the State President.

The separation of the office of State President and the leader of the ruling party set the stage for major conflict between PW and the National Party. De Klerk and the National Party stood for radical reform and negotiations with the ANC, while PW, as the State President, was opposed to such unconditional negotiations. De Klerk was stymied because he did not possess the executive power to execute National Party government policy.

De Klerk and 15 members of the National Party caucus confronted PW on the issue. Botha, however, remained adamant. He was still the president.

Then the National Party caucus, voting 22 to 7, decided that the leader of the governing party would also be State President. A general election was scheduled for September 1989. PW was against it and wanted the election to take place only in 1990. Nevertheless, he eventually, with reluctance, agreed to the September date.

De Klerk immediately set out to inform world leaders of his proposed reforms. He met with Britain's Margaret Thatcher, West Germany's Helmut Kohl, Portugal's Cavaco Silva and Giulio Andreotti of Italy. Tensions mounted between De Klerk and Botha over these travels.

In July 1989 De Klerk met with President Chissano of Mozambique in Maputo.

Pik Botha arranged all these diplomatic initiatives. At the end of 1989 De Klerk and Pik Botha decided to postpone other foreign commitments, including meeting President Kenneth Kaunda of Zambia and other African leaders, until after the election.

On 8 August Pik Botha phoned FW de Klerk who was campaigning in Durban and urged him to meet Kenneth Kaunda as a matter of urgency. Kaunda wanted to discuss the ANC. Pik had been about to despatch a two-man delegation to brief Kaunda on the latest developments in SWA/Namibia and South Africa's efforts to defuse the conflicts in Angola and Mozambique.

There was a serious risk that the United Nations would make arbitrary decisions about the region that could jeopardise South African initiatives in south-western Africa. The opinion of the Frontline States could prove crucial and Kaunda was willing and able to pacify them.

De Klerk agreed to a meeting in Livingstone on 28 August. Two South African Foreign Affairs officials saw Kaunda on 9 August and finalised arrangements. It was agreed that the pending meeting should be kept from the media.

Pik Botha instructed the Director General of Foreign Affairs, Neil van Heerden, to brief President Botha about the scheduled meeting. Before he could do so, however, Botha, who was still recovering from his stroke, found out about it from a media announcement confirming the meeting.

Despite giving his word, Kaunda had deliberately leaked the story to the press.

PW Botha was enraged. On the 10 August he phoned Pik Botha and vented his feelings. He said he had been betrayed by his cabinet and his friends and accused them of working behind his back.

The embattled State President promptly issued a media statement saying that, according to directives for ministerial travels abroad, he had no knowledge of the intended meeting between FW de Klerk and Kenneth Kaunda. He refused point-blank to meet any of his ministers and ordered a special cabinet meeting to take place in Cape Town on 14 August to discuss the matter.

Niel Barnard and Boet Troskie, a close friend of the president, tried without success to broker a compromise between PW and his cabinet. The evening before the scheduled cabinet meeting De Klerk and some senior ministers visited PW at his Westbrook home. They had discussions but failed to reach an agreement.

On 17 July the month before, PW had warned those attending a State Security Council meeting about Kenneth Kaunda.

'Kaunda is a thief', he had said. 'He will draw you into unconditional negotiations with the ANC.'

PW's serious reservations about Kaunda arose because the latter had harboured ANC leader Oliver Tambo for many years. He believed that Tambo was directly responsible for the deaths of many South Africans. So he did not consider Kaunda acceptable as a peace broker. He contended that his only meeting with Kaunda had taken place several years before on neutral ground and on his terms and not on Kaunda's.

At the cabinet meeting on 14 August an embittered PW Botha resigned his presidency. FW de Klerk was sworn in as Acting State President. The last election held on a racial basis was on 6 September 1989. The National Party won and was given a mandate by the electorate to negotiate a new political non-racial dispensation with the ANC.

On 14 September De Klerk was formerly elected State President of South Africa. He immediately lifted the long standing State of Emergency.

After that National Intelligence held a secret meeting with the ANC in Switzerland on the instructions of the State Security Council. Thabo Mbeki and Jacob Zuma — the president and vice-president of South Africa at the time of writing — represented the ANC. The meeting was conducted without the knowledge of President de Klerk.

When Niel Barnard reported the results to President de Klerk afterwards he was furious. He peremptorily banned any further similar initiatives by National Intelligence unless they had his express approval. It was probably only the delicate political tightrope that De Klerk was walking at the time that saved Barnard from the sack.

Not surprisingly, considering this incident in Switzerland, on 28 November 1989 President de Klerk ordered the immediate disbandment of the State Security Council and the National Security Management System. Within weeks he had re-established cabinet rule and drastically reduced the influence of the once powerful inner-circle of Securocrats. He also pulled in the reins of government bureaucrats including Niel Barnard and entrenched safeguards to ensure that the cabinet could not be circumvented again.

On 13 December President de Klerk and Nelson Mandela met in secret for the first time. Present were Ministers Gerrit Viljoen, Kobie Coetzee, General W H Willemse of the Department of Correctional Services (Prisons), and National Intelligence's Niel Barnard and his deputy, Mike Louw.

On 10 January 1990 President de Klerk addressed a meeting of 800 senior police officers in Pretoria. Although his audience was sworn to secrecy, the subjects discussed were widely leaked to the media.

At the opening of Parliament on 2 February, President de Klerk said that only negotiations amongst the representative leaders of all sectors of the *entire* population could ensure a lasting peace in South Africa. He followed up by lifting the banning orders on the ANC, PAC, SACP and other black liberation movements.

On 2 March the President addressed SADF officers and instructed them to play an impartial role in their dealings with the ANC. He also launched an investigation into all secret and covert projects of the Security Forces and by the end of March many had been closed down.

A couple of questions remain. Surely President PW Botha must have known about National Intelligence's recruitment of Kenneth Kaunda and must also have been briefed about his MI6 links. What was the role played by National Intelligence in Kenneth Kaunda's invitation to Pik Botha? And for that matter, what role did the British government, through MI6, play in all this?'

18

Infiltration of the ANC

When a Zimbabwean national, Peter Samushonga, crossed the border into South Africa with a valid passport provided by the ZCIO, no one connected him with the wanted MK operative, Guy Ndhlovu. The black and white mug-shot of the suspect and my note posted at all Zimbabwean and Botswana border posts ordering the detention of the subject and requesting the arresting officer to contact the Service's office in Durban had gone unnoticed. Customs officers and police at the border posts were short-staffed and they found it impossible to compare the faces of the hordes of people flowing into South Africa daily with those on the torrent of wanted notices they received daily.

On 12 February 1989 Guy appeared in the ANC-controlled Kwa Mashu Township on the outskirts of Durban. He linked up with two MK cadres who had already established an underground network in the area.

For security reasons Guy flaunted his bogus Zimbabwean identity with the broader community. After two years in Zimbabwe his fluent Chishona left few doubts about his tribal origins.

Guy and his two comrades, Sibongile Muleya and Chris Chauke, focussed their efforts on the already radicalised youth in an attempt to establish new armed self-defence units (SDUs) in the area.

The ANC youths, known as the Young Lions, had followed the communist example of organising themselves into street and area committees. Their aims were to snuff out *impimpis* (government informers) and to defend the ANC community from armed Inkatha and police attacks. But however noble their efforts and unselfish their commitment, they lacked the training and the arms to make good their intentions.

Vigilantes of the Inkatha Freedom Party (IFP), secretly trained and armed by the South African military and police, were waging a war of terror against the ANC and its supporters. To counter such attacks, the

236

ANC infiltrated trained MK cadres and arms into the townships. This resulted in waves of arson and mass killings that plagued black township populations throughout the country. Reports of faction fighting, township anarchy and, as the authorities quaintly called it, 'black on black violence' began to appear in the international media. Politically inspired murders reached alarming proportions and began to equal the proportions of a full-blown civil war.

Eight weeks after his arrival in Kwa Mashu, Guy and his team completed the training of a group of 20 youths. They were armed with AK47s. The weapons had been smuggled into the country in the upholstered seats of a Bedford truck owned by 'African Hinterland' — a well-known tour operator. Travelling overland down the African continent in the back of a customised truck had become a popular tourist activity. But in reality it was an ANC front used for arms smuggling and its activities continued well into the 1990s.

Guy, a seasoned guerilla fighter, led most of the attacks against Inkatha in Kwa Mashu and Lamontville. His successes didn't end his feelings of guilt for selling out so many of his former comrades. Inflicting losses on the enemy, however, made it easier for him to live with himself.

I struggled to keep up with HQ's escalating demands for information. I was instructed to look for hidden agendas amongst the opposition's leadership and to find evidence that the SACP and MK would hijack the ANC during the negotiation process.

My human sources were sometimes limited and this often resulted in me missing the time-frame set by the government's decision-makers. In this pressure-cooker of agents hunting for information, I could not help but think of Guy. With his access and natural ability as a spy, he would have been a valuable asset in the situation.

But all my efforts to establish his whereabouts failed. My sources found no trace of him and his name didn't appear on the lists of returning exiles that circulated amongst the intelligence community.

On 3 March 1989 at about 18:00 I was driving along Smith Street on my way home when I saw Guy waiting at a taxi stop. I pulled over to the side of the road and called him. He was obviously shocked when he recognised me.

Obviously fearing either arrest by the police or compromise with the ANC, he got in my car. I drove to Brighton Beach near the Bluff and convinced him that he should resume working for me. I could see by his baggy clothing and the weight that he had lost that he was struggling financially. He told me that although he was organising for the ANC in the black townships, he was not on their payroll. We exchanged contact details and I took him to the outskirts of Lamontville.

During 1989 most of the anti-apartheid lobby, including the ANC offices, were in a complex called the Diakonia Centre. It housed several Church groups, NGOs and organisations like the Black Sash and the End Conscription Campaign.

A technical team from National Intelligence's head office installed a bug in the Ukuthula Room of the centre. This device enabled the Service to monitor ANC meetings held there. On 29 of June 1990 they recorded a meeting of MK leaders.

Using my cover as a researcher on liberation theology, I befriended Jenny, a pro-ANC woman involved with the administration side of the complex. She introduced me to Mosiuoa 'Terror' Lekota, then the regional representative of the ANC in Natal and later South Africa's Minister of Defence. Lekota was a jovial and passionate man who wanted to promote the ANC at all costs. He had a vision of establishing an ANC branch amongst Afrikaners in Natal. I encouraged his belief that this was possible so that I could get close to him and enhance my image as an ANC supporter.

On 2 August 1990, I accompanied Lekota to a meeting of the Synod of the Dutch Reformed Church in Durban. It was held at the church of Rev Hennie van Rensburg in Umbilo, Durban. Lekota spoke Afrikaans and made an impassioned speech about the ANC and the value of the Afrikaner in a future ANC dispensation. He invited the Dutch Reformed Church to attend a peace conference being planned by the ANC.

Subsequent to the meeting he mentioned that the ANC's office in Durban was getting threatening phone calls. He also stressed to me the importance of recruiting Afrikaners into the ANC fold. I offered to assist him.

My association and bond with him and my obvious willingness to help gave me considerable access to ANC circles. I gained a lot of intelligence merely by punting my link with him. I always believed that he was impossible to recruit, so I never even attempted it.

Nevertheless, by the middle of 1989 I had established contact with and interviewed most members of the ANC and SACP leadership in Durban and Pietermaritzburg through an unwitting Lekota. I met ANC leaders like Harry Gwala, Sbu Ndebele and SACP youth leader Jeff Rhadebe. Except for Harry Gwala they all achieved high office in the ANC controlled government.

By the end of 1989 I had become well known amongst leftist groups, the ANC and other political leaders in the province. My Afrikaner heritage and in-depth political interest did not appear to be a handicap. To the ANC I was as a man from outside the rigid Afrikaner system and my persistent interest in South Africa's transformation was credible. My veneer of non-prejudiced interaction continued to provide me with numerous contacts within the ANC's political sphere of influence in the province.

The country was in turmoil with mass demonstrations, strikes and stay- aways at an all-time high. In KwaZulu-Natal war between the government-sponsored Inkatha Freedom Party (IFP) and the ANC was running out of control and fighting had spread to the Witwatersrand (now Gauteng). Fearing an escalation in violence during the festive season, the leave of security personnel was cancelled and operational people were placed on standby. I was one of them and my Christmas 1989 leave was put on hold.

By 1990 the ANC had moved its offices to 130 Field Street in central Durban. Guy was part of the ex-MK combatants' organisation, but he still got no salary from the ANC. In July 1990 he provided me with the minutes of a meeting between the ANC and the National Party's Denis Worral. In the main, Guy focussed his attention on the workings and dissatisfactions within MK. He also provided tactical information relating to weapons and the underground activities of the military organisation. I passed this to the local station which in turn liaised with the Security Branch.

National Intelligence enjoyed considerable success in the province, but we also had our share of tragedy when Leonard, a black field officer, was murdered. Responding to a call from an informer, he had left his home at night for an urgent personal meeting. He never returned. Two days later his car and his body were found submerged in a dam. He had been shot several times with an automatic rifle.

With the protracted process of the armed struggle and negotiations with the government dragging on, many ANC and MK members at grassroots level became increasingly impatient and disillusioned. The majority of comrades were unemployed and the ANC was unable to provide them with jobs or financial support to reward them for their efforts in the struggle.

Through Guy, I preyed with notable success on these characters for information. I bought a whole network of casual informers who were prepared to sell out virtually anyone to support themselves and their families.

It became evident by the sheer volume of information provided by *Operation Jaguar* that I was more than pulling my weight. It was true that some of those targeted might have suspected I was an intelligence operative, but in the main they chose to accept my false flag approach. Most of those who had uncomfortable feelings about me continued to feed me information anyway, soothing their guilty consciences by telling themselves that I was only a journalist. It made the acceptance of my money easier.

As we have seen, 1990 brought radical changes to South Africa's political landscape. After President FW de Klerk announced the unbanning of the PAC and the ANC/SACP Alliance, political prisoners were released from prison and the exiles began to return.

Nelson Mandela walk free after serving 27 years in jail.

Thousands upon thousands of cheering people lined the streets outside the prison and in ecstatic frenzy welcomed the most revered leader in all of South Africa's history.

The crowd cheered in jubilation as they watched an aged Mandela walked to freedom and fame. The disenfranchised and disheartened black masses were suddenly radiant with hope. For the first time they expressed defiance in celebrating a long awaited victory. The countrywide celebrations by the black population, however, filled the government and the white citizens with trepidation.

The long-time custodians of political power and their support base were frightened that the rising black tide was about to snatch control from their hands. The country polarised, between black and white, held its breath as it waited for the start of a political battle between the former adversaries.

The ANC and the other liberation organisations faced the major challenge of transforming their guerrilla movements into political parties. The biggest practical challenge faced by the ANC was to entrench its representation at grassroots level and to resettle its dispersed leadership back inside the country.

The National Party government, through its intelligence and security organs, faced the daunting task of staying ahead of ANC planning and concentrating on disrupting and fracturing its strategy and structures on the ground.

We field operatives found ourselves facing something of a dilemma. We had to engage in aggressive collection methods at high risk without compromising the government. It had to be seen as a fair and credible political opponent while it doubled as a peace broker.

During 1990 and 1991, I capitalised on my earlier introductions and forged a close bond with Sbu Ndebele, a rising star in the ANC hierarchy. In the guise of furthering my researches I managed to obtain numerous reports relating to the ANC. The following were of significance:

240

- African National Congress Women's League (ANCWL): Programme for 1991.
- Department of Intelligence and Security (DIS): Identification of intelligence operators.
- DIS investigation against Peter Mokaba.
- Kush Singh: Military training of MK members in India.
- ANC, National Conference 1991: description of licence plates and vehicles to be used.

We field officers were subjected like never before to the so-called eleventh commandment — get the product at all costs, but don't get caught. This was particularly relevant when spying on political parties that were emerging from their chrysalises.

The only alternative to exploiting highly placed sources was to tap into the repository of the ANC's thinking. The only way to achieve that was to lift their records from their offices at 130 Field Street.

In the autumn of 1991 I presented my plan to the head of station at a private meeting held in a Durban nightspot. Neville Höll took the official line in his response to my suggestions.

'We are in a new era, Riaan. The politicians are forcing us to play by the book. Some of the old ways, the bending of rules, the flouting of regulations have to become, as management puts it, more restrained.'

I wasn't put off. I personally believed the system was going soft and conciliatory. Despite this, I was well aware that breaking and entering operations were continuing unabated throughout the country.

'Neville, the president's announcement caught everyone in the field by surprise. The politicians didn't give us sufficient time to prepare for handling a new and radical black political party. Now we have one on our doorstep. But we haven't got enough of the right sources in place to cover all bases. Yet the government is still pressuring us for top secret information.'

After half an hour of bickering, Neville capitulated. He also wanted to impress his superiors by providing high quality product.

'I'll assign you four men, but I don't want to know anything about it. As far as I'm concerned you're on your own.'

We kept 130 Field Street under surveillance for seven consecutive days before making our move. Johnny, the only black operator on the team, visited the ANC offices twice. He assessed the door locks, air vents, alarm systems, the levels of security and possible entry points. His presence amongst the hundreds of ANC supporters besieging the offices daily attracted no attention. They were eagerly applying for membership, enquiring about loved ones last heard of in exile or just collecting the freebie literature available.

On 13 July 1991 we penetrated the place for the first time. The penetration team, in two vehicles, entered a nearby parking arcade at 17:00. A half hour later the arcade was locked up for the night. The owner had given me a key to enable the men to let themselves out

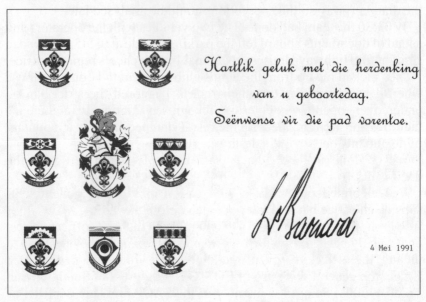

Birthday card from Director General Niel Barnard to the author during the course of *Jaguar* .

when they had finished.

At 22:00 Johnny immobilised the security guard on duty at the entrance to 130 Field Street. Posing as a passing drunk he offered the guard a swig from his bottle. It contained brandy spiked with Dormicum, a pre-anaesthesia drug. The guard was knocked out cold.

Johnny, in constant radio contact, stayed outside the building acting as lookout while the rest of the team broke in. The alarm system had not been activated, so picking the lock on the front door and getting in that way was easy. They swept through the offices with a portable photocopier and copied every document they could lay their hands on. The filing cabinets were unlocked so they posed no problem either. They could not turn on the lights but each operator had a powerful miniature lamp which enabled them go through every drawer and personal diary in the suffocating darkness.

242

The office of the ANC's head of intelligence (and later deputy president of South Africa, Jacob Zuma, surprisingly yielded little of value. His personal diary was virtually blank except for a few cryptic notes of no apparent significance. His apparent lack of activity didn't match his political stature and obviously busy schedule. They copied the diary anyway so the encryptions could be analysed later.

By 03:30 the team had done. The two vehicles with the operators and a load of documents aboard left the parking arcade at 03:45 and headed straight for Highway House — National Intelligence's regional office.

They picked me up from the tennis club adjacent to Highway House where I had been awaiting their return. I ignored the strict ban on undercover operatives entering recognised National Intelligence facilities and went inside with the rest. I dumped literally a mountain of documents on Neville's desk.

'We've done it — Jaguar ', said the note that I left with the documents.

We celebrated our success with free drinks at the government-subsidised office bar and left not much before dawn.

Operation Jaguar repeated its night raids on the ANC offices almost on a weekly basis for the next six months. I expanded the operation to include the offices of several trade unions, particularly that of Alec Erwin, the general secretary of COSATU (Congress of South African Trade Unions), long time member of the SACP and later Minister of Trade and Industry in the Mandela and Mbeki governments.

Erwin took no security precautions whatsoever. His office, in the same building as Military Intelligence, provided a wealth of information. Policy documents regarding the Tri-Partite Alliance which we had not found at the ANC's offices, lay carelessly strewn on his desk. The general disarray was littered with invaluable notes of meetings with senior members of the ANC's national leadership and so on.

The offices and homes of ANC activists and academics perceived to be pro-ANC were also carefully broken into without leaving any telltale signs. Throughout this campaign the regional office also ran an extensive eavesdropping campaign, bugging most of the opposition's fax and telephone lines. The mail section at Highway House collected the opposition's mailbags from the central post office. Letters were opened and the contents copied before they were returned to the post office for onward transmission.

It was at this point in my career that I was awarded the Director General's Merit Award for Excellence. The official ceremony to honour me was held in a private suite in Durban's plush Royal Hotel.

Representing the Service was Phil Vosloo, director of the division; Anton Schutte; Neville Höll, my divisional head; Theron Snyman, his deputy; and, of course, Sonja.

I had been divorced in absentia the month before, so I had no one but my colleagues to share the moment and celebrate with.

The certificate was in my real name and signed by Director General Niel Barnard. It was given to Neville for safekeeping.

Later that night after the top brass had left, I took the opportunity to have a continental piss-up on the Firm's account with Neville, Theron and Sonja.

Theron got talkative and related his most horrific experience in the Service. He had once crossed into Lesotho to meet an agent, an MK executive. He used to cross regularly to debrief him, so most members of the Security Branch at the Ladybrand border post knew he was a National Intelligence officer. For reasons of professional jealousy, a Security Branch officer tipped off the Lesotho Police about his activities in Maseru. As a consequence he was arrested and charged with espionage. He was locked up and severally beaten. While in prison he was tied naked to a flagpole and forced to salute the Lesotho flag.

He was released several weeks later after the intervention of Foreign Minister Pik Botha. Botha threatened to close the border with Lesotho — an enclave within South Africa — end maize exports and cut off electricity supplies. In the end this secured Theron's release. His hearing in one ear is still impaired from the beatings. This highlights the intensity, the distrust and the jealous competition that often existed between the various arms of South Africa's intelligence apparatus.

My success and the operational successes continued without abatement for another two months.

Then disaster struck.

An ANC telephone conversation was routinely intercepted by the Durban office. It was immediately transcribed by the Listeners and shortly afterwards landed on Neville Höll's desk.

It recorded a phone call between someone called Mike Sutcliffe and Mo Shaik, a senior ANC intelligence operative. It only lasted for a couple of minutes.

Neville called the Director Operations in Pretoria on his secure line and gave him a cryptic briefing. Then he buzzed Sonja and instructed her to arrange an urgent meeting with me.

Neville and I met at The Deck like on our first meeting.

He didn't waste time.

'The ANC is suspicious about your relationship with Sbu Ndebele.

They think you're an agent and are warning him to stay away from you.'

He passed me a copy of the intercept.

Neville levelled with me.

'Riaan, the bottom line is that the ANC's intelligence has tumbled to your activities. Your cover has been blown . . . forever.'

I was deeply shocked. I had operated for all that time without anyone tumbling to me. Now I had been compromised. That was the last thing a field officer needed to hear. Fieldwork was my life.

As with the British and other secret services, National Intelligence abhorred media attention. Management continually reminded field officers: 'Just do your job, but don't come back to me in the newspaper.'

It had happened occasionally before in the Service, but had not necessarily adversely affected an officer's operational career. In 1992, though, given the sensitivity of the government's negotiations with the ANC, the NIS could not be seen to be spying on the ANC's leadership. In my case, *Operation Jaguar* 's main thrust had been the infiltration of the ANC. And being compromised posed a danger that the ANC would leak it to the media. If that happened, it would cause considerable embarrassment not only to the Service but to the government as well. Certainly they would have denied I was working for National Intelligence, but it could still jeopardise the ongoing political negotiations.

'How could this have possibly happened?' I asked.

'I can only guess', Neville said. 'It probably came about because of your prominence with the ANC leadership. Your name must have somehow surfaced in the wrong quarters.'

'It doesn't seem possible. No one in KwaZulu-Natal knows me as a NIS officer. What's more none of the ANC people I've dealt with has ever indicated that he was suspicious of me.'

'Get real', Neville said. 'You're an Afrikaner and not a known leftist or ANC supporter. You've been probing and questioning its leadership for a long time. Terror Lekota is the ANC chief in Natal and he's even been to your house. It's quite obvious that sooner or later your name would surface.'

I somehow guessed that it was Guy.

'What do I tell head office?' Neville asked. 'I sympathise, but Pretoria will be furious that you've been blown. They'll blame us even though, indirectly, it's they who have been pressuring us to take chances. They'll definitely shut down *Operation Jaguar* . You may as well pack up your office now. You're on leave from this moment. Stay away from anyone even remotely connected with the ANC. I'll let you know what's happening.'

He left me to face the uncertainties of my future alone. I knew the drill. Suddenly I would be treated like a leper. As everyone ran for cover to avoid blame, the volumes of intelligence I had produced would be conveniently forgotten. I could be certain it would not be used to balance the scales in my favour.

I lazed away my days on Durban beach without a word from my superiors. Guy Ndhlovu, meanwhile, grew in prominence and stature with the ANC. He was given a salaried position in its Durban office as co-ordinator of returning ex-combatants. A position in a future ANC government seemed a certainty.

In Pretoria my future was being fiercely debated by everyone in the know. A meeting to decide what could be done with the 'unfortunate' field officer was held in the Concilium Building. In attendance was the head of personnel, the Chief Director Operations, the director of Division 041 and a member of the 'headshrinkers.' Anton Schutte, the former regional representative in Durban, now my divisional head, presented my case.

Anton made an emotional plea on my behalf.

'That's why there are so many unsuccessful officers in the field and only a few true operators. Operators are becoming a dying breed in National Intelligence. It's the handlers, spymasters and their sources that make us an intelligence service. These bloody rigid rules that bind us nowadays are making it impossible for us to operate in the field.'

His audience showed signs of discomfort at this obvious truth.

'It won't be long before you find yourselves working with a bunch of academic farts who will be incapable of going into the field to get product. Who will you have left who'll take the chance of dirtying his hands to get information for you? Do you think that with another government coming in, this will be the end of the road? Do you think there will never be another threat?'

The Chief Director of Operations frowned at the insubordination by a senior member of his staff.

'Our deep cover projects and operators like Riaan, are bound to become anachronisms and an embarrassment to the Service. We have special projects and undercover personnel from the old school spread out all over the world. In these changing times it's a recipe for disaster. It's an operational style that's becoming obsolete the world over. With the collapse of international communism and the end of the Cold War, the CIA has pulled the plug on scores of covert officers. The British have done the same. They are putting their rogues up for early

246

retirement or shifting them to desk jobs.

'It's a new era and we have to adapt or be sidelined. Anton, don't take it personally but we must face facts. We have little control over those boys in the field. They play the game as they see it on the ground, but we cannot afford that in the present political climate. These men have adopted a game plan over the years that's not in line with management's vision for the new service.'

'And what's this new vision?' Anton asked sarcastically.

'Bluntly, I fear, we'll simply be unable to retain some of our more colourful characters. In the past they were acceptable because of the circumstances of the times. In the new service, however, they will stand out and cause offence. I'm sure you understand that?'

Although a man with a college education, Anton had worked his way up to the top through the ranks and he found the Chief Director's line of reasoning insulting. He still regarded himself as a field officer, as did those serving under him.

'Sir, if our field officers are unaware of management's change of direction, or its new vision for the future, it's hardly their fault. It seems that management has deliberately kept the field officers in the dark as to their likely future and the future of the Service as a whole. *Operation Jaguar* , you'll recall, was recommended by you and approved by Director General Dr Barnard himself. Everyone knew we were taking a chance and that the time span of such an operation was likely to be limited.

The Chief Director became coldly official.

'Are you suggesting, Mr Schutte, that the Service is deliberately misleading its staff?'

'I don't know, but I never thought I would see the day when Operations turned its back on one of its own . . . not for failing in the job, but for taking the risks to produce the product.'

Anton Schutte was a man's man, a man moulded by the principles that the Service had taught him. He was the sort you could happily go to war with, a leader who stood by his men at all costs. For him the issue was no longer about me. It was about this so-called new service that had become a threat to all operators, including himself. He was speaking for us all.

He realised what was happening. The National Intelligence Service that he served as a divisional head and as an operational agent, was playing for the benefit of the political world. He was ashamed of the changes that were suddenly becoming apparent in what had once been uncompromising and proud leadership.

'You are getting ready for your new political masters, the ANC

247

alliance.' Schutte had no intention of remaining silent. 'You're cleaning house to save your arses. You're denying actions launched against the ANC that you personally approved. That's why you want to get rid of field officers like Riaan. I've been watching this process of so-called re-evaluation — the shredding of documents, the deleting of data from the mainframe computer and this recent ban on spying on the ANC because it now happens to be a political party. You want to come up smelling of roses instead of shit, to ensure the salvation of your personal empires.'

'Shut up, Anton, I'm not going to allow this', the CDO said. '*Operation Jaguar* has ceased to exist so just find another posting for Riaan. Give him a desk job away from the action.'

'He will not take it.'

'Then he must opt for early retirement', the CDO ruled

On the late afternoon of the eighth day of my unexpected leave, Neville told me I was being transferred to the Port Elizabeth regional office. I reported there for duty on 5 August 1992.

19

Port Elizabeth

National Intelligence continued its programme of 're-evaluation' for months on end.

Thousands of files were destroyed. Members of Division 062 entered regional offices at night, raided members' offices and searched filing cabinets for classified documents. Officers were ordered to destroy all personal files and mementos. Many of the field operatives had communist flags, ANC T-shirts and all sorts of other souvenirs to remind them of the victories they had achieved against the erstwhile opposition.

The Service had a sophisticated personal reference database on virtually every leftist and anti-government activist in South Africa. It contained personal details, addresses and telephone numbers and it tracked the movement of targets. Often vehicle descriptions and registration numbers were noted. Most of this data, particularly anything the ANC might find the least bit embarrassing was deleted from the database. This made the day-to-day operations of field officers extremely difficult. Without proper records it was extremely difficult to identify people mentioned by agents in their reports.

Documents relating to secret projects were also destroyed. Complete erasure was difficult as financial records relating to expenditure on projects had to be retained for audit purposes. Hasty alterations were made to such records to conceal the fact that the expenditure related to operations concerning the ANC alliance. This difficulty was overcome when on 3 July 1992 the Minister of Justice and Intelligence authorised the destruction of all the Service's financial and related records.

Some source and agent files were also amended or destroyed as certain of those individuals became ministers in President Nelson Mandela's new government. Then there were the senior ANC-aligned individuals who were on record as working for foreign intelligence services like MI6 and the CIA. Most had been recruited while studying abroad. In some cases, though, clever clues were deliberately left in the system.

This re-evaluation programme began as early as 1991.

*　　*　　*

I arrived in Port Elizabeth on a Friday afternoon. The city was in chaos. Black protest on this occasion had taken the form of civil disobedience. Taxi drivers had disrupted traffic flow by blocking the access routes to the city as well as the streets in the central business district.

This prevented me from reaching National Intelligence's Eastern Cape Regional Office in Brister House, Main Street. Black smoke was billowing from beneath the flyover bridge that led to the beachfront. Angry protesters had set the contents of large city refuse bins alight. The blockage prevented fire engines and the police from getting to the scene. Defiance and rebelliousness was palpable amongst those blacks that I passed on my way to the Humewood Hotel where I would be staying until I found a house.

The Eastern Cape had always been a politically volatile region with the local tribes displaying a high level of resistance to white governance. Even as far back as the 19th century, the Xhosas — the predominant tribe in that area — had mounted raids on settlers farming in the Kei River basin. There had been nine frontier wars — the so-called Kaffir Wars — fought in the region from the end of the 18th to the middle of the 19th centuries.

The Xhosa ethnic grouping, to which Nelson Mandela and most of the current ANC cabinet belong, had been the backbone of resistance that finally ended white domination.

By Monday the situation had calmed down and I was able to get to the offices on the 8th floor of Brister House. A year later they were moved to the top floor of a new building in Ring Road, Greenacres. I was met by the regional representative who introduced me to the rest of the staff and showed me to my office. Once the door was closed, he told me that jeans and a T-shirt were unacceptable dress and that in future I should wear a tie. It was clear that things were going to be very different from what I had been used to.

The region was a cauldron of civil unrest and political activity, but the regional office was the epitome of inactive incompetence. Although I was a seasoned field operative, I found myself stuck behind a desk editing the reports of junior field officers. The quality of their reports was poor and without depth. There was nothing that even remotely gave advanced information of what the ANC was planning in the region. It seemed they were following an ANC trail that had long gone cold.

For the first time in my life I found myself in the true public service. It was an archetypal eight to five job involving hardly anything that resembled an intelligence service. It did not take long for me to assess my work environment which, to say the least, did not compare favourably with the one I had come from.

There were two main reasons for the office's dismal performance. First was the poor leadership qualities of the regional representative and his deputy. Neither were particularly efficient either. The regional representative had been appointed because of his strong Afrikaner background and his friendship with Phillip Vosloo, the divisional director. He hardly ever left the building during working hours and had never worked in the field.

His deputy, who was responsible for the office's operations, was out of his depth. He was a former bodyguard who had never recruited an agent of significance. He got the job on a platter by toadying up to the right people. He was also not one of the world's workers. He used to lock his office for an hour every afternoon to take a nap. Even the junior officers laughed at his ineffectualness. Regardless, he was promoted to regional representative when his chief was transferred to head office. He would eventually retire to his house in the upmarket Cape Town suburb of Clifton with a generous pension of close to R2 million.

Another contributing factor was that only a few officers had experience in the field. They were mostly new recruits so it was a case of the blind leading the blind. The exception was Etienne Shamley, who became the new deputy. The newly promoted chief delegated virtually all his responsibilities to Shamley.

Under the new political dispensation Shamley later became the regional representative — a position he held until 2001. By then he was one of only a few white officers of the former National Intelligence Service who held such a senior position. Things were about to change, however. At the annual conference of regional representatives, the new senior management dominated by the ANC, asked him to join the organisation.

He declined, saying that he was a professional intelligence officer who had served the new dispensation loyally for several years and was disinterested in politics. Shortly afterwards he was told he was being relocated to Bisho in the former Ciskei. He refused on the grounds that his children were in high school in Port Elizabeth and it was

251

unreasonable to demand he consider an educational change at that stage of their schooling.

Without further ado he was arbitrarily stripped of his powers as the regional representative, told that he would retain his pay and his rank, but he would effectively be reduced to field officer again.

Not surprisingly, Shamley resigned.

My appointment to Port Elizabeth was still as a field officer. I started a drive to recruit agents. I was a false flag specialist, but the office management bogged me down with administration. It seems likely they had been filled in by head office about my previous exploits — making the head and his deputy neurotically afraid that I would attempt a recruitment that would publicly fail and drop them. The head was not prepared to take the risk of having a single blemish against his name and he refused to take responsibility for any actions in the field. He preferred that the job was simply not done.

During my time there I was ordered to investigate a former military officer who had been involved in *Operation Katzen* in 1985. It was a year when the United Democratic Front (UDF) had succeeded in making the Eastern Cape ungovernable.

The failure of the Security Force to contain what had become unacceptable levels of civil unrest led to a high level meeting in August 1985 in Port Elizabeth. Amongst others, Defence Minister General Magnus Malan, the Minister of Police Louis le Grange and the members of the Joint Management Centre (JMC) led by Brigadier Joffel van der Westhuizen, attended the meeting.

Malan threatened the military and police officials present that they would be relieved of their commands if they failed to stabilise the situation.

In the first half of 1986 Brigadier van der Westhuizen summoned Colonel Pieter Hall, his Senior Staff Officer Operations and Colonel Lourens du Plessis, his Staff Officer Intelligence.

Van der Westhuizen issued a command directive for them to prepare an operational instruction based on his ideas of how the unrest in the Eastern Cape could be quelled.

He suggested the amalgamation of Transkei and Ciskei as the means by which the Xhosa nation could be united as a pro-government group. To execute this plan, Ciskei President Lennox Sebe would have to be assassinated and a Xhosa resistance movement established to combat the unrest. They would deal with the dissidents by intimidation or assassination. Van der Westhuizen chose General Charles Sebe to head a Xhosa resistance movement to be called *Iliso Lomzi*.

Unfortunately, Charles, the former head of the Ciskei Central

252

Intelligence Service (CCIS), had been arrested in July 1983 and imprisoned for plotting to overthrow Ciskei's President Lennox Sebe. So for him to play a part in *Operation Katzen*, he first had to be bust from prison.

Hall and du Plessis drafted the plan as instructed. Brigadier Ferdi van Wyk, Director of Communications Operations at Army HQ in Pretoria named the plan *Operation Katzen* after the 'Kat' in General Kat Liebenberg and the 'zen' in Brigadier van der Westhuizen.

Van der Westhuizen added final touches to the draft and on 13 June 1986, he submitted his paper showing a plan designed to achieve President Botha's desired order in the region.

In July 1986 the Chief of the Army, General Kat Liebenberg, approved *Operation Katzen*.

The involvement of National Intelligence at this stage was limited as became clear at a meeting in Cape Town to discuss *Operation Katzen*. In attendance was SADF Chief, General Jannie Geldenhuys; the secretary of the State Security Council, Lieutenant-General P van der Westhuizen; the Commissioner of Police, General Johan Coetzee; the Director General of National Intelligence, Dr Niel Barnard; the Natal representative of National Intelligence, Neville Höll — the project officer and my former boss; and Colonel John More.

Dr Barnard said he was not prepared to involve his department in the operation as it was a 'non-executing' body. Nevertheless, he asked to be kept informed and Neville Höll continued to attend meetings as the NIS representative.

National Intelligence had again played its hand with stealth and deception using its lack of executive powers as an escape route from crimes of murder. The fact was that the Service would not involve itself in assassinations and other dirty tricks if there was the slightest chance of compromise. It preferred to keep an eye from a distance and let other branches of the Security Forces do the dirty jobs.

The sub-plan of *Operation Katzen* — the assassination of Lennox Sebe — was codenamed *Operation Duiker*. The South African-inspired assault involved men of the Transkei Defence Force and members of the so-called Xhosa Resistance Movement. They were led by ex-Selous Scouts military advisers under the command of Lieutenant-Colonel Ron Reid Daly. The assault against Sebe's palace in Bisho was launched on 19 February 1987. The operation was badly planned, poorly executed and it failed dismally. Reid Daly and his men were later unceremoniously ejected from the Transkei by General Holomisa who had taken over as the leader of the Transkei Military Council. Military Intelligence, who before that had always called the shots in the homelands, paid off the 'ex-Rhodesians' with a suitcase containing R2,25 million in bank notes.

The top echelon of the Security Forces and members of the State Security Council tried to wash their own hands of any involvement. Central to *Operation Katzen* was Colonel Lourens du Plessis, secretary of the JMC.

On my arrival in Port Elizabeth I was told that sensitive information about military and police operations was being leaked to the ANC and the press. Questions about the deaths of Matthew Goniwe, Fort Calata, Sparrow Mkontho and Sicelo Mhlawuli were being asked in the media.

Goniwe and the others were school teachers in the Eastern Cape and were committed UDF activists. The State Security Council, on the recommendation of Brigadier Joffel van der Westhuizen approved their assassination (euphemistically called permanent removal from society). On the 27 June 1985 they were ambushed by the Security Police while en route from Port Elizabeth to Cradock and murdered. The officers responsible were later convicted of the killings and sentenced to long prison terms.

With the leakage of information Security Forces personnel began to realise for the first time that they could be tried for criminal acts committed on the behalf of government during the course of their official duties. Operatives did everything they could to hide their involvement in any dirty tricks in the past.

Colonel du Plessis, of all the Security Forces personnel with the required access, was thought to be the weakest link in the cover up chain.

On 10 August 1992 Du Plessis was placed under surveillance. We followed him to the Sunridge Park Post Office close to his residence where he used a public phone to make a call. He was driving his wife's vehicle, a metallic blue Honda with registration CB274758.

On the second day of the operation we discovered that Du Plessis was leaking sensitive information to Major-General Bantu Holomisa, head of Transkei's Military Council. He revealed details of *Operation Katzen* and other military and Security Branch operations that he knew from his position on Port Elizabeth's Joint Management Centre (JMC). Holomisa warned him not to call him from his home telephone as it was probably bugged.

In fact, the Port Elizabeth office had just arranged for his home telephone to be tapped to determine his bona fides. The procedure for telephone tapping was a circuitous operation. Section 118A of the Posts and Telecommunications Act made provision for the intercept of mail and telephone conversations under certain circumstances. As field officer, I made a submission to National Intelligence's head office asking for the installation of a device at Du Plessis' home.

Each of National Intelligence's regional offices had a permanent contact at Telkom (the public telephone company) who was responsible for all legalised bugging in the region. Telkom had made the necessary adaptations at each of our regional offices to give us the technical wherewithal to arrange bugs within the comfort of our offices. Each regional office had a room specially equipped to tap up to 50 lines. In some areas it was technically impossible to feed a tapped line into the Service's offices. In such cases the lines were bugged at the telephone exchange. Usually female officers, dubbed operational assistants, handled all telephone tapping and mail interception operations. Occasionally, when a field officer was being punished, he was sent to work in the mail room.

The understanding between field officers and Telkom officials was that devices should be installed in advance of any approval. In the case of Colonel du Plessis I arranged for the public phones at Sunridge Park Post Office bugged on the same day that du Plessis made his first phone call from there.

In many cases field officers did their own bugging. The target's phone line was intercepted at the telephone pole or at the underground cable and the recorder hidden underground or in the ceiling of the building concerned.

In the early 1990s a law to control the tapping of telephones was passed. Under this new law the Security Forces have to get approval from a judge before a line can be tapped. It has made little difference in practice, however, and many of the same Telkom officials who ran bugging for National Intelligence are still doing it for the new National Intelligence Agency.

For a time Du Plessis refrained from using his home telephone to contact Holomisa, other than on two occasions when he appeared to have had rather a lot to drink. As expected, though, he otherwise used one of the two public phone booths at Sunridge Park Post Office. He was obviously unaware that both were bugged. Transcripts of his conversations were sent to National Intelligence's head office. They were then passed on to Military Intelligence and the Security Branch.

In the last week of the operation, I could hear by his voice that Du Plessis was stressed and close to breaking point. On 13 August he requested a personal meeting with General Holomisa to hand over certain documents. He also asked for money as he feared he might lose his pension. Perhaps he suspected by then that he was being monitored. I think he feared for his life and believed that his military colleagues might want to kill him.

General Holomisa suggested they meet in secret at a venue close to the Ellis Park Rugby Stadium in Johannesburg. He is a big rugby fan and a former player. He had booked to watch a rugby match there on that Saturday. I passed the information to the Service's head office and requested that the meeting be placed under surveillance.

However, a few days later the operation was terminated for reasons unknown to me.

Colonel Lourens du Plessis later publicly testified to the Truth and Reconciliation Commission regarding the criminal activities of the military and at various criminal trials of Security Police officers in connection with *Operation Katzen* and other matters.

The greatest influence that National Intelligence had as an institution was the secret role it played as the key government negotiator — a function arising from its close proximity to the ruling National Party and the *Broederbond*.

In 1987, the National Intelligence Service, and specifically Niel Barnard, was tasked to make contact and handle the opening phases of negotiations with the ANC. The mandate, in fact, was not limited to the ANC, but also included governments and heads of states traditionally opposed to South Africa.

The power base of the National Party government was religiously and fervently anti-communist. In essence it totally opposed the concept of an ANC-controlled government. Until the 1990s it publicly and absolutely rejected the possibility of black majority rule and resolutely voiced its opposition to communism and the ANC.

To satisfy international pressure for a negotiated settlement with the liberation movements, the NIS was used secretly to fulfill the role that the government could not publicly adopt because its political constituency would undoubtedly have kicked it out of office. It might even have led to a military coup. So it became the job of the Service to negotiate with the communists.

Those in the loop at National Intelligence had to, for the same reasons, keep their knowledge of what was going on from their own rank and file. Their subordinates, like the general run of the mill white Afrikaner electorate, would not have stood for it. Inevitably, it resulted in the Service's inte'ligence priorities being subtly adapted towards aiding the National Party government in a quest for a settlement. National Intelligence no longer served the government of the day — it became an extension of the government of the day.

In the early 1990s management began the process of mentally preparing its members for the political change to come. The mere thought that the Service, that everyone regarded as untouchable, was about to change came as a shock to many.

Seminars explaining the Service's new direction were held at regional offices across the country to stem the tide of confusion and panic. The intellectuals from head office used a new buzzword to describe the process — they called it a 'paradigm shift'. The seminars propagated two main themes.

In the first place, senior management tried to soften the blow of the Service's change of direction by explaining its new methodology. National Intelligence would not target organisations anymore, it would concentrate instead only on individuals.

The ANC alliance including its military wing plus the smaller liberation movements like the PAC (Pan Africanist Congress), BCMA (Black Consciousness Movement of Azania) and AZAPO (Azanian African People's Organisation) would shortly become legitimate political parties. Officers would not engage those entities, but would focus solely on individuals posing a threat to the constitutional negotiations. This shift from organisations to individuals was more than strange to most members because they had been focussing on groups for as long as anyone could remember. Even the line functions of the Service were geared towards dealing with organisations. Besides, how could one collect intelligence regarding members of an organisation without collecting intelligence on the organisation itself. Many officers, in any case, protested that the threat still lay with those organisations.

The second theme on the senior management's agenda was to make members aware of the pending arrival and absorption of former enemies into its ranks. Suddenly there was much talk of values. The enemy had changed. It was now those opposed to the peaceful process of negotiations and individuals with different values to ours. It was an echo of the National Party stance, verbalised by President FW de Klerk, that the ruling party sought co-operation with everyone who believed in the same principles, regardless of race, colour or creed.

In National Intelligence it was not quite so simple. We were a close knit secret society rife with fiefdoms and private empires. Accepting field operators from the ANC's Department of Intelligence and the intelligence services of the independent homelands into the organisation posed an unacceptable threat to most of us. It was like inviting strangers into the privacy of your own home and giving them the keys.

Top management made an all-out effort to soften the blow. They swore high and low that nothing of the Service's culture would change.

257

The elements of the old NIS would remain the dominant force within the new Service. The chief directors and directors promised not to resign and assured us that their positions were not under threat. The worst case scenario, they rationalised, would be the appointment of an ANC Deputy Director General and a few junior operatives. They believed they had done their homework into the transition and even emphasised that Nelson Mandela himself had been impressed by the Service and had assured them it would be retained it in its current form.

Notwithstanding this flannel, things would soon change.

When a political settlement with the ANC became a looming reality, there was a whittling down of professional objectivity. Most of the Service's officers were both Afrikaners and National Party supporters. Their future careers depended on the ruling party retaining political power. Added to this unhealthy situation was the fact that most of the Service's senior managers were serving cheek by jowl with their political masters in the Afrikaner *Broederbond*. Its philosophy had filtered right down to the lowest levels of the Service. Not even fellow Afrikaner officers were promoted to senior positions unless they were fellow brothers in that secret organisation. This policy inevitably resulted in the promotion of many incompetents, making the delivery of a high standard of intelligence product increasingly difficult.

But regardless of management efforts, field officers continued on the ground as usual without a change of pace or method. The simple reason was that operatives could only report on what they received from their agents and sources. Such individuals within an organisation like the ANC or MK, had become accustomed to what they were doing and they also relied on the money. The changes seemed bizarre to the field officers since they could only report on the activities of the organisations their sources were serving in. In any case, most sources lacked the ability to determine which individuals in their organisations were a threat to the process and which were not.

So they continued to report on everybody as before and the field officers forwarded the material regardless. As far as the field officers were concerned, head office could sort out what information they wanted and what they didn't want.

For a long time head office ignored the lack of direction change and passed the information on to the government who presumably reaped the benefit of having insight into the politicking of the opposition. Then they tightened up.

Many informers were angry as well as confused when their reports were rejected. It also impacted negatively on their income. When they finally began to understand the narrow parameters of what was required, they began to fabricate information on individuals to show they were threats to the negotiating process. Suddenly, we discovered there were more people around who posed a threat to the process, than there were who didn't. This led to the whole operational force having to realign and find new sources of information.

As should have been anticipated by a professional organisation like NIS, by the time Nelson Mandela took power as president, collection of information had ground virtually to a halt. National Intelligence no longer had any enemies — and apparently nor did the country — so they switched their attention to crime — a task they were ill-equipped to tackle.

20

An explosive relationship
AZAPO/AZANLA and Directorate K

I finally managed to establish a safe house in central Port Elizabeth. Making use of a false flag operation, I recruited an executive member of AZAPO (Azanian People's Organisation). This agent, Pat, served on the organisation's national executive and had insight into its military structure, AZANLA (Azanian National Liberation Army). He was also friendly with senior members of the ANC and reported on their activities. Pat remained an agent long after my departure from the Service. By then he was probably controlled by Shamley who was his alternative handler.

With Pat's recruitment, I felt alive for the first time since arriving in Port Elizabeth. I was back in the field and controlling an agent of substance.

During the ongoing constitutional negotiations in the 1990s, AZAPO became dissatisfied with what was going on. They believed the ANC was capitulating on key matters and conceding far too much to the government. So they vowed to continue the armed struggle.

To understand the role of AZAPO in the South African political scene during the 1990s, it's necessary to go back and deal with the co-operation that existed between elements of AZAPO/AZANLA and the Security Forces in the 1980s.

AZAPO's origins lay in the creed of Black Consciousness developed by the late Steve Biko. It was a relatively small organisation and proved to be easy meat for the *agents provocateurs* of the state.

The fundamental disagreement between the UDF/ANC/SACP alliance and AZAPO centred on the land issue. The former professed adherence to the non-racial Freedom Charter which called for the land to be shared by all those who lived on it. The latter's objective, contrarily, was to repossess all land owned and occupied by whites and use it for the exclusive benefit of the black indigenous peoples. Dissension between the two groupings soon surfaced publicly.

In September 1984 AZAPO criticised the pro-ANC United Democratic Front Mandela Committee for calling for a work stay-away without first consulting all sectors of the community. Yet, along with 15 other Black Consciousness inclined organisations, it did exactly the same thing at a meeting in Soweto in November 1984. This action epitomised its ambivalent attitude towards the countrywide UDF-inspired eruptions of township violence that were directed against government authority. While it professed to support such methods in principle, AZAPO invariably took a stance that opposed the UDF's methods.

The Security Police in Port Elizabeth took advantage of the situation by printing and distributing bogus pamphlets in AZAPO's name containing allegations that the UDF was being 'manipulated by liberals'.

The Security Police formed a covert alliance with Rev Ebenezer Muzondile Maqina who ran the Black Crisis Centre, an affiliate of AZAPO. With the help of the police who supplied it with finance and weapons, the organisation soon gained control from the UDF of some of the most radically inclined black areas around Port Elizabeth.

When it became apparent that Maqina had gained the upper hand in the constantly swaying battle for supremacy in the townships, the UDF appealed to MK for assistance.

Chris Hani was in favour of throwing in cadres to fight Maqina, but both Joe Slovo and Joe Modise opposed it. The question was referred to the ANC's Political Military Council (PMC) for a decision and they decided 'the powerless should not be encouraged to fight the powerless.'

*   *   *

Divisions between AZAPO and the UDF were first exposed publicly during Senator Edward Kennedy's visit to South Africa in January 1985. The UDF hosted him at various centres, but AZAPO condemned his visit and staged public protests.

Violence between AZAPO and UDF erupted in April 1985 when the UDF refused to allow AZAPO to play a role in the funerals of victims of police shootings in Langa and Uitenhage.

In May 1985 UDF supporters attacked 19 AZAPO members in the Eastern Cape killing four. They also burnt the homes of 33 AZAPO supporters.

In January 1986 AZAPO and the UDF managed to hammer out a peace agreement. Needless to say, this suited neither the Security

261

Police nor Rev Maqina and in February the latter splintered his recently formed Azanian National Youth Unity (AZANYU) away from AZAPO.

The UDF in Paarl near Cape Town claimed that AZANYU was receiving support from the police in its fight against the UDF. Needless to say, this was denied by both the police and AZANYU.

Rev Maqina expanded his organisation into Uitenhage near Port Elizabeth where he took control of another Security Police surrogate, the Ama-Africa vigilante group. Like AZANYU it was in violent opposition to the UDF. For 18 months the black township of Kwanobuhle in Uitenhage became a violent battleground between the opposing gangs of AZAPO and the UDF.

On 4 January 1987 armed groups of Ama-Afrika vigilantes ordered the residents of Khayelitsha and Tent Town to march on Kwanobuhle and rid it of UDF supporters. The police followed the procession but made no attempt to interfere with the activities of the vigilantes. With police help, Ama-Afrika gained temporary supremacy.

Many believed that despite the deaths and injuries, the community as a whole approved the outcome. The Comrades had gotten out of hand. With Ama-Afrika in control, people could continue their normal life. They could go to town safely, trucks and buses could come and go, people could go to work and children could attend school. It was a fragile peace, though, and in efforts to maintain it, violence escalated. Kwanobuhle was soon plunged into a protracted period of Ama-Afrika inspired violence.

Colonel Lourens du Plessis, running Comops (Communication Operations — effectively propaganda operations) in the SADF's Eastern Cape Command, Port Elizabeth, later said that Rev Maqina became an embarrassment to the Security Police. They asked him to take over from the SAP's Major Herman du Plessis as his handler, but he refused.

For a brief time Rev Maqina dropped from sight, but he reappeared in 1991/1992 and opened offices for his Peace Foundation for Youth in North End, Port Elizabeth. It was likely that various state departments funded the organisation. With this historical background, it will be easier to understand the next saga in AZAPO's history.

In mid 1993 two bombs exploded at Torego Flats in Uitenhage causing a fire. The Uitenhage Security Branch investigated and discovered that a commercial explosive, SMX, had been used in the attack.

In November 1993, the Port Elizabeth bomb squad was called to the scene of two explosions at Jasmyn Flats in Algoa Park, just outside

Port Elizabeth. While the police were attending the crime scene, two further explosions rocked an area of residential flats in Swartkops, approximately ten kilometres away. Fortunately, there were no casualties in any of the bombings. The bomb squad discovered another six unexploded devices at Jasmyn Flats and two more at Swartkops, all of which it disarmed.

On the same night a fire broke out at the Easigas storage facility in Port Elizabeth harbour. Underground feeder lines from the facility provide gas to the hospitals and most of the restaurants in the city. The Humewood Fire brigade rushed to the scene and quelled the fire, unaware at the time, that the fire had been generated by an attempt to bomb the facility. If the attack had been successful, the secondary explosion of the gas and fuel storage tanks would have caused death and destruction in a radius of two kilometres.

This bombing spree, I subsequently discovered, took place against the sinister backdrop of a high-level conspiracy to reintroduce AZAPO as an *agent provocateur* for Directorate K of the National Intelligence Service.

The preliminary police investigation found that, like the case at Torego Flats, SMX had also been used in all the explosive devices used at Algoa Park and Swartkops.

It was only several weeks later that the investigating officers discovered by forensic analysis that the Easigas plant had also been bombed. SMX had once again figured in the attack.

The Easigas bombers, Andile Samuel Solo, an AZANLA unit-commander, Benjamin Skosana, AZAPO's Eastern Cape regional chairman and Nkutsoeu Skaap Motsau, AZANLA's National Commander had failed to breach the electrified fence that protected the facility to place their explosive charges on the tanks as planned. Seeing no alternative, they lit the safety fuses of the two devices and threw them from outside the security fence in an attempt to get them onto the top of the nearest liquid gas storage tank. Their throwing lacked range, however, and both devices bounced off the side of the tank and exploded harmlessly a few metres away. This generated the fire. The attackers did not realise that if they had succeeded in detonating their bombs on the tanks, they would all have been vaporised.

The police had no idea who the perpetrators were.

A police dog brought about the first breakthrough. Andile Samuel Solo was arrested in New Brighton Township, Port Elizabeth for an unrelated case of pointing a firearm. His house was searched by the New Brighton police. They found an unlicensed firearm and a plastic bag containing what was thought to be normal window putty and a length of rope.

The suspect was taken to the New Brighton station for questioning. One of the black arresting officers decided to 'liberate' the putty for himself as he needed to replace some broken windows at his home. On his way out of the station when going off duty he passed the police dog and its handler.

The dog identified the 'putty' as explosive by its smell and reacted in the way it had been trained. It lay flat on its belly and blocked the departing policeman's path. The handler confronted his colleague and found the explosives in the bag. The 'rope' turned out to be safety fuse and the 'putty' SMX.

The Port Elizabeth bomb squad and Security Branch officers were called to the scene. Solo was taken to the Security Branch cells at Mount Road for questioning. After rigorous interrogation and on being confronted with the explosives, Solo confessed to the bombing at Torego Flats and the Easigas storage facility. At that stage the police was still unaware that Easigas had been bombed. Solo was taken to the harbour to make indications and at the scene he pointed out to the investigating officer what he had done. He also named Skosana and Motsau as having been involved with him.

The investigating officer discovered that a warrant for the arrest of Motsau had been outstanding since 1990. He was being sought in the independent homeland of Bophuthatswana for murder and the unlawful possession of weapons.

Both Motsau and Skosana were arrested in a night raid on the latter's house in Kwamagxaki Township outside Port Elizabeth. The next morning the arresting officers were confronted by their commanding officer, Colonel Dick Hattingh, and sternly criticised for the arrest of Motsau. The policemen were astonished by the colonel's attitude as the subject had been properly arrested in terms of a legal warrant issued by the courts. But Colonel Hattingh went even further and absolutely forbade them from arresting anyone connected with AZANLA and AZAPO. He explained that he was under pressure from Pretoria to leave these organisations alone. Prior authority had to be sought from Pretoria if further arrests were considered. Motsau and Skosana, however, remained in custody for the time being.

The investigating officer was an experienced policeman and certainly no fool. He knew that the hands-off policy could mean only one thing — a covert government agency was deeply involved with AZAPO/AZANLA. It did not want its agents arrested or its level of involvement revealed.

Although National Intelligence, Security Branch and Military

Intelligence shielded the identities of their agents and sources from other intelligence organisations, most senior field officers had a pretty good idea which agent worked for which department. The field officers of the various intelligence organisations were frequently in contact and they shared information about common problems. The information itself was often a useful pointer in identifying its source.

I had a personal involvement in the bombings as one of my registered agents took part in the attacks. He had been arrested and was being held in St Albans Prison. I was also friendly with one of the police investigating officers.

I saw my agent in prison and he provided me with details of the attacks which I passed on to the investigating officer. As a result, I managed to secure my agent's release because I wanted to keep him in place within AZAPO. The investigators accordingly turned the focus of the investigation away from him.

The life of an agent is a complex one. To gain access to intelligence targets, an informer had to participate in the actions of the group he belonged to. The problem with this was that if he was involved in an action that broke the law we usually could not protect him against prosecution. There were a few general exceptions and a pardon could be arranged if the informer turned state witness and testified in court. Normally, this was not a viable option, however. Blowing an informer's cover immediately placed his life in jeopardy. Very occasionally, as in the case of my source, it could be arranged on the q.t. as a favour by colleagues in other services.

During the interrogation of Skosana and Motsau it soon became apparent that the latter was an agent working for one of the intelligence bodies. Security Branch and Military Intelligence were soon ruled out. This left National Intelligence as the most likely handler of AZANLA's national commander.

Motsau confessed he had brought the explosives from Johannesburg by road. This made sense as my informer had told me several weeks earlier that AZANLA was transporting explosives to Port Elizabeth by this means. He even gave me details of the route and probable dates that consignments would be despatched.

I had liaised with my colleagues in the Security Branch and roadblocks were set up on all the access routes to Port Elizabeth. Skosana and Motsau, however, somehow made it through the roadblocks with the explosives. The investigators deduced from this that someone in the Security Forces had been assisting them. Fingers continued to point at National Intelligence.

The forensic examination of the explosive concluded that the SMX's chemical composition had been tampered with and desensitised. This explained why the devices had failed to explode. Only the detonators went off, blowing the devices apart and starting the fires. It was obvious that someone with technological knowhow had been involved.

Meanwhile, the investigating officers were making progress in breaking Motsau. They mentioned the possibility of turning him to work for the Security Branch. The next day, however, orders arrived for Motsau to be moved immediately to Bophuthatswana for further investigation into the case for which the 1990 warrant had been issued. The investigating officers offered to transport the prisoner themselves. It was an 11-hour trip which would have given them sufficient time to break Motsau and get answers to all the unanswered questions regarding his involvement in the bombings. However, Port Elizabeth's murder and robbery unit, which was uninvolved in the investigation, was ordered to provide the personnel to escort the prisoner to Pretoria.

This ended the bombing investigation as far as Motsau was concerned. The investigating officers were furious. They felt certain that National Intelligence had pressured their superiors into removing Motsau from the investigation. But I knew nothing about it.

The first accused, Andile Samuel Solo, was convicted of the bombings and sentenced to eight years imprisonment. He served very little prison time and after applying to the Truth and Reconciliation Commission for amnesty, he got it and was freed on 8 October 1996.

Motsau also applied for amnesty and was not even put on trial. He was granted amnesty as early as 1994.

Despite the setback to his investigation the investigating officer continued his probe regardless and focussed on tracing the origins of the explosives. He discovered that the SMX had originated from African Explosives in Modderfontein, Johannesburg. After sustained pressure, personnel at African Explosives admitted that they had desensitised the explosives with the full knowledge and consent of the company's management. The material was supplied to a Major D Steenberg of the Witwatersrand Intelligence Unit of the South African Police.

The investigators discovered that Steenberg had connections with NIS. He had conducted intelligence and tradecraft courses for members of the Security Branch using the Service's training material. One such course attended by members of the Security Branch was conducted at a Directorate K safe house in Midrand.

Although the evidence of Directorate K's involvement in the AZANLA bombing attacks is inconclusive, the circumstances raise certain questions.

- Why were the towns of Swartkops, Uitenhage and Algoa Park — known for their strong Afrikaner right wing sympathies — targeted by AZANLA?
- Was it to provoke a similar response from the AWB (Afrikaner Weerstandsbeweging)?
- How did AZANLA obtain the desensitised SMX? Clearly, if they had known it had been tampered with, they would not have used it. This fact, in my opinion, excludes the possibility of an own source.
- Who pressurised the police, in particular Colonel Dick Hattingh, not to allow any further arrests of members of AZANLA and AZAPO?
- Why were the investigating officers hindered so that they could not complete their investigations against Motsau?
- Why was Motsau protected by the authorities?

My own agent also received an 'unofficial pardon' in that no criminal prosecution resulted for his involvement in the bombing. This arose because I had made a specific request to this effect.

In the transitional phase leading up to the 1994 elections, National Intelligence intensified its collection efforts on the Afrikaner right wing. It was a task allocated to only certain trusted officers within each region. In each office it was handled separately to normal collection activities. Special projects were established to infiltrate right wing extremist groupings that had mushroomed throughout the country, especially in the Transvaal. The Service had problems with this procedure as most of its officers did not want to be seen as working against their fellow Afrikaners. Another aspect was that with the volatility of the political situation, the Service did not know which of its members it could trust. Conservative right wing sentiments were common in the organisation. The government was equally concerned about right wing links among the police and the military, especially in Special Forces.

In 1990 a commemorative reunion was held for all Special Force operators at the 1-Reconnaissance Regiment base on the Durban Bluff. Each operator was presented with a commemorative medallion. The function was attended by serving personnel and most ex-members of the unit. National Intelligence, probably through Directorate K, secretly videotaped the proceedings. What they discovered is unknown.

In February 1992 the Conservative Party Deputy Leader, Ferdi Hartzenberg, accused National Intelligence of spying on the right wing.

The Service denied the claim, but they would have wouldn't they?

There seems little doubt that Afrikaner right wing extremism with its acts of violence aided the National Party government in its negotiations with the ANC. The National Party clearly used the possibility of an Afrikaner revolution as a bogy during the negotiating process.

I believe that National Intelligence through Directorate K provided Motsau with the explosives for him to commit serious acts of violence in white right wing centres like Algoa Park, Uitenhage and Swartkops. The motivation would have been to create a definite rise in the political temperature of the area. Provoking the extreme Afrikaner right wing into violent action was a strategic move designed to contain the ANC's demands at the negotiating table. Using AZAPO as a catalyst removed National Intelligence and its political masters from any blame for instigating violence in the country. Desensitising the explosives would prevent loss of human life, but still achieve the objective. It was unlikely that those who survived the bombings would ever realise this. They would just think they were lucky.

The whole turn of events, to my mind, had National Intelligence written all over it. The Service, after all, was responsible for strategy, disinformation and the manipulation of the political situation to suit the NP government.

As predicted by National Party politicians and the press on many occasions, the Afrikaner right wing responded to perceived provocation by the liberation movements. In the first few months of 1994, the AWB and allied Afrikaner right wing groupings, exploded bombs at a shopping complex in Worcester, at Nelspruit, Hoopstad and in many other centres.

In contrast to the AZAPO/Directorate K's campaign, the AWB's bombings claimed numerous lives. On 24 April 1994 a car bomb exploded in front of the Monte Carlo Hotel on the corner of Bree and Von Wielligh streets, midway between the ANC's national and regional headquarters in Johannesburg. The blast, the largest in the country until then, killed nine people and injured 92. On the following day the AWB exploded another bomb in Germiston. Ten people were killed and many injured. On the morning of the first democratic general election, 27 April 1994, another device was detonated in front of the terminal building at Jan Smuts (Johannesburg International) Airport, injuring 21 people.

The right wing organisations responsible had been deeply penetrated by the Security Police and probably National Intelligence as well. Their top leadership was riddled with paid informers — and inform they did. They planned bombing missions and ordered their subordinates to carry them out, then passed details of the operations to their handlers. Afterwards, they collected rewards of up to R250 000 per bomber they had fingered for arrest. Many of those right wing bombers are still languishing in gaol and are likely to remain there for some time to come.

In the end there was not much difference between the white right wing leaders who sold their men out and certain senior officers in the MK who likewise betrayed their own men — leading to many of them being shot as they crossed the border into South Africa.

*   *   *

In 1993 Pat reported that AZANLA was planning more armed attacks in Uitenhage. He was unsure of the targets, but passed on the names of the cadres who would be conducting the operation.

I warned him not to get personally involved as I would probably be unable to protect him. Two days later in the early hours of the morning, AZANLA launched an arson attack against Levan Service Station in Durban Road, Uitenhage.

I immediately passed Pat's information to the Security Branch. National Intelligence's Port Elizabeth office enjoyed an excellent working relationship with the local Security Branch. We automatically passed on tactical information collected by us that related to suspected terrorists or weapons. Within a matter of hours AZAPO's regional publicity secretary, Benjamin Skosana, and the organisation's Uitenhage branch chairman were arrested.

Pat was later promoted to the movement's national executive from where he continued to provide me with information. Of particular importance were details of joint talks held by AZAPO, the PAC and the ANC regarding negotiations with the government.

Ironically, just before the March 1994 election, Rev Maqina re-emerged on the Port Elizabeth political scene, this time as a re-invented National Party supporter.

*   *   *

Jerry (*nom de guerre*), was a serving member of the SADF's Permanent Force stationed in Port Elizabeth. He was also a covert AWB member serving under the direct command of Fred Day, the AWB's head commandant in the Eastern Cape. It was given out that Day was a former Special Forces operator, but his only military experience was as an infantryman during his national service.

269

Boasting for the purpose of enhancing one's military status was not uncommon in the AWB.

AWB's national command, Jerry said, had decided that any attack on whites by the liberation movements would be met with a violent response. This was confirmed in January 1993 in a media statement by AWB leader Eugene Terre'Blanche. He said he had information that 'revenge units' of AWB supporters had been formed to attack black terrorist groups who targeted whites. He emphasised that he had merely heard of the units and had no personal knowledge of them. The obvious purpose of this lie was to protect himself from arrest and prosecution. He believed, he said, that it was his duty to warn black terrorist groups that there were whites around who would strike back at them back hard.

Port Elizabeth's AWB command, according to Jerry, decided to bomb the businesses of the supporters of the liberation movements. They didn't care if they supported AZAPO, PAC or the ANC — as far as they were concerned they were all terrorists.

The first target was the farm store of Malcolm Hepburn, a white farmer who belonged to the ANC's local branch executive in Patensie — a small farming community 150km west of Port Elizabeth. An AWB strike force was detailed for the job. They had generous supplies of commercial and military explosives obtained by members working on the mines or provided by sympathisers in the army or police. The device chosen for the attack comprised a combination of military and commercial explosives. Hepburn's store was devastated by the blast and the bombers escaped without detection.

On 4 January 1993, after the blast, the SAPA-Reuters news agency reported: 'It was unclear if the bombing was linked to a spate of racial attacks on whites by black guerillas which have prompted revenge attacks by white extremists.'

Fred Day ordered the bombing of other targets in the rural centres of Hankey and Kirkwood. In Kirkwood a cafe opposite the police station was selected, because it was believed the owner was giving money to the ANC. Before anything could materialise, though, the Hepburn Store bombers Barend Mosterd, Abraham Younge, Petrus Lombaard and Andre Vorster were rounded up, charged and sentenced to ten years imprisonment. They were released after seven years.

AZANLA's bomb attacks in the Port Elizabeth region drew little response from the AWB. Its leadership was far too involved in making plans to disrupt the April 1994 election to bother with AZANLA's (and Directorate K's) ineffective actions. This did not stop the organisation from preparing for war. Its members got down to roaming their home neighbourhoods at night in motorised gangs. Their targets were blacks, perceived satanists and known 'moffies' (homosexuals) whom they might find wandering around. Their focus, though, was to prepare to take over the country by force by election day.

In January 1994 Fred Day ordered the bombing of a black taxi rank at the bottom end of Russel Road, Port Elizabeth. Phosphorous grenades were acquired from the local military base. They planned to park a car on the freeway that overlooked the rank and toss grenades onto the black commuters below. While driving to the target, the three-man assault group including Jerry, noticed they were being tailed by a Security Branch vehicle. They continued on the freeway and passed above the taxi rank. That was the end of that plot, but they continued their acts of assault on blacks and the others out of favour. The main focus of the regional AWB, though, was to prepare to take the country over by force on election day.

On the night prior to election day, the Port Elizabeth, Uitenhage and Dispatch units of the AWB fielded a combined force of almost 250 people. They were armed with a great variety of firearms, mostly of non-military type. The plan was to sabotage the main power plant at Coega, enter the black townships and kill as many blacks as possible. They expected to be deployed in the field for several months and a small motorised force was detailed to raid the Pick and Pay supermarket at Hunters Retreat to gather in supplies of food.

Jerry and a section of soldiers was patrolling Port Elizabeth in a Buffel infantry fighting vehicle that night. His was one of many police and army patrols. Jerry, having a foot in both camps, was aware of the AWB plan and also knew that the job of the Security Forces was to prevent acts of violence and uphold the law. Jerry and his men, however, were all members of the AWB or sympathised with its objectives. They did not intend to do much for the cause of law and order that night. They were waiting for the AWB forces to launch their armed attacks. When they did, they intended to throw in their weight in support. They would also fight to prevent their Security Force comrades from responding effectively.

The heavy Security Forces presence abroad in Port Elizabeth that night made the AWB generals nervous. They knew that some policemen and soldiers would be coming over to their side, but they could not be sure how many of them that would be. There was also a danger of them ending up fighting their fellow white Afrikaner in the army and the police. That could seriously damage their cause. In facing up to the army they might also end up coming off seriously second best. It was probably this that decided them to abort their plans and send their members home.

But Jerry told me enough to convince me that the violent attacks on whites by the liberation movements, had triggered the AWB into retaliating. AZANLA's National Intelligence-backed attacks in and around Port Elizabeth stirred up strong emotions in the local AWB ranks. The incidents, however, took place so close to the election that retaliation lost its priority. It was obscured by the bigger picture of the white Afrikaner right wing grabbing their country back.

It is accepted that many of the white extremists' acts of violence were motivated by racial hatred. The liberation movements, like the right wing, also committed unprovoked acts of violence against whites. *Agents provocateurs* of Directorate K, nevertheless, played a significant role in stirring up violence both to the left and the right of the political spectrum.

On the night of 27 January 1997 Fred Day's car careened of the road at high speed between Grahamstown and Port Elizabeth and overturned. Fred Day, his driver and a passenger were killed. There were no eye witnesses to the accident.

I was surprised to discover that the AWB was still active at the time. Day was still head commandant of the AWB in Port Elizabeth. According to the AWB's then head of logistics in Port Elizabeth, the three were returning home after an important meeting in Grahamstown with the AWB's national leadership. They were planning a terror attack against Gelvendale coloured township on the city's fringes. There are two huge water storage reservoirs on a hilltop overlooking the township. The opening phase involved an electricity blackout, which would be achieved by AWB men working for the Port Elizabeth municipality. The walls of the reservoirs would have been blasted with explosives, the water would have gushed out and flooded the communities below.

The purpose of the planned operation is a mystery, unless it was to prove a point that the white man was still in charge. Day's death put an end to all that.

Many of his former comrades are convinced that Day's vehicle was run off the road. Others suggest that drink played a role in the accident. Day was carrying a black attache case containing everything relating to the operation. When the police returned the briefcase to his family it was empty.

What happened to the documents is a matter for conjecture.

And did Day's car leave the road accidentally or was it run off?

As they say, the more things change, the more they stay as they are.

Barend Mosterd took command of the local AWB after Day's death, but resigned shortly afterwards. Five years later there is little evidence left of the movement in Port Elizabeth. Some of its members are still serving in the army and others can be found propping up the bars of MOTH clubs (Memorable Order of Tin Hats) across the city in the evenings.

The right wing political ambitions of former AWB people seems to have evaporated. Personal survival in a struggling economy where unemployment is endemic has become their focus. Jerry shuddered when he discussed the past and the things that he and his AWB colleagues had got up to. 'We must have been mad', he said, 'but we were so stirred up that we honestly believed the "kaffirs" were about to take our houses'. Many still claim to hate blacks, but oddly enough in Sidwell where Jerry lives, blacks and whites now live together harmoniously with few signs of racial intolerance.

21

End of an era

On 4 May 1993 I was dining at home when my phone rang. It was Arlene, the regional director's secretary. She made an unusual request. The personal physician of former President PW Botha, with whom she was acquainted, had phoned and asked for National Intelligence assistance. A friend of the former president had important information that he wanted to bring to the urgent attention of the Service.

She gave me the telephone number of a Brian Cohen. I phoned him just after 20:00. The man who answered was extremely agitated and said he was in personal danger. He feared assassination because he had certain documentation that would expose the government. He intended passing it to the media the next morning. He gave me directions to his game ranch near Lake Mentz in the Jansenville district. It was approximately two hours drive from Port Elizabeth.

I summoned a fellow field officer to accompany me and phoned the regional director. Arlene had asked that I say nothing about the man's connection with the former president. I merely gave the regional director a brief outline of the situation and told him that I was leaving for Jansenville to meet a source. He told me to keep him informed, but not to phone after 23:00. I thought this was pathetic. At Division 061, when field officers were on a sensitive job, they always informed their immediate superior of their safe return — regardless of the time.

The property was ten kilometres along a rough dirt road off the national road. We were met by the caller, Brian Cohen, a frail looking man in his fifties, and his personal assistant, a male law student from London. Cohen was appreciative that we had driven all the way from Port Elizabeth to see him.

He said he was very angry with the National Party government, in particular Minister Pik Botha and Antonie Guldenhuys, chairman of the National Peace Structures. Cohen, an international businessman, owned Tuna Marine, a large fishing concern in Cape Town. In the late

274

1970s he allied himself politically with the National Party and became friendly with several senior government ministers — Pik Botha in particular.

Confirmation of these friendships was prominently displayed on the walls of the large farmhouse. These were photographs of himself hunting with PW Botha, Pik Botha and other cabinet ministers. In an effort to prove his credibility to me and being angry, Cohen probably revealed more about his connections with the government than he had intended.

To substantiate his high level cabinet contacts and to demonstrate how he was being ignored, he tried to phone Pik Botha then and there. The minister was not available, so he left a rude message for him to return the call.

In an act of desperation, Cohen had asked PW Botha's physician to put him in touch with someone in National Intelligence — which is how I came on the scene. His problem, he said, was that his former friends in the cabinet, particularly Pik, had shut him out. They had obviously experienced a political change of heart, he told me. Because of Cohen's past anti-ANC stance, they were trying to deny links with him but he did not intend to let this happen. In his capacity as chairman of the interim Border Peace Structure, he had threatened to hold a press conference at 08:00 the next morning. His intention was to publicly expose Pik Botha and certain cabinet colleagues for their pretence of being opposed to the ANC when, in reality, they were capitulating to them.

Cohen had made preparations for my visit. Numerous documents were neatly stacked on the dining room table. He had no copying facilities and neither did I have time to go through such a massive pile. Nevertheless, I soon came to understand his gripe.

The interim Border Peace Structure was composed of members of the SADF, the South African Police, the Ciskei Defence Force, the ANC and representatives of the Border Farming community. The region's farmers had been suffering from many incidents of arson and a serious increase in stock theft. The Border Peace Structure had managed to assist and improve the situation with the co-operation of the local community. The National Peace Structure's Antonie Guldenhuys, however, had ordered Border Peace Structure to be disbanded and replaced by an ANC-dominated structure with a communist chairman. The move had been approved by the government and his friend Pik Botha.

Cohen demanded that National Intelligence do something to restore sanity in the government, failing which he would expose them to the media for what they were. He was under the impression that National Intelligence was Big Brother and that it still adhered closely to former President PW Botha's policies. But by then it was the co-author of change — which neither he nor I knew at the time.

He handed me a document which had been produced by the Rockefeller Foundation as a guideline for use in the South African peace talks. Copies had been handed secretly to South African government officials in Europe with the suggestion they use it in the negotiating process with the ANC. It presented a cleverly constructed argument and was used in the talks. However, it had also been handed to the ANC without the knowledge of the government. The upshot was that both sides, without being aware of it, used similar reference points throughout the negotiations.

Cohen revealed the depth of his involvement with the South African government. It had started in the 1970s. The government was making every effort to break the stranglehold of international sanctions and, as an international businessman, he made his companies available for use as trading fronts. Many substantial deals were facilitated by his interests and he had made substantial profits. The government, as a reward for his co-operation, granted Tuna Marine generous and valuable fishing quotas.

His game ranch of almost ten thousand hectares was his prized possession. It became clear to me that it had frequently been used by certain cabinet ministers. Cohen owned a private aircraft and his own pilot was always on standby. The farm had a tarred runway long enough to take an executive jet and was obviously built to fly in his high-powered friends for rest and recreation.

He related how he and his guests often flew to Cape Town for fresh oyster starters and returned to the farm for the main course of kudu steaks. Money and political influence were abundant in Cohen's life.

It was clear that his revelations would cause the government considerable embarrassment.

I asked him to postpone the press conference and said that someone would contact him in the morning. I got back to Port Elizabeth after 01:00 and as instructed I did not call the deputy regional director. Nevertheless, I regarded the situation as a crisis. I phoned a personal friend, a senior National Intelligence Service analyst, at his home in Pretoria and asked for advice. He said we should activate damage control immediately. I should send a signal containing all information as soon as possible. He would alert his director and the director of my division and arrange a meeting at Concilium Building for 02.30. They would prepare a brief for Director General Niel Barnard's attention

276

later in the morning. I summoned a typist and the cryptographer to my office and prepared an urgent signal.

By 09:00 the next morning all hell had broken loose around me. The regional director scolded me for not advising him of the situation, conveniently forgetting that he had ordered me not to call him after 23:00. The director of the division phoned personally and reprimanded me for bypassing Operations and contacting the analyst direct. He was highly offended and accused me of disgracing Operations in the eyes of the DG.

At the very least my actions saved the day. It provided government with a forewarning and time to put measures in place to minimise whatever Cohen said. This was what an intelligence service and a field operative were supposed to do.

In the end Cohen did not even call a press conference.

My irritation turned to disgust a few days later when head office instructed me to have no further contact with Cohen. He had been blacklisted and the Service wanted nothing more to do with him. I realised then that National Intelligence as I knew it, was falling apart — and probably my career along with it. The Service's professional objectivity had been traded to suit the wishes of the ruling National Party and certain privileged officials. Head office had no desire for its field officers to bring to light the behind-the-scenes dealings of certain politicians.

Many years later I accepted an invitation by Cohen to hunt on his farm. He spoke of current links with the Kennedy family — the famous ones. Two weeks before my visit John Kennedy Junior and his girlfriend, Daryl Hannah, had stayed at the farm for almost a month. Cohen showed me photographs of himself with the couple. He had the unlisted phone numbers of most of the Kennedy clan in his address book.

Pik Botha had introduced him to the Kennedys, he told me. It was evident that his political differences with Pik were long forgotten and the broken fences of his relationship had been mended. They were apparently even involved in a business venture together.

The time had come. I told the regional deputy director I was unhappy in the Service. I told him I could see that National Intelligence was on the verge of change and that top management was being less than truthful about the organisation's future and the career prospects of serving personnel.

A few days later I was instructed to talk with the Divisional Head, Anton Schutte. We met the following evening at 19:00 sharp in

Saddles Restaurant on Port Elizabeth's beachfront. He was waiting for me at the bar, dressed casually in slacks and an open neck shirt and nursing a scotch-on-the-rocks.

'Good to see you Riaan.'

He extended his hand. We went back a long way together.

I accepted a double scotch and water from the barman.

'Thank you, sir.'

'Call me Anton tonight. This is not an official meeting.'

We had a few more rounds of drinks, discussed life in general, the impact of my divorce on my life and the political changes taking place in the country.

We studiously avoided anything that related to our profession or the Service until we were seated at a quiet table in the corner by a window.

'Forget the Cohen incident', he said eventually. 'You have a great future ahead of you and nothing is going to change that.'

I could see that it pained him to lie so blatantly.

I knew I could not waste any more years of my life aboard a ship that was slowly sinking. I also knew it was impossible for Anton to tell me the complete truth or share his own insecurities.

'We'll retain control of the Service,' he said unconvincingly. 'The ANC will just have to adapt to our way of doing things.'

I've had a good innings, I thought. I had always been in the right place at the right time. I had worked on the most elite and exclusive projects in the Service. I was fortunate to have been the protégée of some of the finest operators — true characters, men who had always flown by the proverbial seat of their pants — real intelligence professionals. In the new Service I would be out of place. There was no enemy anymore and intelligence gathering had become a farce. No one even knew what intelligence could be collected nowadays. I thought of my undercover work with Division 061, being a desk officer with 031 for a few months, my service at the Zimbabwe Trade Mission and the skin-of- my-teeth stuff with *Operation Jaguar* in Durban.

I was an intelligence operator. I had not been taught. What I knew had come the hard way from experience in the field. I was proud to be an intelligence professional.

Anton, I knew, was patronising me. Perhaps he was trying to persuade himself into a false sense of security. It was a security that I knew did not exist.

'Sir, tell them they can shove it', I said with finality.

Agitated because he was acting against his personal beliefs, Anton lashed out at me as an operator whom he respected and one he knew was right. He also knew it was the end of an era, but was not prepared

278

to accept it.

'Don't be angry at me, young man. When you joined the Service you agreed to serve anywhere in South Africa without question.'

'Anton I'm really sorry. You know that I've got the greatest respect for you, but what you are telling me is bullshit. It's all finished. The game is over.'

Tell them', I paused and chose my words carefully, 'that I love the sea and I love the Eastern Cape. I'm sure I'll be able to make a success of my life here. Their offer for me to stay with the Service is generous, but . . .'

I shrugged.

'Well, well', Anton said shaking his head. 'I rather expected you to come up with something foolish like this. Do you need more time to reconsider?'

'No, I don't think so.'

We both knew what was happening to all of us. It had been a long journey but it was rapidly coming to an end . . . it was the end for a generation of National Intelligence's best and most loyal operators . . . men who had risked their all in the field for *volk en vaderland*. Some had family interests that prevented them from saying what I had. I knew, though, that it would not be long before they would have to go as well, whether they chose to or not. I guessed it was the same for all those guys in the Rhodesian Security Forces who had found themselves out of job — and a country — when Mugabe came to power.

National Intelligence was obsequiously courting its new political masters. Its top management did not seem to realise that the ANC's top intelligence dogs would never agree to serve for long under the command of incumbents left over from the apartheid days. The Service was looking at the present, not at the future, and dreaming it could come out of the country's turmoil without a trace of tarnish. It was also intent on damage control to ensure that the villains of the assassinations, violence and dirty tricks would be Military Intelligence and the South African Police — and not the National Intelligence Service.

Gambling that they would be able to carry the Service into the future with their own images intact, the seniors were prepared to sacrifice anybody and everybody. If it was the likes of me and other high performing field operatives of the apartheid era who made it difficult for the Service to maintain its unblemished image, then we would have to take the fall.

Further talk seemed unnecessary, so we changed the subject. The east coast lobsters polished off at the Service's expense were exquisite. We identified with each other in an unspoken silence. The cognac in balloon glasses and a bill of R580 put the seal on an honest last encounter.

We walked outside to be met by a gentle sea breeze.

'Thanks for the dinner. I appreciate you coming down from Pretoria to speak to me.'

I reached into my back pocket and slipped out a sealed envelope.

'It's my resignation. Give it to them, Anton. I know that's what they want. It's easier for all of us this way.'

He accepted it without a word and looked away in embarrassment.

I left my car at the yacht club and strolled along the pier. Hundreds of glittering lights were bobbing on the swell. The familiar rattling and creaking of ship's rigging drifted gently in the evening breeze. The moon was a disc floating in a hazy limbo.

It's going to be nice out at sea tomorrow, I thought. Maybe I should take my boat out. It's a good time to start diving again.

Maybe I could start a small diving charter outfit. I thought of my children. They were still so young and innocent. I wished I had spent more time with them. I had been away on too many missions and I was too engrossed with my work to be a proper father.

A ship's horn sounded somewhere in the harbor. I turned my National Intelligence car around and headed for home. They would soon be after me to get that back. The headlights played on the dirty T-shirt of a street kid scuttling into a darkened alleyway.

It bore the words: *Viva Mandela*.

Yeah, I thought.

22

Aftermath

In evaluating the National Intelligence Service in the 1980s it's necessary to consider the internal forces that guided its operation. From inception the Service mainly focussed its attention on intelligence gathering. They achieved only limited success. Although a number of high-level spies were recruited, most of the information collected was overtly available anyway and did not involve the use of covert agents.

The Service was technically impaired in many ways. It lacked many of the sophisticated electronic resources necessary for establishing clandestine communications with its agents in the Communist Bloc and certain African states.

The Counter-Intelligence Division failed to detect a highly placed Soviet mole in the SADF. It was only after a tip-off from the Americans, that Commodore Dieter Gerhardt of the South African Navy was arrested and jailed for espionage in the early 1980s. Gerhardt leaked information not only on South Africa, but also NATO secrets to which the South Africans were privy. It's only logical to deduce that there must have been other hostile infiltrations of the SADF and the South African Police.

Likewise, in the eight years of NIS' existence, nothing came to light that revealed treacherous activity in its own ranks or within the core of the government itself. As with other security establishments, there must have been at least some infiltrations. The presence of cuckoos in the nest is always accepted as a worrying probability. But no such agents were ever compromised or caught.

The secret Afrikaner empire did not last long after the 1994 election.

Niel Barnard, Director General of National Intelligence, together with most of the top structure unobtrusively exited the stage. Barnard's deputy, Mike Louw, replaced him as DG.

There was a general exodus of white officers from the Service throughout the 1990s. A few still cling to their jobs in the new National

Intelligence Agency and the South African Secret Service, despite being continually leapfrogged by new entrant black operators, for the sake of the money and their pensions. The majority, though, have drifted off into the shifting sands of private life.

There will be no call for an encore of their services.

They decided, as I did, that politics and the espionage game have lost their importance. The cause seems no longer worthy of dedicating one's life to. Besides, their new political masters were hardly showing an eagerness to keep them on. So by the millennium the National Intelligence function was primarily in the hands of black operators.

Nelson Mandela became the first democratically elected president of South Africa in May of 1994 and by his office, became the head of South Africa's intelligence services. Joe Nhlanhla became the Secretary for Intelligence and Security. The Directorate of Military Intelligence, which falls under the Minister of Defence, was reined in so that in future it would be restricted to military matters. The function of the police newly named Crime Intelligence (CI) was similarly limited to criminal intelligence.

On the 1st January 1995 the National Intelligence Service ceased to exist. It re-emerged as an amalgamation of the intelligence bodies of the former liberation movements and the former 'independent' homeland states of Transkei, Venda, Bophuthatswana and Ciskei as the National Intelligence Agency (NIA). Its foreign collection arm was named the South African Secret Service (SASS). The US government donated R283 million to smooth and complete the process of integration.

The NIA assumed the mantle of being the supreme intelligence body in the country. Regardless of its new political masters and the general changes within the intelligence community, the art of spying continued as before. Moe Shaik, the top security advisor to the ANC, said at an IDASA (Institute for a democratic alternative for South Africa) conference in November 1993: 'There's a place in a future non-racial and democratic South Africa for covert military and intelligence operations.'

In the end, nothing about the profession or its methods has ever or will ever change. Those of us who were part of it know that unpublicised and unseen intelligence services will always be present amongst us, watching and listening, whether anyone likes it or not. It's the way of the world. The inescapable fact is that those in power will always need that secret product to give them the edge over those whom they perceive as threats.

Covert operations against the enemies of the state still continue.

282

In January 1996 bugging devices were found in the offices of Gauteng Police Commissioner Sharma Maharaj and other provincial police commissioners. Dirk Coetzee, a former Vlakplaas commander and now a NIA operative, told a reporter that he had been tasked to spy on the National Police Commissioner George Fivaz and other senior police officers. His allegations were denied. Coetzee later also denied he had said it. A formal inquiry was instituted on 12 February 1996 by the Standing Committee on Intelligence. Nothing happened.

The intelligence saga continued. An electronic bugging device was discovered in the car of the then Land Affairs Minister, Derek Hanekom. The NIA denied involvement. Is it significant that Hanekom no longer holds a ministerial portfolio in President Thabo Mbeki's government?

In February 1996 a public row erupted when it was revealed that the National Intelligence Agency was engaged in satellite intercepts of domestic phone calls. It responded with the following statement: 'Technical Intelligence gathering is an accepted method used by sophisticated countries throughout the world.'

*   *   *

In recent years the NIA's Port Elizabeth office have lost six officers from premature deaths. Two of them, Squash and Clive Mngadi, died from HIV/AIDS and another from cancer. Corrie, a female officer formerly with NIS, was brutally murdered by her jealous husband. Three other officers died of gunshot wounds, two of which are still unsolved at the time of writing.

In September 1996, field officer Nicky Vanqa shot a man dead outside a Port Elizabeth township tavern after an argument over a woman. Vanqa, a former MK member who had received extensive military training in exile, was grabbed from behind and shot in the chest at close range. He died at the scene.

A large crowd witnessed the shootings, but no one volunteered to step forward and identify the shooter. Vanqa was with a NIA colleague, Lulamile Shakes Mkalipi, who ran away when the bullets began to fly.

Vanqa's death prompted a wave of anger amongst his former MK comrades. They blamed Mkalipi for cowardice in deserting his comrade. It compounded a rift between the former exiles and those who had stayed behind during the liberation struggle. The former exiles regarded the stay-at-homes, who not received the same training or suffered the same hardships as they, with disdain. Yet many of

283

them, because of superior educations, were being appointed to plum senior government posts in preference to those who had sacrificed their educations for the cause.

It did not help that Mkalipi, who had not been in exile and whose struggle roots lay in the United Democratic Front (UDF), had run away and left his partner and comrade to die in the dirt. Mutterings to this effect began being heard in NIA circles, particularly in the Port Elizabeth office.

On 30 December 1997 Mkalipi and his girlfriend Nomvuzo Mqatazana, were sitting in his car that was parked in front of her house. Mkalipi got out to retrieve a gift for her from the boot. He found himself confronted by two men who spoke to him. A third man appeared and stood a few paces away. There was a shot and Nomvuzo ducked from the car and ran into the house to phone the police.

On her return she found Mkalipi dead on the ground. He had been shot in the back and his car was gone. A 9mm CZ pistol registered in the name of the ANC and the keys to his vehicle were the only things missing. His brother Boy Mkalipi, currently the Regional Director of the Department of Public Works in the Eastern Cape, claimed to be the responsible person for the firearm.

It was strange that his vehicle was found abandoned less than a block away. Even stranger was that the autopsy revealed that he had been shot nine times from different angles with two different weapons — a 9mm parabellum and a 9mm short. His aorta had been severed and both lungs had collapsed. He had effectively been shot to pieces. According Ballistics, one of the murder weapons had been used in another murder in neighbouring New Brighton Township six months earlier.

Perhaps coincidentally, one of the first people to arrive at the scene was Linda Mti — a former head of the National Intelligence Co-ordinating Committee (NICOC).

A month later in January 1998 a suspect was arrested. He was identified by Nomvuzo as the third man at the scene. Unfortunately, the case was thrown out in court because the police had failed to follow the correct identification procedures.

The unsolved case is still under investigation by the police's Serious Violent Crimes Unit of the Eastern Cape. It is a matter for conjecture whether Mkalipi was murdered in a revenge attack for abandoning Vanqa in his time of need the year before.

*   *   *

In April 2002 the NIA created a stir in media circles. They wanted to vet members of the press for 'top secret' clearance before they could be included in the Presidential Press Corps. The Agency required journalists to complete a questionnaire in which they were asked about their sexual habits and preferences. After an international media outcry, the Agency accepted that sexual behaviour had no relevance to a person's security clearance. NIA director Vusi Mavimbela, explained that the incident was attributable to the misguided actions of an overzealous officer.

Minister of Intelligence Lindiwe Sisulu pledged to investigate the matter and said she had already ordered the removal from the questionnaire of some questions relating to sex.

Later, however, when the press storm had abated, Lorna Daniels, the ministry's spokesperson, said that after consultations with Director General Mavimbela, it had been decided the questions would remain — despite South Africa's new constitution banning discrimination on grounds of sexual preferences. It seems that the ghosts of Burgess and Maclean are still refusing to lie down.

An assertion that the questions were routine and officially approved was a lame excuse for what we old intelligence professionals knew to be the truth. Those who believe otherwise can stand on their heads and whistle *Die Stem* for all I care, but homosexuality and promiscuity will always be viewed by an intelligence service as a risk factor. There is always the inherent risk of blackmail arising from such practices.

The government's right to lie about such matters has always been reserved and passed from one government to the next, no matter what its political inclination. This is the way it was in my day, this is the way it is now and this is the way it will always be.

*　　　*　　　*

In June 2002 an advertisement appeared in the media under the name of National Intelligence Agency Director General Mavimbela. It contained a rambling historical background to the tradecraft of intelligence, commencing with Moses in the Bible and ending with the operation of intelligence services under former Prime Minister John Vorster and President PW Botha.

Mavimbela reviewed the Agency's existing role and said that national security should be extended through all tiers of governance and that every private citizen has a duty to assist the Agency with intelligence.

The advertisement was headed by the agency's logo — the 'all seeing eye' on the male peacock's feathers. The device has been adapted from the logo, symbols and colours of the former National Intelligence Service. It seems to me that along with the symbols, the NIA has also adopted most of its predecessor's philosophy, methodology and involvement in political matters.

The call for the involvement of private citizens in intelligence matters when there's no current threat to the country's national security is reminiscent of the National Security Management System during the total onslaught days of PW Botha. More ominous parallels can be found in Nazi Germany under Hitler, the Soviet Union under Josef Stalin and recently in Iraq under Saddam Hussein. If such a culture is allowed to become entrenched, it can end with sons denouncing parents and parents denouncing daughters.

*   *   *

On 5 March 2002 a sophisticated, electronic listening device was discovered in the office of Pierre Beneke, the office manager of the former provincial director general of the Western Cape Province, Dr Niel Barnard. Barnard had been dismissed as the provincial director general in January 2002 when the new ANC/NNP coalition had taken over the provincial government. Barnard denied allegations of espionage activities in the Provincial Legislature building at 4 Dorp Street, Cape Town. He said the device, a Watchdog WS100, was installed as a defensive measure in September 2001 to create a so-called bunker room to counter eavesdropping in the legislature building because he had become concerned about leaks. This sophisticated device, according to a technical expert, can also be used in an offensive role because it has the capability of intercepting conversations at a distance of up to four kilometres.

The bunker room was created, Barnard said, to enable senior officials and politicians in the administration to conduct meetings on sensitive subjects without the fear that they were being bugged. The need had arisen because of suspicions that the provincial offices had been bugged although Barnard had no physical proof. If they were bugged, he said he suspected gangsters, Pagad (People against gangsterism and drugs), international intelligence agencies or private companies were the culprits.

He told the Desai Commission of Enquiry that he had himself featured on gang hit lists. Provincial Police Commissioner Lennit

Marx, he said, had told him that gang leaders were holding 'better *bosberade*' (bush conferences) than the government and that they hired private consultants to address them. They also possessed sophisticated technical abilities.

In answer to reports that he had formed a special intelligence unit staffed by former National Intelligence Service members, Barnard conceded that he had established an intelligence capability and had appointed experienced people to run it. His organisation was called the Western Cape Information Unit. He again denied allegations that he had engaged in espionage activities directed against Western Cape politicians and administrators.

Appointments, he said, had been made in terms of the provisions of the Public Service Act. His unit had been tasked to provide intelligence over a broad spectrum to assist the provincial cabinet in making informed decisions. The unit had a co-operation agreement with the NIA reached two years before after negotiations when the agency had approached Barnard, former Western Cape premier Gerald Morkel and former minister of community security, Hennie Bester. The Agency asked for access to the province's intelligence on health issues and issues of community security. The Agency was asked as a *quid pro quo* for a written commitment that it would not engage in eavesdropping operations within the province. It failed to respond.

Allegations of eavesdropping began to resurface and the new Western Cape premier, Peter Marais, referred it to the National Intelligence Agency. Arthur Fraser, the Agency's provincial manager, said that his office had conducted an investigation into all the ministerial departments and the 12 councillors in the building.

Captain Renier Strydom of the SAPS' protection services revealed that on 8 November 2001, in the early hours of the morning, two men had been discovered in the premier's office. The pair, Niehaumer and Lorenzo Lombard, claimed they were engaged in sweeping the offices for bugging devices. They said that Louis Steyn, an advisor to Niel Barnard, had given them permission to do it.

Lombard and Steyn were both former National Intelligence officers. Steyn was the first secretary at the South African embassy in Paris, who was expelled from France for attempting to buy the British made Blowpipe ground-to-air missiles in the 1980s.

What was the truth? Was it an attempt by Barnard's intelligence unit to keep the Democratic Alliance in power in the Western Cape because it was the last bastion of power not controlled by the ANC?

What's the true relationship between Barnard's operatives and the National Intelligence Agency? Has the Agency's covert collection ability deteriorated to such an extent that it needs an outside body to do it for them? Did Barnard and the Agency play open cards with one another? I somehow doubt it. There are a few people around who know the truth, but they're not telling.

Controversy about the involvement of former National Intelligence Service operators in the Western Cape government continued with startling allegations emanating from former NIS operative, Piet Smit. Smit had commenced his intelligence career with BOSS in 1975 and stayed on with National Intelligence when they came into being. He served in Portugal and the United States. He moved to SASS after the 1994 elections and remained with it until 2000 when he was drafted into Niel Barnard's provincial intelligence unit in the Western Cape.

It emerged that Niel Barnard had been kept well informed in National Intelligence Agency circles. Liaison contacts between him and President Thabo Mbeki on intelligence-related matters had been taking place regularly.

By mid 2001 the Western Cape Information Unit became aware of moves to establish a presidential intelligence unit. On 6 July, Piet Smit said that Nel Marais — a former NIS operator hired by Barnard as a security consultant — had spoken to him about a request by President Mbeki, directed via ex-SASS Director General, Billy Masetlha to help set up a system that would provide him with reliable intelligence. Former SASS director, Super Moloi, was tasked to assist Barnard. A presidential intelligence agency was officially formed in November 2001, but a formal announcement about it was made only in 2002.

In January 2002 Niel Barnard attended the Palestine/Israeli summit chaired by President Mbeki at Spier Estate outside Stellenbosch.

Piet Smit left his employment with the Western Cape Provincial Government in December 2001. He recalled how he used to make 15 copies of provincial cabinet briefings, one for each MEC (Member of the Executive Council) and for members of the cabinet secretariat. Afterwards, he wiped the hard drive of his computer clean for 'good housekeeping' reasons.

There are more questions than answers.

'Why does President Mbeki require a private intelligence service when he has the National Intelligence Agency and the South African Secret Service at his elbow? Is it that he does not regard them as competent and trustworthy, or is it because he needs 'off the record' information?'

Does Niel Barnard have the ear of the current president as he did with PW Botha and FW de Klerk?

Is President Mbeki's presidential intelligence service a rehash of the old Directorate K?'

Was President PW Botha's reliance on an cabal or inner circle of Securocrats similar to President Mbeki's own over-dependence on government officials?

No one will say . . . we can only guess.

Bibliography

BOOKS

Dorril, Stephen. *MI6: 50 years of Special Operations*, (Fourth Estate, London, 2001); **Steenkamp, Willem**. *Borderstrike*, (Butterworths, Durban, 1983); **Stiff, Peter**. *Nine days of War and South Africa's final days in Namibia*, (Lemur, Alberton, 2nd edition, 1991); *The Silent War: South African Recce operations 1969-1994*, (Galago, Alberton, 1999); *Warfare by other Means: South Africa in the 1980s and 1990s*, (Galago, Alberton, 2001)

WEB SITES:

www.geocities.com
www.lib.sun.ac.za/army/army-talk
www.anc.org.za/ancdocs/history
www.mg.co.za/mg/news
www.truth.org.za
www.hartford-hwp-com/archives

NEWSPAPERS:

City Press, *The Eastern Cape Herald*, *Rapport*, *Sunday Times*, *The Star*, *Weekly Mail*

Picture Credits

The following are credited for the use of photographs and illustrations: Riaan Labuschagne, Riaan Labuschagne collection, Peter Stiff, Peter Stiff collection and *Rapport*. Some photographic contributors have asked to remain anonymous. The copyright holders of a few photographs are unacknowledged, although the publishers have made every effort to establish the authorship which have been lost in the mists of time or blown away by the winds of war. However, the publishers will gladly amend or add credits in subsequent editions and make the necessary arrangements with those photographers who were not known or who had not been traced at the time of going to print.

Index

224, 228, 234
Division 032, NIS, 170, 174, 175
Division 041, NIS, 250
Division 051, NIS, 221
Division 06, NIS, 177, 183
Division 061, NIS, 80, 164, 282
Division 061/01, NIS, 82
Division 062, NIS, 152, 253
Dolincheck, Martin, NIS, 56, 57, 61
Doorewaard, Pieter, mercenary, 56
DRC (Democratic Republic of Congo), 95
Du Plessis, Barend, National Party, 235
Du Plessis, Col Lourens, SADF, 256, 258, 259, 266
Du Toit, Capt Wynand, 4-Recce, 68, 69
Du Toit, Layla, NIS, 72, 73
Duffy, Peter, mercenary, 56
Dutch Reformed Church, 24, 164, 242

E
Easigas Storage, Port Elizabeth, bombing at, 267, 268
Egypt, 230
Egyptian Intelligence Service, 223
Els, NIS, 177
End Conscription Campaign, 242
Engelbrecht, General Krappies, SAP, 15
Entabeni, SADF training base, 84
Erwin, Alex, COSATU, 247

F
FAPLA, 45, 113, 117, 128, 205
Fivaz, George, National SAPS Commissioner, 287
Flaam, Robert, yacht skipper, 38
Fourie, Neil, NIS, 153
Fourie, Piet, NIS, 171

Fraser, Arthur, NIA, 291
Freedom Charter, ANC, 264
Freemasons, 177
FRELIMO (Front for Liberation of Mozambique), 84
Fritz, Johan, killed, mercenary, 55

G
Gaborone, Botswana, 88, 113, 148
Gaddafi, Pres Muhamar, of Libya, 117, 157
Geldenhuys, Gen Jannie, SADF chief, 230, 257
Gerhardt, Commodore Dieter, SA traitor, 197
Germiston, car bomb, AWB, 273
Goatley, Charles, mercenary, 56
Godlo, Stelfox, ANC, 166
Goniwe, Matthew, murdered by security police, 258
Gorbachev, Mikhail, Soviet Pres, 108, 114, 234
Grahamstown, 276
Gröskopff, Heinz, MK soldier, 217
GRU (Glavnoye Razvedyvatelnoye Upravlenie) — Soviet Military I, 99, 104, 198
Guldenhuys, Antonie, National Peace Structure, 278
Gunter, Col Herman, STASI, 160, 162
Gwala, Harry, ANC, 242

H
Hall, Col Pieter, SADF, 256
Hamman, Brig Daan, Military Intelligence, 55
Hanekom, Derek, ANC, 217, 287
Hanekom, Kallie, ANC, 217, 220
Hani, Chris, SACP and ANC, 265
Harms Commission, 92
Hartzenberg, Ferdi, CP leader, 272
Hattingh, Col Dick, SAP, 268, 271

Schutte, Anton, NIS, 248, 250-252, 282-284

SDECE (*Service de documentation étrangère et de contre-espionage*), French Intelligence, 175

Seabelo, Moris, ANC, killed in raid, 90

Sebe, Gen Charles, Ciskei, 257

Sebe, President Lennox, Ciskei, 256, 257

Security Police, 23, 55, 88, 89, 181, 194, 207, 215, 227, 243, 248, 258, 259, 265, 269-271, 273, 275

Selous Scouts, Rhodesia, 125

September, Dulcie, assassination of, 233

Seychelles, 17, 25, 30, 44

Seychelles Movement de la Resistance, 43

Shaganovitch, Soviet General Konstantin, 112, 113, 118

Shaik, Moe, ANC security adviser, 286

Shamley, Etienne, NIS, 77, 99, 255, 256, 264

Shope, Peter, ANC, 167

Sibeko, Archie, ANC, 108

Sierra Leone, 171

Silva, Cavaco, Portuguese leader, 236

Singapore, 170

Singh, Kush ANC, 245

Sisulu, Lindiwe, Minister of Intelligence, 289

Skosana, Benjamin, AZANLA bomber, 267, 268, 270, 273

Slovo, Joe, SACP leader, 182, 206, 215, 232, 265

Smit, Piet, ex-NIS, 292

Smith, Eileen, 212

Smith, Michael, CCB, 211, 212, 224

Snyman, Theron, NIS, 248

Solarz, Stephen, US Congressman, 183

Solo, Andile Samuel, AZANLA bomber, 267, 270

Solomon Mhlangu Freedom College (SOMAFCO), 166

Sonja, NIS, 248, 249

South African Air Force (see SAAF)

South African Airways, 54

South African Communist Party (see SACP)

South African Navy, 65, 285

South African Secret Service (See SASS)

Soviets/Soviet Union, 54, 58, 66, 99, 104, 108, 116, 127, 168

Special Forces, 67, 89, 113, 181, 183, 215, 271

State Security Council, 23, 54, 88, 90, 112, 174, 180, 237, 258

Stealth (NIS agent), 213, 214, 218-222

Steenberg, Major D, SAP, 270

Steyn, Douw, Recce officer, 114

Steyn, Louis, NIS, 175, 176, 291

Strydom, Capt Renier, SAPS, 291

Sverdlovsk, Major Gregor, Soviet KGB, 160

SWA/Namibia, 45, 66, 87, 92, 230, 236

SWAPO (South West Africa People's Organisation), 45, 66, 91, 128

Swart, Phillip, NIS, 60, 62, 73, 77-79, 86, 99, 101, 103-105, 109-111, 118, 147, 151, 153-157, 159, 168, 169, 186

Swartkops, Port Elizabeth, 267, 272

Swartkops Air Force Base, 193

Swaziland, 174, 184

Minister, 15

Voortrekkerhoogte Military base, proposed MK attack on, 193

Vorster, John, SA premier, 21, 22, 290

Vosloo, Phil, NIS, 248, 255

W

Watchdog WS100, 290

Watchers, NIS, 73, 94, 99, 117, 120, 155, 157, 206

Waterkloof Air Force base, 13, 206

Webster, Dr David, assassination of by CCB, 233

Western Cape Information Unit, 291, 292

White, Ant, Military Intelligence, 59

Whitehead, Peter, NIS, 77, 82, 86, 87

Wilemse, Willie, Director Prisons, 234

Williamson, Col Craig, 58

Windhoek, Namibia, 91

Withers, Ian Douglas, NIS, 58

Woods, Kevin, prisoner in Zimbabwe, 212, 224

Worral, Denis, NP MP, 229, 243

XY

Younge, Abraham, AWB, 275

Z

Z-squad, BOSS, 232

Zaïre (now Democratic Republic of Congo or DRC), 96, 128, 171

Zambia, 87, 95, 101, 105, 108, 164, 166, 168, 172, 198

ZANLA (Zimbabwe African National Liberation Army), 191

ZAPU (Zimbabwe African People's Union), 219

ZCIO (Zimbabwe Central Intell Organisation), 83, 188, 189, 191, 194, 195, 197, 201, 202, 204, 219, 221, 224, 226

Zimbabwe, 87, 95, 101, 108, 125, 176, 186, 194, 217, 219, 224

Zimbabwe Central Intelligence Organisation (see ZCIO)

Zuma, Jacob, ANC, 247